D1566249

LOW LIVING AND HIGH THINKING AT MODERN TIMES, NEW YORK

UTOPIANISM AND COMMUNITARIANISM

LOW LIVING AND
HIGH THINKING AT
MODERN TIMES, NEW YORK

Roger Wunderlich

SYRACUSE UNIVERSITY PRESS

First Edition 1992
92 93 94 95 96 97 98 99   6 5 4 3 2 1

On the title page: Enlargement of A. J. Macdonald's pencil sketch of Josiah Warren's "Mechanical College."

The paper used in this publication meets the minimum requirements of American National Standard for Information Sciences—Permanence of Paper for Printed Library Materials, ANSI Z39.48-1984. ∞™

Library of Congress Cataloging-in-Publication Data

Wunderlich, Roger.
    Low living and high thinking at Modern Times, New York / Roger Wunderlich. — 1st ed.
        p.   cm. — (Utopianism and communitarianism)
    Includes bibliographical references and index.
    ISBN 0-8156-2554-5
    1. Modern Times (Collective settlement)—History.   2. Collective settlements—New York (State)—History.   3. Utopian socialism—United States—History.   I. Title.   II. Series.
HX656.M63W86   1992
307.77′4′0974725—dc20   91-24490

Manufactured in the United States of America

To Fran

Roger Wunderlich is a Research Assistant Professor of history at the State University of New York at Stony Brook and is founder and editor of the *Long Island Historical Journal*.

The name "Modern Times" was chosen as most fitting for the under-taking—in view that the principles we hoped to embody were wholly new and the name distinctive from all other Social Experiments.

—CHARLES A. CODMAN,
"A Brief History of 'The City of Modern Times'"

CONTENTS

ILLUSTRATIONS

ACKNOWLEDGMENTS

At the State University of New York at Stony Brook, Wilbur R. Miller and Eric E. Lampard constructively criticized my work. Bernard Semmel shared his knowledge of Mill and Spencer. Hugh Cleland, Ned Landsman, John W. Pratt, Michael H. Schwartz, William R. Taylor, John R. Williams, and Nancy J. Tomes provided insight and helpful suggestions. Margaret M. Schrage encouraged me to tackle the subject of Modern Times. Oscar A. Haac increased my understanding of Henry Edger and Auguste Comte. Taylor Stoehr of the University of Massachusetts, Boston, generously sent me rare microfilms pertaining to Mary Gove Nichols and Thomas Low Nichols.

Doris Lewis Sargeant and Martha E. Stepsis, of the Brentwood Public Library, went out of their way to help me and furnished most of the book's illustrations. I also received the cooperation of David Y. Allen, Helen E. Dorre, Donna Sammis, and Evert Volkersz, of the Frank Melville, Jr. Memorial Library, State University of New York at Stony Brook; George Wagner and Ronne Cosel, of the Port Jefferson Free Library; Vera Toman, of the Smithtown Library's Long Island Room; and the Long Island librarians at the Brooklyn Historical Society and the Queens Borough Public Library.

I benefited from the friendly cooperation of Mary Aline Cook and Rosemary Alsop, of the Library of the New Harmony Workingmen's Institute; of Joyce Ann Tracy, curator of newspapers and serials at the American Antiquarian Society; and of the rare book and document libraries of Yale University, Harvard University, the University of Michigan, the University of Illinois, and Syracuse University.

I am grateful for the use of the deed and map archives stored in the record rooms of the Suffolk County Clerk, and for the assistance given to me by the Suffolk County Historical Society; the Suffolk Marine Museum; the Islip Town Museum; the Town of Islip's Community Develop-

ment Agency; the Office of the Superintendent of Schools of Brentwood; and the Sisters of Saint Joseph, Brentwood.

I commend Lyman Tower Sargent and Gregory Claeys of the University of Missouri–St. Louis for initiating this series on Utopianism
and Communitarianism, and to the staff of Syracuse University Press
for their creative presentation of my contribution to it.

I appreciate the advice of my daughter and son-in-law, Elizabeth
and Stuart Ewen; my sons, Roger and Michael Wunderlich; and my
grandsons, Paul and Sam Ewen. Most of all, I thank my wife, Frances C.
Wunderlich, for her counsel, patience and love.

LOW LIVING AND HIGH THINKING AT MODERN TIMES, NEW YORK

1

Scale Model of Liberty

LIBERTY is the vital principle of human happiness; and human nature seeks its liberty as the magnet seeks the north, or as water seeks its level . . . but it can never be realized under any organization of society now known to us, nor can it ever be attained upon any of the theories upon which societies are now acting.

—JOSIAH WARREN,
Practical Details in Equitable Commerce

THIS BOOK BRINGS BACK TO LIFE the obscure village of Modern Times, a libertarian laboratory of individual sovereignty. Dispensing with formal organization, the settlers consorted spontaneously, as if each were a sect and a nation. Forty-one miles from New York City and four miles inland from Great South Bay, Modern Times was a clearing in the wilderness that covered inland Long Island during the middle years of the nineteenth century. Never more than a hundred and fifty strong, on a plat of ninety acres, here was a haven for nonconformists, its currency words, its religion discussion, its standard of conduct free and easy. During its thirteen-year demonstration of an unorthodox counterculture, it acquired a controversial and somewhat immoral reputation. In September 1864 the settlers stepped out of the limelight by giving the village its present and unprovocative name of Brentwood.

Modern Times was one of ninety-one model communities created in the United States between 1780 and 1860.[1] The programs of these communities ranged from communal to private ownership, religious to secular orientation, group marriage to celibacy, and universal to nuclear families. But no matter how varied the species, each belonged to the genus communitarian, hoping that by its witness a golden age of harmony would save the nation from worship of Mammon. Albert

1

Brisbane, one of the movement's leading ideologues, defined the common goal: "If we can, with a knowledge of true social principles, organize one township rightly, we can, by organizing others like it, and by spreading them and rendering them universal, establish a true Social and Political order."[2]

The largest and longest-lasting model communities consisted of believers in the Second Coming, who patterned themselves on the early Christians by pooling their assets and living communally, taking their wages in room and board and the certainty of salvation. Oddly, or perhaps logically, these bands of Bible communists triumphed economically, successfully trading with the "world's people" in the markets they chose to enter. Although far from the centers of traffic, the Harmonist, Shaker, Oneida, Amana, and other communal experiments prospered for generations, long after the passage of time had refuted their millenarian expectation.[3]

Modern Times, however, a secular, individualist cog in a mainly religious, collectivist wheel, featured nuclear families, separate housing, and private property. Its founders were a pair of philosophical anarchists: the fifty-three-year-old Josiah Warren and his writing partner and editor, Stephen Pearl Andrews, sixteen years his junior. The formation of Modern Times in 1851 climaxed Warren's lifetime of work for collaboration of equals without coercion, authority, or any arrangement except the kind that left "every individual at all times at liberty to dispose of his or her person, time, and property in any manner in which his or her own feelings or judgment may dictate, WITHOUT INVOLVING THE PERSONS OR INTERESTS OF OTHERS."[4]

The community was a living test of Warren's dual principles—sovereignty of the individual and cost the limit of price. Sovereignty of the individual meant that everyone had a right to live as he or she pleased as long as this freedom did not impair the right of another to do the same. To believe in any religion or none, to cohabit in or out of marriage, and generally to conduct oneself as one chose were personal decisions, subject to no other rule than reciprocal toleration. The object, in Warren's words, was to have "no organization, no indefinite delegated powers, no Constitutions, no laws nor bye-laws, 'rules' or 'regulations' but such as each individual makes for himself and his own business."[5]

Cost the limit of price implied an economy based on exchange of labor without the incentive of capital gain—a benevolent order of barter, with goods and services swapped at cost instead of sold at market value. They could also be paid for with labor notes, the self-coined circulating medium written by individual sovereigns and promising payment in hours of work at the issuer's occupation. At the hub of the system was Warren's "time store," where he sold merchandise at cost plus a small markup to pay for his time in transacting a sale. The time store also served as employment office and clearing house, with offers posted by makers and users accomplishing "adaptation of the supply to the demand."[6]

Warren and Andrews fused sovereignty of the individual with cost the limit of price and called it "equitable commerce." No goods or services were to change hands at a penny more than cost—precluding profit, speculation, usury, inflation, and that "foundation evil of the world," the general "insecurity of condition," which Warren held responsible for the "universal scramble for property and money."[7]

To mental or manual workers alarmed by the rise of industrialism, equitable commerce offered an alternative, friendlier order by which "competition is rendered cooperative instead of antagonistic."[8] Its practice empowered cash-poor pioneers to acquire land and build homesteads. Homes for the homeless was Warren's slogan: people who never before owned land and houses suddenly did at Modern Times.

The community's indifference to whether couples lived in or out of wedlock added a lurid overlay to its image of eccentricity. Compounding this notoriety was the crusade for sexual liberation led by Dr. Thomas Low Nichols and his wife, the flamboyant Mary Gove Nichols. Although Warren and most Modern Timers refused to enlist in the free-love army, the campaign of the militant vanguard magnified the aura of sin that already illumined the village.

The model societies of Harmony, New Harmony, Brook Farm, the Shakers, Oneida, and Amana attract many more scholars than does this unpreserved and all-but-forgotten hamlet. It is time to rescue Modern Times from limbo by defining its program, reassembling its people, examining its problems, and interpreting its history. My aim is to complete what Charles A. Codman—the village's oldest male survivor—began with his "Brief History of 'The City of Modern Times.'" I can

say figuratively, as Codman did literally, that "I am glad to give testi-
mony to the Motives of the pioneers and to rescue their reputation
from any imputations put forth by those who had no just conception
of their Motives and Aspirations . . . 'Tis my purpose to give an inside
view as unbiased as possible, from a personal knowledge of the aims
of the projectors and acquaintance with nearly all the first settlers."[9]

We have many sketches of Modern Times, but this book is its
first full-length portrait. To the extent allowed by sparse and elusive
data, I hope to recreate the 250 people whose lives touched the village
as settlers, visitors, neighbors, or critics. Of special concern are the
pioneers who carved a community out of the wilderness. My purpose
is to retrieve the outlines of their existence from land deeds, censuses,
gravestones, muster rolls, maps, newspapers, minutes of town and school
board meetings, and frequent inspections of the site, enhanced when-
ever possible by eyewitness memoirs, letters, and reports.

Attention also focuses on the champions of causes attracted to
this freewheeling hamlet, a sounding board, in Codman's words, for
"Every kind of reform . . . from . . . Abolition of Chattel Slavery, Woman's Rights, Vegetarianism, Hydropathy (and all the pathies), Peace,
Ante-Tobacco [sic], Total Abstinence, to the Bloomer Costume." The
sovereigns enjoyed discussing reform as much as or more than working
for it. "Every new and strange proposition," wrote Codman, "was welcomed by a respectful hearing—debated and considered—and the latest 'Anti' was often thought the truer as being the result of latest experience or riper knowledge."[10]

At a time when the nation moved west, the testers of equitable
commerce opened an eastern frontier, a reverse movement of pioneers
whose settlement proved the value of the pine barrens and the Long
Island Railroad when neither was well regarded. All the pioneers were
rebels, but not all the rebels were pioneers. Tension developed, partly
because of friction between rival reformers, but mainly as a result of
the conflicting goals of transients, to whom the village was only a stop-
over on the road to societal reorganization, and settlers to whom it
meant homesteads and the companionship of fellow freethinkers.

Labor exchange—for example, a carpenter's trading skills with a
tailor—sufficed for transactions in handmade products or self-performed
services. However, it could not keep step with the new regime of commodities made in factories, on machines, for a burgeoning national

market. The gap between reformers' goals and settlers' needs widened until the homesteaders renamed their village and merged with the local culture.

"From the usual standards," muses Codman, "the attempt was a failure, in that we attracted neither numbers nor capital." But in spite of all the privations and missed opportunities visited on its settlers by the rigors of equitable commerce, he concludes that "we had the moral compensation which flows from altruistic effort, and the cheering hope that our lives had not been entirely for self—that our Social Experiment might be a factor in the moralization of Humanity and that we had assisted in keeping alive the aspiration for Social Progress."[11]

The practice of individual sovereignty linked with private but profitless enterprise is an extremely ambitious hypothesis to put to the test of daily life. The significance of this eccentric enclave and incubator of social change is not that it failed but that it tried. Its method of swapping labor at cost enabled people of limited means to own land and build houses. Self-governing refugees from conformity treated women as equal to men, and conversed with each other more than they worked. Before the market-based, corporate system reached a point of no return, this genial commonwealth of principals gave proof that a free but noncompetitive style of life was possible in the United States. An alternative course, preserving private ownership but forswearing the exploitation of labor, spun into motion at Modern Times, a scale model of liberty.

2

The Site and the Founders

I N 1841, AFTER LOSING A DAUGHTER TO CHOLERA, Dr. Edgar Fenn
Peck moved his family from Brooklyn to the uninfected village of
Smithtown forty miles to the east. A physician with an eye for
real estate, Peck came to Suffolk County sharing the common mis-
conception that "no considerable portion of land in Long Island that
could be cultivated but what had been cultivated." For three summers
he roamed south of Smithtown, spade in hand, where crews of workmen cut through the wilderness, laying the tracks of the Long Island
Railroad. Peck's research convinced him that "the surface of these lands
is smooth, and entirely free from stone or swamp. The soil is a fine,
warm yellow loam, in many places from two to four feet deep, adapted
to the finest culture." With the proper cultivation, the area could rise
to the level of other farming sections of Long Island, the garden of
New York. Peck challenged the prevailing opinion, expressed by such
authorities as the historian Nathaniel S. Prime, that the pine barrens
had no use except for "'the timber they bear, (after which) they become absolutely worthless, at least to the present generation.'" Referring to the area that became the site of Modern Times, Prime asserted
in 1845 that "'the sand increases in fineness, even in some places to
fluidity, for there is no soil.'" Peck noted the concurrence with Prime
of an equally respected Long Islandist, Benjamin Franklin Thompson,
who wrote off the wild belt that marred inland Suffolk County from
Farmingdale to Riverhead as "'a vast tract of barren land, so entirely
composed of sand, as to be unsusceptible of profitable cultivation by
any process at present known.'"[1]

Although poorly rated, for more than one hundred years the soil
produced huge stocks of cordwood used for heating houses before the
advent of anthracite coal. A 1986 study reports that before the Civil
War, Suffolk County suppliers—New York State's leading source—cut

THE SITE AND THE FOUNDERS

100,000 cords of firewood each year for shipment to New York City "as well as to voracious brick kilns on the Hudson River at Haverstraw, Newburgh, and elsewhere."[2] Clearly, "barrens" was a misnomer.

Timothy Dwight, a past president of Yale College, described the zone more precisely in a travel guide published in 1822. Except for some land rescued for farming, he found the region heavily wooded: "Formerly, four fifths of the County of Suffolk were considered barrens: i.e., not literally, but tracts of poor land; left to nature, and regarded as incapable of cultivation . . . One-half at least, of these forests . . . is yellow pine: the rest is . . . oak, chesnut [sic], hickory, &c."[3]

Although its reputation suffered from the charge that the soil was sandy, verging on fluid, an agricultural expert judged that because of its adhesive qualities, "no intelligent person . . . would mistake the soil of the plains for sand, or hesitate . . . to pronounce it a clayey loam."[4]

The groves observed by Timothy Dwight were first depleted by cutting and then all but destroyed in the 1840s by fires kindled by sparks from the smokestacks of the Long Island Railroad's primitive locomotives. The resulting "vast opening of the forest canopy"[5] gave the sunlight needed by the surviving tangle of pitch pine (Pinus rigida), a tree endowed with loose and fire-resistant bark, and scrub oak (Quercus ilicifolia), a shrub whose roots resume growth after fire. In one of many polemics against the diagnoses of Prime and Thompson, Peck contended that the semblance of desolation quickened because of the "fire road," a twenty-foot clearing alongside the track to contain the blazes ignited by puffer-bellies called Post-Boy, Hicksville, and Ariel: "The space between the railroad and these fire roads is burnt over every spring and fall, with a view to kill and destroy all vegetation and all vegetable matter on it . . . to prevent the recurrence of fires, and this fully accounts for the extreme barren appearance along the borders of the road."[6]

As a member of the American Institute of the City of New York, Peck joined an 1847 fact-finding mission assembled to explore the chances of tilling the so-called wastelands on the right-of-way of the railroad. "As a general prejudice prevails against these lands we must be certain of our facts," explained an official, "or we may be liable to ridicule." To avoid any hint of a conflict of interest because of his real estate dealings, Peck declined his nomination to the evaluation committee, but accepted an invitation to speak at a meeting in Greenport after the field trip. His address on "the improvement of the immense

plains now lying waste and sterile in the centre of the Island, on each
side of the railroad" blended history with husbandry. Had not Daniel
Denton, the first Englishman to write about Long Island, described
it in 1670 as of a "'very good soyle, and very natural for all sorts of
English grain'"? Was not the Hempstead Plain, the earliest prairie known
to Americans, long held useless except for grazing? To Peck, the stunted
woods that bordered the tracks in no way negated the soil's produc-
tivity; they were rather the consequences of a Gresham's Law for trees,
under which the bad survivors of fires, cuttings, and charcoal making
drive out the good. This lode of fertility lies untapped because people
think it is barren. To counter such an impression, Peck asserted, it is
up to the great American Institute, patron of agriculture, arts, and science, to "roll back this dark cloud of error . . . that has so long over-
hung, and obscured so large a portion of this beautiful Island . . . let
[it] waken into new life its patent energies and powers."[7]

Although many speakers endorsed Peck's position, the Institute
took no action, not even to implement its plan to buy land in Suffolk
County on which to build a college of agriculture. This sort of bias,
protested a later observer, inhibited settlement of "the pine forest of
the island [that] occupies the portion between the central range of hills
and the south shore, six to eight miles in width, and extends for sixty
miles through the whole length of Suffolk County . . . There is no other
evergreen forest of equal size in the State of New York short of the
Adirondacks."[8] Not until 1912 did Farmingdale Institute (a future branch
of the State University of New York) become the first agricultural school
on Long Island.

Edgar Peck the speculator influenced Doctor Peck the scientist,
but the heavyset, square-faced man never wavered in his insistence that
the vast tracts called the "plains or barrens – did not differ in soil and
geology, at all, from the cultivated lands on their borders, that the
soil . . . was and is suitable in every way for culture."[9] According to
Charles A. Codman, Peck proved the soil would blossom if properly
treated by starting "experimental farms, one at Brentwood, which today [1904] is owned by Dr. W. H. Ross who has little fault to find with
his farm or fruit crops." Most persons, thought Codman, were ruled
by "traditional prejudices of the natives that 'a grasshopper would starve
to death on the "Barren Plains" . . . Give a dog a bad name, etc.' Dr.
Peck died in the early nineties, maintaining until the end the correct-

ness of his opinion; as to the fertility of the soil, Mr. John Ryan told me that he raised 33 Bushels of wheat on one Acre. And the Summary of Experience to date Shows that under right treatment good results are obtained."[10]

In spite of Peck's forty-year mission to promote the barrens for settlement, and for all of Modern Times's demonstration of the fertility of the inland soil, most Long Islanders still prefer to reside on or close to the North or South Shores. As for Peck's maligned pine barrens, eighty thousand acres (one-third of the original number) still evade the tract-builders' grasp. They continue to "form the protective cover and natural recharge system for vast reservoirs of pure fresh water lying just beneath their surface."[11]

THE SITE

Soon after arriving in Smithtown, Dr. Peck began dealing in pine barrens real estate. Advised and encouraged by his friend George B. Fisk, the president of the Long Island Railroad, he bought several hundred acres hewn from the wilderness at Suffolk Station, a mile and one-half to the east of the future Modern Times. However, three developments spoiled his plan to form a settlement for his own and several associates' use: the death of his mentor, Fisk; the "faithless and false" character of his colleagues; and the refusal of an owner to sell, unless for "three times its fair market value," the additional land Peck required for the success of the undertaking.[12]

Buoyant as always, the doctor decided not only to keep the property rather than sell at a loss ("which I ought to have done"), but to look for more land in his crusade to vindicate the pine barrens and to civilize the backwoods in the northwestern reaches of Islip town. Disclaiming the motive of personal gain, he stated his aim as nothing more than to "bring in new owners and new interests." For this purpose he "purchased by contract most of the land between Thompson [the future depot for Modern Times] and Suffolk Stations"[13] from two squires of ancient Long Island lineage—Francis Moses Asbury Wicks, the laird of Thompson's Station, and Nathaniel O. Clock, a farmer with relatives ticking all over the township. The tract of which Modern Times was part was "something over 400 acres," bought from Wicks "without the wood for $2.75 per acre." Peck sold these lands to a syndicate of investors from New York City, who, Peck assumed, would remove the stumps and improve the land.[14] They did not. Disheartened by the old refrain of the barrens' sterility and heedless of Peck's denial of it, the buyers lost interest, convinced that the land was not worth improving. "It was not until the land had passed through several hands, and several years later," wrote Peck, "that any considerable improvement was made on it. My old friend, the late Samuel Fleet, then Editor of the Am. [American] Artisan rendered through his paper, essential service in making these sales."[15]

The "considerable improvement" was Modern Times. Josiah Warren came to New York in 1850 to test the viability of an eastern village of equity. Writing in 1873, a year before he died, he recalled his reasons for choosing a site for his model community close to, but not within, the metropolis: "If our efforts do not secure homes to the homeless, we work to no purpose: and these homes cannot be had in the cities now built."[16] However, in April 1853 "A Card – to the Public," an advertisement in the New York Tribune soliciting settlers at Modern Times, explained that "The vicinity of the largest market in the country is of greatest importance as respects selling the product of the land and the workshops."[17]

Taking over the lands from which the disappointed New Yorkers were willing to part for what they had paid, the founders obtained easy terms of purchase. One reason for selecting the site, wrote Codman, was that the owners were willing to sell on a "very small cash payment and take a 5 years bond for any balance due – a matter of importance to all whose capital was limited and needed for improvement."[18]

The map of Modern Times shows a grid of eight avenues running west to east crossed by seven streets running north to south; the track of the Long Island Railroad forms the diagonal northern border of the otherwise rectangular village. Avenues and streets are numbered beginning with "First" and proceeding in order. There are 220 lots, all one acre square except for seven sliced smaller by the angle between the railroad track and First Avenue.[19]

Codman remarked that Modern Times was "laid out on a generous scale, the streets being 56 ft. and the avenues 82½ ft. in width which shows a clear foresight of future and convenience. [P]lotting was so arranged that each acre was a corner lot having a frontage on a street and avenue; and [not] until 1890 was there more than one house on an acre, a great desideration in the matter of light air and disposal of sewage."[20]

With Andrews handling the legal papers and Warren "on the ground" as an early resident, the sale of lots began in the spring of 1851 on the premise of cost the limit of price. Applicants required approval by Andrews, William Metcalf, or, in their absence, any one of the first ten pioneers—a practice soon dropped because screening and sovereignty did not jibe. Each square block contained four of the one-acre lots; no buyer could purchase more than three, "as the object is not agriculture on the large scale, but a town of diversified occupations. The amount of land thus limited is ample for gardening purposes, play and pleasure-grounds, retiracy [sic], fresh air, etc. Those who desire to procure farms can do so in the neighborhood of the town."[21]

The expounders of equitable commerce preferred truck gardens to sizeable farms, and a closely knit community to the isolation of rural life. The price of $20 to $22 an acre (covering land, roads, surveys, deeds, and other expenses) was, in Warren's words, "the whole price—nothing in the shape of profit or speculation has any place in the operations of the 'Cost' principle."[22] Breaking up and removing stumps and roots, the backbreaking work called grubbing, was a chore that underfinanced but sinewy sovereigns did themselves or contracted with Curran Swaim, "the one who undertakes that business. The price per acre . . . to make all clear, ready for cultivation, is thirty dollars."[23] "A Card—To the Public" announced to all "who are desirous of bettering their conditions in life by escaping from hostile competition and obtaining *and retaining* for themselves the full results of their own labor, that an opportunity is presented, at this point, such as we believe exists nowhere else."[24]

The sale of the lands that became Modern Times requited Peck's devotion to "the improvement of the immense plains now lying almost waste and sterile in the centre of the Island, on either side of the railroad."[25] His purchases, wrote the doctor, gave "the first market value to these lands, that they ever had beyond the value of the wood on them."[26] Ironically, his vindicators practiced cost the limit of price, an economic system that repudiated market value in favor of even exchange.

THE LONG ISLAND RAILROAD

When invited to spend a weekend at Modern Times in 1858, Moncure Daniel Conway resolved to find the village, starting out "with the mere knowledge that it was on Long Island, not being sure whether a place where people attended to their own affairs and did without money was to be reached by railway or rainbow."[27] In Conway's vivid phrase the "railway" for reaching Modern Times was as air-built as its inception as was the "rainbow" of equitable commerce.

The Long Island Railroad's promoters dreamed of filling the New York–to–Boston gap in the chain of railways stretching from the Carolinas to Maine. They did not anticipate competition after their engineers assured them that "no direct rail line could ever be built along the Connecticut shore between Boston and New York because of the numberless bays, inlets, rivers, and hills."[28] When the line incorporated in April 1834 by special act of the New York State Legislature, investors snapped up the capital stock of $1,500,000 at $50 a share.[29] The company commenced to lay a single track from South Ferry, Brooklyn, to Greenport ninety-five miles to the east. Stalled at Hicksville in 1837 because of a nationwide financial crisis, construction resumed in 1840, revived by a $100,000 loan secured by the credit of New York State.

Once pushed through the forest from Hardscrabble (Farmingdale) to Deer Park, the track reached Thompson's Station on 24 June 1842, and Suffolk Station (North Islip) three weeks later. On 29 July 1844 a crew of laborers driving eastward met another working west from Greenport, to hammer home the "golden spike" at Punk's Hole, an inelegant name quickly upgraded to Manorville.[30] From the terminal at Greenport, palatial steamers rented from "Commodore" Cornelius Vanderbilt ferried passengers and freight across the Sound to Stonington, where the New York, Providence and Boston Railroad whisked them off to Boston. A fortune awaited the bold investors: the trip that took sixteen hours by water was reduced to eleven and one-half, or less.[31]

To the delight of the stockholders, business flourished. Suddenly, the New York and New Haven Railroad, ignoring reports that it could not be done, constructed a line on the mainland. Opened for traffic on 28 December 1848, it ran west from New Haven through Bridgeport, Stamford, Greenwich, Rye, and Mount Vernon to Williams Bridge (a part of Westchester County later annexed to the Bronx), where it merged with the New York and Harlem line to run south to its Manhattan terminus at 27th Street and Fourth Avenue.[32] The new route did not reduce traveling time, but was so much more convenient that "the tide of traffic at once turned." Whether the cause of the Long Island Railroad's downfall was competition, inefficiency, loss of its ferry leases, or general financial incompetence, "by 1850, the Long Island Railroad had been forced into receivership."[33]

When planning the route of the Long Island Railroad, the promoters ignored the needs of Long Islanders. Almost all of Suffolk County's 37,000 people lived on or near Long Island Sound or Great South Bay. Linked to the outside world by a few single-lane dirt roads — rutted at best or mudlogged at worst — and dependent on their boats to transport themselves and their products, they made ideal prospects for train service. But the company, beguiled by visions of easy wealth, regarded Long Island not as the reason for its existence but only as a conduit from one source of revenue to another. Rejecting the route of the North or South shores where the people dwelt, it built the line four to six miles inland from the southern coast because this was the fastest and easiest course: "It would follow the northern edge of that smooth apron of glacial outwash that slopes gradually from the hills of the terminal moraine to the sea . . . The handicap of passing through an unsettled region would be more than counter-balanced by the increasing speed that could be developed by fast trains in passing over flat country with neither hills nor rivers to obstruct."[34]

Not only did management disdain its natural clientele, it enraged the people who lived near its tracks, especially where they emerged from the barrens onto the settled farmlands of Riverhead. Nathaniel S. Prime told of engine-sparked forest fires "eight or ten miles in length, and from two to four in breadth . . . [that devoured] . . . every vestige of vegetation [plus] thousands of cords of wood . . . cut and piled . . . and . . . hundreds of deer and rabbits, and other game."[35] Angered by losses of fuel, livestock, and game on which they depended for meat, many residents turned to sabotage, halted in 1845 by the company's partial payment of damages. This begrudged concession eased but failed to erase hostility for the railroad desperately in need of good will, now that it abruptly had changed from a through to a local carrier.

From Hicksville to Greenport the only regular stops were Farmingdale and Manorville — to replenish fuel and water. All others were flag stops, with mail dropped and passengers let on or off, by request. Such a whistle-stop was Thompson's Station, four miles east of Deer Park in the frontier wilds of the town of Islip. Leased, not built, by the railroad, Thompson's Station was the bailiwick of the local land baron, Francis Moses Asbury Wicks, the grantor of Dr. Peck's purchase. Named for the Thompsons of Sagtikos Manor,[36] this large farmhouse "served as Railway Depot, Post Office, Telegraph Office, Tavern and store." Wicks, a seventh-generation Long Islander, "was also Justice of the Peace and County Treasurer."[37]

It took ten years from the receivership of 1850 until a reorganized Long Island Railroad mounted a serious drive for settlers along its empty line. But at the beginning, as a result of the chain reaction set off by Dr. Peck and his land sales, Josiah Warren and Stephen Pearl Andrews stopped off the train at Thompson's Station one autumn day in 1850 to contract for Modern Times. The land was available, the price was right, the climate was healthful, and the soil, although disparaged, was tillable. Thompson's Station was near enough to the city for possible settlers to reach it easily, but far enough not to become a mere satellite of the metropolis. In the words of Peck, the positive thinker,

> The Long Island Railroad passes directly through the uncultivated parts of the Island—thereby affording easy and certain access during the whole year, having, in this respect, a great advantage over even those places on the coast or bays that are esteemed the most valuable—for by the Railroad the market can be reached at all seasons and at all times, without reference to wind or tide, and unobstructed by ice, as the bays and harbors are for three months in a year.[38]

In his study of individual anarchism in America, James J. Martin observes Warren's acquaintance with "prominent land reformers in New York"—among them George Henry Evans and Lewis Masquerier. Their ideas may have helped him to detect the usually ignored fact that "the rush of land-hungry to the new areas of Iowa and Minnesota now and then by-passed pockets of relatively inaccessible soil which the railroads subsequently opened up . . . Long Island was one of them, an incident which followed this expansion of transportation."[39]

Impressive to prospective sovereigns was the founders' claim to one hundred acres, with an option on six or seven hundred more, "lying across the track of one of the railroads running from this city, within four miles of the ocean, and about forty distant from New York."[40] "A Card—To the Public" pointedly stated that "the undersigned are citizens of 'Modern Times' . . . two hours ride from New York upon the Long Island Railroad."[41]

The placing of Modern Times in a remote and empty woodland near the whistle-stop of Thompson's Station served three separate but simultaneous interests. It was the first new community on the track of an bankrupt railroad hungry for passengers, freight, and settlements now that its moment of interstate glory was over. By their cultivation of lands rejected as useless, the sovereigns of Modern Times proved Dr. Peck's faith in the region's fertility, even if their demonstration made little impression on the shoretropic residents of Long Island. Finally, at a time when the tide of emigration flowed west, Modern Times was an eastward movement of pioneers to the inland forest opened serendipitously by the failure of the Long Island Railroad.

JOSIAH WARREN

Josiah Warren was not a charismatic father figure like George Rapp, Robert Owen, or John Humphrey Noyes. Low-key in style, he put projects in motion and left them once they were on their feet. Nonetheless, Moncure Conway was struck by the sovereigns' respect for the founder, "to embody whose ideas the village had been established. He was a short, thick-set man, about fifty years of age [Warren was fifty-nine], with a bright, restless blue eye . . . He was fluent, eager, and entirely absorbed in his social ideas."[42]

With his Yankee bent for making things work, Josiah Warren could as easily build a town, a house, or a printing press. The creator of equitable commerce and the prime mover in both of its working models was also an inventor of stereotyping and printing devices, a player and teacher of music, and the developer of two systems of shorthand for musical notation.[43]

A seventh-generation New Englander, he descended from Pilgrim and Puritan first-comers—Richard Warren, a passenger on the *Mayflower*, and John Warren, of Watertown, who arrived on board the *Ar-*

bella with the Furitan fleet in 1630. Lyman O. Warren, M.D., a first cousin, three times removed, compiled the ancestry of the man he called "Josiah the Reformer."[44] Josiah would admire his kinsman's three years of research but balk at the nickname "Reformer," a designation he assigned to supporters of combined, not individual, efforts. The Peaceful Revolutionist wanted to rebuild society, not repair it. "I really object to being called a *Reformer*," he wrote in 1854, "for no word is less calculated to place me in the position which I now choose to occupy." Equitable commerce is "*not* like any thing heretofore known or proposed as a *Reform* movement—it is exactly opposite to Community of property or partnership interests of any kind."[45]

He was born in Boston on a day in 1798 as obscure as that on which he married Caroline Cutter twenty years later. According to a biographical sketch by George William Warren, his only son, all that is known of his early years is that Josiah and his brother George "joined the 'Old Boston Brigade Band' while very young." Josiah and Caroline Warren left Boston in 1820 to make their home in Cincinnati, at that time a frontier outpost. There Josiah taught music and manufactured a lamp of his own invention that burned lard instead of the more expensive oil or tallow.[46]

In 1824 the Harmony Society—its members known as Rappites in honor of George Rapp, their leader—decided to sell its Indiana village and move to Pennsylvania. Robert Owen, a British textile magnate with a vision of social democracy, paid $150,000 for Harmony, the Rappites' thriving community on the banks of the Wabash River. Owen took possession of 30,000 acres of rolling downs, ideal for wine-growing, grain, or grazing, and endowed with timber, a quarry, water-power, and 150 houses.[47] Promptly renaming the village New Harmony, he proposed to build "a halfway house on this new journey from poverty to wealth," a temporary residence until "we . . . can fully prepare ourselves for . . . that period when there shall be no artificial inequality among the whole human race."[48]

At his mill at New Lanark, Scotland, Owen proved that a capitalist could prosper as much as or more than his greedier peers while eschewing the low wages, long hours, excessive child labor, and harsh conditions considered part and parcel of the early industrial revolution. Europe's elite sought his counsel but recoiled at his proposal for Villages of Cooperation, the self-sustaining units of eight hundred to twelve hundred people that he hoped to organize, along socialist lines, to abolish all forms of oppression. After deciding to sell his New La- nark holdings, he set out for the United States, where the power of birth and rank was not chiseled in stone: "I am come to this country," he proclaimed, "to introduce an entire new state of society."[49] The im- portance attached to his mission resulted in Owen's addressing two joint sessions of Congress in March 1825, also attended by President James Monroe and his cabinet, President-elect John Quincy Adams, and the justices of the Supreme Court.

Warren heard the persuasive reformer speak in Cincinnati, late in 1824. Owen's invitation to the "industrious and well-disposed" so impressed Josiah that he sold his lamp factory, and, "with about eight hundred other persons went to New Harmony . . . with Robert Owen, to assist in reconstructing society upon the the the plan of *common prop- erty* proposed by that gentleman."[50]

Together with Owen, Owen's capable sons, and a team of scien- tists and educators known as the "boatland of knowledge,"[51] Warren enlisted in the task of changing the former model of Bible communism into a secular New Jerusalem. For two years he served the New Har- mony Community of Equals as its music teacher and orchestra leader.

No other ideal community began as auspiciously as New Har- mony, endowed with the funds and genius of the world's leading lib- eral industrialist, and listing among its settlers a brilliant assortment of intellectuals from the schools and laboratories of Europe and the United States. Unfortunately, the settlement foundered two years later, wrecked by internal dissension. Robert Owen's stated belief in equal- ity conflicted with his stubborn retention of ownership and decision making; moreover, too many of "the eight hundred other persons" were sloths seeking the founder's bounty, rather than beavers with the will and training to form a self-sufficient township. The very success of New Lanark, Scotland, presaged the opposite outcome in Indiana, U.S.A. Scottish peasants turned factory workers became a docile and easily-managed constituency, expecting little and happy with any im- provement over the deprivation they took for granted. The New Lanark mill hands, not inclined to question their social superiors, were grate- ful for favors, unlike restless frontier Americans bred on revolution and emerging into the age of Jackson—a time when common folk de- manded the benefits of equality on an unprecedented scale. Owen kept the title to land and paid all the bills, digging constantly deeper into his dwindling fortune to feed his flock and keep them supplied when debits exceeded receipts. He came to Indiana with assets of $250,000, four-fifths of which he lost because of the gap between premise and performance.

The workshops and fields of the Rappites were never used efficiently; unlike the resourceful Harmonists, the new owner gave too little thought to recruiting the farmers and mechanics needed for trading with the outside world. In addition, the more affluent and mentally gifted minority—who tended to look down on the uneducated rank and file—kept bickering with Owen over ownership and control, resulting in seven different constitutions and three separate subcommunities parallel to the central settlement. As an exercise in communalism, New Harmony survived only from the spring of 1825 until it self-destructed two years later.

At New Harmony, Warren whetted his interest in ideal villages, inspired by Owen's passion for social justice but repelled by his mentor's paternalism. An Owenite innovation that Warren adapted for wider use was the concept of the labor note, used at New Harmony as a medium of exchange between the several subcommunities. The vocational school, another New Harmony breakthrough, may have given Josiah the idea for the Mechanical College—or trade school—that he introduced at Modern Times.[52] But communism, to Warren, was a blueprint imposed upon subjects by managers self-endowed with infallible knowledge of what to do. Whatever its ideology, any community run by leaders and governed by rules threatened liberty. Warren charged New Harmony's failure to Owen's top-down style of leadership, and to the principle of combination which stifled personal initiative. "Where all the interests of life are involved in a combination," he stated, "*there* will be found the minimum of individual FREEDOM . . . as harmony and progress are impossible without *freedom*, neither . . . can be attained in any other proportion than as interests are *disintegrated* or *Individualized* . . . directly opposite . . . to the plan of combined or united interests in which we had just been defeated."[53]

Although "most of the [New Harmony] experimenters left in despair of all reforms," Warren resolved to spend his life in search of equity through individual, rather than delegated, sovereignty. John Humphrey Noyes hit the mark when he wrote that Warren, after witnessing New Harmony's confusions and downfall, eventually "sprang off into the extreme of anti-Communism. The village of 'Modern Times,' where all forms of social organization were scouted as unscientific, was the electric negative of New Harmony."[54]

With New Harmony in the throes of disintegration, Warren returned to Cincinnati in 1827 to open the first of a series of time stores, which he proceeded to test as building blocks for the equity villages he later created. At the same time he learned the printing trade and resumed the teaching of music. In the course of his business, he took a long-term lease on a tract of land in the heart of the city and might have "lived and died a rich man," wrote his son, George W. Warren. However, Josiah by now was well into formulating his doctrine of cost the limit of price. Declining to hold this valuable land for a profit, he "returned the 99 year lease to Mr. [Nicholas] Longworth,"[55] a well-known real estate operator who went on to wealth and political fame. Warren took this action, wrote William Bailie, his first biographer, because of his belief that "the only legitimate title to property is labor," and therefore that money made by a rise in land value "due not to action of the individual owner but to social causes beyond his control, is opposed to the principle of Equity."[56]

Robert Owen's teaching convinced Josiah that people are molded by circumstance and not by the whim of God. But the book that most profoundly influenced Warren was *A Treatise on Language*, an 1828 work by the semanticist and commonsense philosopher, Alexander Bryan Johnson.[57] Johnson's nominalism reinforced Warren's. In 1833, the "Peaceful Revolutionist" informed his readers that

> I use language with a constant regard to its principles as developed by Mr. Johnson . . . I do not intend to enter into any argument where the language does not refer to some sensible "phenomena" . . . Mr. Johnson's elucidation of language is a bridge over which I have escaped from the bewildering labyrinths of verbal delusions called arguments and controversies . . . and I do not expect to recross it but as a free child of a peaceful village would approach the uproar and confusion of a noisy city on a holiday in pursuit of variety.[58]

Warren's first publication, *The Peaceful Revolutionist*, was a newsletter issued in 1833 and sporadically thereafter, which he wrote, printed, and mailed to a short list of subscribers. Ten years later he attempted to widen his influence by disseminating a pamphlet describing the time store he ran at New Harmony (the pleasant little town that succeeded the Owen colony's failure). He also sent an account of the "Cost Principle" to a list of some fifty newspapers culled from a roster of "two hundred (so-called) reform papers." Years afterward he recalled that "never to this day has the author seen the first word of notice of either from any of these leading papers of Reform!" This lack of response convinced him that the reform press could not be relied on to publicize either the time store or the idea behind it, "because none of the newspapers could *make money* by advocating 'Equitable Commerce,' and the author had entirely given up any attempt to get it before the public through the ordinary papers, and depended on disseminating the subject by the means of *Amateur* printing."[59]

Warren himself was no "amateur" printer. His advancement of printing and stereotyping technology would have earned him a fortune had he elected to go into business. Instead, the man who urged people to be their own nation and church encouraged anyone with something to say to be his or her own publisher. The printing press that Warren invented in 1840 for the *Southwestern Sentinel*, of Evansville, Indiana, made it the "first newspaper probably in the world which was printed in a continuous sheet."[60] When the pressmen objected because they feared the invention would cause unemployment, Warren broke up the press and carted the pieces home to New Harmony, where his son later used the stone for his doorsill. The commercially successful Hoe press was similar to the innovative rotary press, which Warren never patented. On 25 April 1846, however, the year in which plates made of rubber first appeared in the United States, the "first American patent on rubber stereotyping plates" was granted to Warren.[61] This stereotyping device, mixing shellac, tar, and sand, combined with gum arabic, beeswax, stearine, tallow, and oil as a substitute for type metal, was used by the Smithsonian Institution for its first book catalog in 1851, the year Modern Times was founded.

He continued to publish books and newsletters on his homemade equipment, but his writing gained scant recognition until, under Andrews's editorial guidance, his books were published by Fowlers and Wells, the underground press of its day.[62] The disdain or outright hostility of most editors for his ideas and activities soured Warren toward the newspapers: the *Circular*, issued at Modern Times in September 1852, warned prospective settlers not to rely on the blundering and inaccurate press for information about the village.[63]

James J. Martin traces the progression of *Equitable Commerce*, from its issuance in 1847 (dated 1846 on its title page) when Warren lived at New Harmony, through a second edition in 1849 datelined Utopia, Warren's equity village on the Ohio River frontier, to the 1852 edition edited and with a preface by Andrews, which at once became the standard version. According to Martin, the book was "the first important publication of anarchistic doctrine in America, and with minor deletions, additions, and revisions, went into more editions within the next thirty years than any other product of native anarchist thought to this time."[64]

Also in 1852, Fowlers and Wells published Warren's *Practical Details in Equitable Commerce*, a "how-to" companion to the more theoretical *Equitable Commerce*. *Practical Details*, a key source for the study of Modern Times, contains a preface by Andrews explaining the terms for becoming a settler and reprints the text of *Circular*, with the names of the twenty-six pioneers who signed it. As a learner's guide to equity, *Practical Details* records Warren's doings from the opening of his Cincinnati time store in 1827 to the eve of Utopia's founding, twenty years later.

These decades witnessed both the demise of Owenite villages in the United States and the sunburst, followed by the swift decline, of Fourierist Association. Warren observed that the average Phalanx lasted for "about two years and a half." Now that the spate of secular ideal villages "commenced in the last impulse had been given up, and the field of reform appeared again to be almost unoccupied," the time had come to demonstrate equitable commerce: "such was the evident and frightful progress toward inevitable confusion, that it seemed almost criminal not suddenly to disengage from all other pursuits, and plunge into the arena, and do whatever might be done.[65]

Editors of reform periodicals shunned his ideas for decades, during which many potential sovereigns, thought Warren, were deflected to Fourierism. Now, at last, "simple *Equity* might obtain a hearing, provided it were not too late to offer it." The "Peaceful Revolutionist" vented his passion for justice: "Remedy is the demand of the age! Remedy will now be listened to, but it must be REMEDY! Words alone will no longer supply the demand—Homes for the Homeless! food for the starving! clothing for the naked! EQUITY for all!"

In Warren's judgment, Fourierism, Owenism, and all kindred movements that aimed for this remedy erroneously proceeded on the "false basis of Combination." Impossible. The task of "a few pioneers" was to mount a new solution "based on INDIVIDUALITY" and set it in "practical form before the public."[66]

The gospel of equitable commerce, with Modern Times as a living model, was spread by the *Periodical Letter*, the sale of books, and the presentations of Warren and Andrews at lectures and parlor gatherings in New York City and Boston. Because he suspected the editors' objectivity, Warren refrained from sending his literature to newspapers for review. The final lines of *Practical Details* address that handbook "to the other end of society—to the followers, rather than to the leaders—to those who wish to learn, rather than to those who profess to know enough already."[67]

At the age of fifty-two, Josiah left the Midwest to test a model village of equity close to a major eastern city. Although his "formulas were the rock on which [Modern Times] was founded," reflects Codman, "Mr. J. Warren was a poor leader. He had no magnetic qualities so needful in persuasion or gaining converts. Also, he was a timid man and hated to wrangle." Were he a more gifted leader and public speaker, "the fortunes of this village and its founders would have been very different." But Codman fails to explain that the concept of "leader" was foreign to Warren, that the "Peaceful Revolutionist" presented his views more effectively in living rooms than in meeting halls, and that his past unhappy experience convinced him not to trust the press. Warren aimed to shield Modern Times from an increasingly sinful reputation as the pulpit of free-love fundamentalism. "Mr. Warren deprecated this phase of agitation," notes Codman, "mainly from fear that this Equity movement might be burried [*sic*] out of sight by that of Freedom [free love]."[68]

The Warrens ceased to live together when Josiah left their New Harmony home. After thirty years of marriage to a peripatetic activist, Caroline tired of wandering. She chose to stay in their comfortable house, near her son who resided in Evansville, while Josiah roamed the countryside sowing the seeds of equity. Perhaps the pressure of the times "has had considerable to do with the breaking up, as it were, of our early association," she wrote to her absentee husband in 1855. "When I most willingly consented to be your wife, and came out West, I gave up relations, friends, acquaintances—all, for the (to me) greater pearl, and never do I remember having a lingering longing look behind . . . for I was fortunately and most happily married." Now the ties with the friends of her youth were cut. If she went back "by a desire to please you" she would feel out of her element, just as one of the "large old trees that grow on the common in Boston" would die if transplanted. Josiah would not fully appreciate this sentiment "because you have for years been a citizen of the world, and in fact, been receding from my views and habits, mentally, morally, and physically: we have receded from each other in most things, and our judgments must be individual."[69]

Far less poignant was a letter of Caroline's written during the following summer. Commenting on Josiah's plan to expand the *Periodical Letter*, she tartly remarked that "Your P. L. is good; but your proposition to enlarge it etc. meets with my—objections, as usual. *You* are not *made* of the right material, to even *make* it pay cost, *it*, that is, a paper of any kind or book either, with you is an *out*lay, not an *income*." Call this judgment whatever you please, she added, "I think it is sensible."[70]

Separated but never divorced, the Warrens remained on distantly friendly terms, each giving the other the power of attorney for real estate dealings, Caroline in New Harmony and Josiah in the East. Warren's marriage to his work undoubtedly took precedence over his loyalty to Caroline. Little is known of his romantic life apart from his wife, but if he had a feeling for any woman at Modern Times, it was probably for one Mrs. Jane Cran.

On the 1852 *Circular*, linking names of spouses or housemates, the final two signers were Jane Cran and Josiah Warren. In a letter of 5 January 1852 from Warren at Modern Times to Andrews in Manhattan, Josiah was pleased to inform his partner that he had "just been treating myself and Mrs. Cran with another reading of your first glorious work, and what a treat it is!"[71] Five days later came the news that "Mrs. Cran is reading your work on the "*Cost principle*, and is exceedingly interested in it. She has paid it several compliments—Last night she said with a great deal of emphasis, looking up from the book.

'Well, I am sure whoever reads *this* will get paid for their time.'"[72]

People who read at night together tend to be more than casual friends. On the strength of the letters—the only proof of her existence—Mrs. Cran was divorced, separated, or widowed, with several grown children. On 31 March, Warren announced that she wanted to purchase back-to-back lots—"one for her children to be divided among them," which he thought was "a very pretty and desirable thing."[73] In spite of his efforts to help her, he complained a month later that both acres had been sold to Mr. [Peter] Blacker, with the connivance of Mr. [William] Metcalf. "Mrs. Cran is so hurt at the injustice she has received in different ways from Mr. Metcalf" that if maneuvered out of the property "she will leave the place." Laced with hostility for Metcalf, who apparently wanted to be Modern Times's official "screener" of applicants during the phase in which charter householders had this option, the letter ended with the determined postscript "Peace for the peaceful—'fight' for fighters."[74]

By 4 July, Mrs. Cran scaled down her bid from two lots to one, because of her "uncertain prospects here." Warren hoped that someone would reimburse him for the $20 he had advanced for the cost of opening "the avenue" so that he could use it "to pay for a lot for Mrs. Cran."[75]

What happened from then on is shrouded in darkness: no deed, census, or other record links Jane Cran to Modern Times. If she lived with Warren during the first winter and second spring, her stay was short and their union uncertain. In any case, it would seem that the real romance in Josiah's life was with equitable commerce.

During his years at Modern Times, Warren traveled—mainly to Boston—but kept returning to Long Island until he packed up and left for the last time in 1862. His health declined in his later years, but he maintained his interest in typography, music, and equitable commerce. After several quiet years at Cliftondale, near Boston, wrote William Bailie, Warren moved into the home of "his friends, Mr. and Mrs. [Ezra] Heywood, at Princeton, Massachusetts" in 1873. Warren suffered from dropsy late in life and was forced to curtail his movements. He spent his final months in Charlestown, across the river from Boston, "at the house of his early friend Edward H. Linton," where he died at the age of seventy-six on 14 April 1874. Josiah was nursed in his final illness by Kate Metcalf, a Modern Times pioneer.[76]

STEPHEN PEARL ANDREWS

Stephen Pearl Andrews (1812–1886), the radically unconventional son of a nonconformist Baptist minister, grew up in western Massachusetts and was educated at Amherst College. In 1850 this erudite lawyer, abolitionist, reformer, linguist, phonologist (shorthand expert), philosopher, and defender of woman's rights met Josiah Warren, converted from Fourierism, and became Warren's editor and partner in the promotion of equitable commerce and the founding of Modern Times.

Andrews was more learned than Warren, with broader interests. He lent his talents to many causes other than equity, including freethought, the abolition of slavery, and the teaching of freedmen to read (with the aid of the Pitman method of shorthand, which he was the first to bring from England and promulgate in the United States). The master of thirty-two languages, he created one of his own called Alwato, which he intended to be a world-uniting language for his philosophy of "Universology."[77]

Andrews was not cut out to play second fiddle in Warren's band — or anyone else's. Although he was indispensable to the formation of Modern Times as a speaker, writer, and attorney for real estate transactions, he and his wife Mary chose to remain in their Manhattan home instead of living at the village. In 1855 he opened the League of the Men of Progress, a secret club of men — and women — who paid admission to meetings at which they debated controversial subjects from equity commerce to free love. According to Madeleine B. Stern, his biographer, "Every member was an individual sovereign though the sovereign of all the individuals was Pearl Andrews."[78]

The Grand Order of Recreation, a subgroup split off from the League, was a social club where people met, danced, and held discussions at 555 Broadway, three flights over Taylor's Saloon. Both the *Times* and the *Tribune* assailed the Grand Order for its consideration of lawless principles "known by the general name of Individual Sovereignty," and then putting them into practice "especially in the sexual relations." On a night when Andrews chanced to be at home, sick, and his friend Albert Brisbane was in the chair, the police raided the club, seized its receipts, and arrested its patrons on grounds of disorderly conduct and other trumped-up counts. All charges were dropped on the following day, but the organization was done for. "The Grand Order of Recreation, tarred with slander, had gone the way of Modern Times,"[79] wrote Ms. Stern somewhat hyperbolically; Modern Times, although tarred with slander, was far from "gone" in 1855.

Andrews, the would-be philosopher-king, conceived another way to realize his dream of freedom and brotherhood five years later. "On the ruins of Modern Times and the Grand Order of Recreation he would build yet another community of individual sovereigns," not deep in the woods, or over a barroom, but on East 14th Street near Union Square. The Unitary Home, a complex of four connected brownstones, was a cooperative boarding house run on the precepts of individual sovereignty and cost the limit of price. It soon evolved into the Pantarchy, "a Grand Composite Order of Government, reaching with its influences every department of human affairs."[80] J. T. Trowbridge, a popular novelist of the time, recounted Andrews's vain attempt to recruit him for the Pantarchy, that "'infinite Republic . . . [constituting] organized and orderly operation in all the affairs' of all the nations of the earth," by the power vested in one central person, "the Pantarch; and the Pantarch was Mr. Stephen Pearl Andrews."[81] Grander in scope than number, the Pantarchy, in which society would be a chain of industrial and social groups and series, was founded on the work of "earlier sociologists, and especially upon the far abler writings of Fourier," Andrews's primary mentor.[82]

Later on, Andrews served both as an editorial writer and as a columnist pleading the Pantarchy's cause in *Woodhull and Claflin's Weekly*, a muckraking, suffragist newspaper published for six years beginning in 1870 by the impassioned Victoria Woodhull and her equally feisty sister, Tennessee Claflin. Andrews advised and wrote speeches for "The Woodhull" during her short but colorful campaign for President of the United States in 1872. Andrews translated the *Communist Manifesto* and, in December 1871, gave it its first American publication in *Woodhull and Claflin's Weekly*; after he and the dynamic sisters helped to form Section Twelve of the First International, they clashed with Karl Marx and were promptly expelled for heretically giving "precedence to the women's question over the question of labor." Marx personally denounced Victoria Woodhull for agitating "'the woman's franchise and . . . all sorts of nonsense,' such as free love."[83]

In support of the separation of church and state, Andrews and a group of his freethinking colleagues, in 1875, prevailed on President

Ulysses S. Grant to include in his message to Congress "the famous . . . paragraph [suggesting] taxation of all property equally, whether church or corporation."[84]

Charled Codman ranked Andrews ahead of Warren as Modern Times's "best advocate, both with his voice and pen for some years, but his interest waned";[85] the restless Pantarch was too self-centered to stay in a movement peripheral to his purpose. At issue are neither his brilliance nor failings, but whether he helped or hindered the village's growth. His *Science of Society* gave equitable commerce the intellectual content that Warren's homespun writing lacked. Presenting sovereignty of the individual as the love child of Protestantism and democracy, Andrews endowed it as the rightful heir of Luther, Locke, Paine, and Jefferson (as shown in chapter 5 below). But his linking of Warren's system to socialism was awkward and inappropriate, stemming from Andrews's allegiance to Fourier, his first and always mentor. For all of his casuistry, not even the Pantarch could dovetail lthe Associationist mode of combination with anarchism. By inviting the Nicholses to come to Long Island, and choosing anti-marriage as the paramount cause for which Modern Times stood, he exposed the young village to public censure it never lived down.

Andrews outdid Warren in formal learning and worldly knowledge; his editorial, speaking, and legal skills served Modern Times well in its formative years. But if Warren needed a partner—a relationship which seems contradictory to that of uncombined individualism—he needed one whose commitment to equitable commerce superseded all his others. The volatile Andrews varied his interests rather than hewing to only one.

Although a staunch spokesman for the village, he narrowed his vision of Modern Times from a model village of social justice to a specialized community formed to defy the institution of marriage. Thus, the forceful and eloquent Andrews sometimes worked at cross purposes from Warren. Before Modern Times could sink its roots, it wilted under the glare of scandal. The Pantarch of the Grand Pantarchy might have offered to come out for or against the Peaceful Revolutionist, whichever would do his colleague more good.

3

Homes for the Homeless

THE FIRST FIFTEEN ACRES OF MODERN TIMES were spoken for on
30 January 1851, in a sparingly punctuated agreement between
"Mrs. Catherine Fleet of the City and State of New York wife
of Samuel Fleet the first part and Josiah Warren of Utopia Clermont
County Ohio Mary A. Andrews Henry Wilson William Hayward and
Samuel R. Wells of the firm of Fowlers, Wells, and Horace Greeley all
of the said City of New York and William Metcalf of the City of Brooklyn of the second part."[1]

Mary Anne Andrews (Mrs. Stephen Pearl Andrews), William Metcalf, Josiah Warren, Samuel R. Wells, and Henry Wilson contracted
for one acre each, William Hayward for three, and Horace Greeley for
seven. The seven charter buyers received a five-year option on one hundred acres at $15 an acre, plus an "extra charge for streets and proving
their deed"; subsidiary agreements extended the option to seven hundred acres. A sprightly, informative feature story on Modern Times
appeared in the fall of 1853 in the *New York Sunday Dispatch*. "B. D. J.",
the reporter, quoted Metcalf on the terms arranged with the grantors:

> S. P. Andrews, of New York, is our agent—the parties who own
> the land live in New York. Mr. Andrews has their bond, condi-
> tioned to execute good and sufficient deeds to members on pay-
> ment of the original price, $15 per acre. The other charges will
> bring the price up to $17 per acre—next year it will be $18, and
> so on. Each member purchases one half the street or avenue op-
> posite his property which will further enhance the price [to] about
> $20 per acre. We think this cheap.[2]

Pearl and Mary Andrews neither resided nor spent much time "on
the ground." There is no further record pertaining to their lot number
28

74, on the northwest corner of Fifth Street and Second Avenue, for which they paid Catherine Fleet $18.875 (fractions of cents were common in Suffolk County deeds). In the fall of 1854, Mary Andrews paid $23 for lot 139, on the opposite corner, only to sell it the following spring for the same sum of $23, a classic illustration of cost the limit of price.[3]

Two of the charter buyers defaulted: Samuel R. Wells, of Fowlers and Wells (the firm that published Warren's and Andrews's books), and Henry Wilson, whose name does not reappear in connection with Modern Times. It is possible, however, that another friend of equity commerce took up one of these acres. Lot 64, at the corner of Second Avenue and Fourth Street adjoining the Andrews's lot 74, was bought by "Edward N. Kellogg, of New York City" on 4 April 1851, the same day that Hayward, Greeley, Metcalf, Warren, and Mrs. Andrews fulfilled their purchase contracts of 30 January.[4]

Verne Dyson, Brentwood's historian, describes William Hayward as a well-to-do business man, "a prominent resident . . . who was not in sympathy with the ideals and practices of the founders." By stating that Hayward retired to Modern Times in 1860 and "bought four acres on Third and Fourth Avenues at Fifth Street," Dyson seemed unaware that Hayward was a charter buyer who acquired his two (not four) acres—lots 68 and 78—in 1851.[5] Perhaps his friend, William Metcalf, informed Hayward of the projected village, impelling him to buy the lots in hopes of making a sound investment.

The Metcalfs and Haywards were English. Mrs. Sophia E. Hayward, the wife of William Hayward's brother, separated from her husband and crossed the ocean to Long Island "to meet her wealthy kinsman; but he did not take kindly to her. He, however, was friendly with William Metcalf, her suitor."[6] Suitor is a euphemism because Mrs. Hayward and William Metcalf lived together from the day they arrived at Modern Times when he was thirty-four years old and she was ten years older. With them lived his spinster sisters—Jane, thirty-seven, and Sarah, thirty-six—and his younger brother John (who became Henry Edger's acolyte in the quixotic mission of making Modern Times the American shrine of religious positivism). At long last Sophia and William appear as husband and wife on a deed recorded in 1887, thirty-six years after the village's birth.[7] Their long and stable cohabitation shows that the charge of promiscuity often leveled at Modern Timers is not necessarily so.

HORACE GREELEY

Curiously, no historian or biographer cites the name of Horace Greeley as a charter buyer at Modern Times. Not even in their debate in
his paper, the *New York Tribune,* does he or Andrews refer to his purchase of seven acres.[8] It is puzzling why Greeley, without an anarchistic bone in his body, decided to be a ground-floor investor in an
antistatist experiment. Perhaps, like Hayward, he bought land at Modern Times because he knew a good buy when he saw one. Another
explanation is that this spokesman for democratic reform was, in the
mid-1840s, an ardent supporter and publicist of the ideal village movement. He and Albert Brisbane imported Fourierism from France and,
with Greeley's *Tribune* as their organ, promoted it in the United States
under the name of Associationism.[9] By the time of Modern Times's
creation, Greeley's zeal for Fourierism cooled, his prodigious energy
harnessed to the cause of land reform, especially to the enactment of
legislation giving public land to homesteaders.

Although he favored organized rather than individual action, he
may have invested in Modern Times in sympathy with Warren's goal
of enabling settlers of limited means to own land and a house. In *Hints
Toward Reforms*—published by Fowlers and Wells in 1851, the year of
Modern Times's formation—Greeley trumpeted his belief in equal opportunity for the poor and lowly: "A single law of Congress, proffering
to each landless citizen a patch of the Public Domain . . . would promote immensely the independence, enlightenment, morality, industry,
and comfort of our entire laboring population evermore."[10]

Greeley shared Warren's belief in homes for the homeless and
sought to achieve it by passage of the Homestead Act, which he was
the first to introduce while serving an interim term in Congress in 1848.
The bill was moot on Long Island, which had no public domain; in
any case, Modern Timers did without governmental solutions in favor
of do-it-yourself initiative of individual sovereigns. Yet their aims, if
not their methods, coincided with Greeley's condemnation of selling
land "as mere merchandise, like molasses or mackerel." They surely
would have given a resounding "Yes" to his rhetorical question, "And
is the time not at hand when every free citizen shall have his own home
if he will?"[11] There is nothing inconsistent in Greeley's silent partner-

ship in a settlement of "Go east, young man [and young woman]" pioneers.

The baffling aspect of Greeley's purchase of seven lots at Modern Times is that none of the outspoken people involved took public note of his presence on the list of primal grantees. On 4 April 1851 he completed his agreement by paying Catherine Fleet the sum of $133 to cover $105 for land, $21.62 "for avenues," and $6.125 for the survey certificate and records—in "lawful money of the United States of America"—for which she "granted, bargained, sold, aliened, remised, released, conveyed, and confirmed . . . Lots 6, 7, 31, 32, 33, 71 and 81 . . . in said village of Modern Times."[12]

THE PIONEERS

Of the seven present at the creation, only Metcalf and Warren braved the hardships of frontier life in the spring of 1851. In his memoir, Warren recalled the beginning: "One man [William Metcalf] went on the ground alone, and built a little shanty, ten or twelve feet square. There was not, at that time, even a cowpath in sight, among the scrub oaks that were everywhere breast-high."[13]

This confirms Charles Codman's account of the tract, "from which all the wood, shortly before, had been removed and hardly a tree over 6 ft. in height was in sight, but scrub oaks were plentiful, taking the place of the original growth of Pine and Oaks." Building material was scarce, but Warren's ingenious method of making bricks out of sun-dried mortar, combined with the savings accomplished by swapping instead of paying for labor, brought the cost of constructing houses within the means of people who otherwise could not afford them. There was, recalled Warren, nothing on the land to make lumber of, and even the winter fuel (coal) had to be brought from the city. Even with these drawbacks, "houses seemed to go up . . . without means: and *those who never had homes of their own before, suddenly had them* [emphasis added]."[14] The provision of homes to the homeless was the Law and the Prophets of Modern Times.

Codman, too, recalled the first building, a log cabin put up by the Metcalf ménage in the early summer of 1851 on the southeast corner of Fifth Street and Fourth Avenue. "In the course of the following year," he went on, "a Dozen or more families had joined."[15]

In a letter to the London *Leader*, Henry Edger shared with English readers his knowledge of Modern Times, which he carefully inspected long before he decided to join. Soon after the first house was begun, he reported, "Mr. Warren went down and built a house, subsequently sold 'at cost'—*i.e.*, money for what cost money (120 dollars, I believe), and labor for labor. The purchaser is a good practical mechanic, a smith and boilermaker; but like most Yankees, able to turn his hand to anything, and in particular is a well-skilled carpenter."[16]

The buyer was Benjamin Franklin Bowles, another jack-of-all-trades and one of the "two clergymen who had left the pulpit to assist in the Equity Movement."[17] His name appeared in a "A Card—To the Public," an 1853 advertisement in the *Tribune* referring potential settlers to Warren at Modern Times, Andrews at 49 Dey Street, New York, or any of its four signers, all residing at Modern Times:

Robert Gray, late Congregational Pastor, Boonton, N.J.

William Metcalf, late merchant, Brooklyn, N.Y.

B. F. Bowles, late Universalist Pastor, Southbridge, Mass.

T. C. Leland, Phonographic [shorthand] Reporter.[19]

Edger's estimate of the price was wrong: Bowles and his wife Mary Ellen paid $200, not $120, for lot 76 with "all premises," on the corner of Third Avenue and Fifth Street.[19] Warren at once set to work on a new building on the eastern part of lot 59, at the corner of Fourth Avenue and Fourth Street (one of the few transfers of less than an acre) for which he paid Catherine Fleet $11.0625.[20] Here he lived, ran his time store and print shop, and conducted the "Mechanical College," an early vocational school at which he gave hourly lessons in trades that ranged from printing, stereotyping, bricklaying, brickmaking, and carpentry to the art of instrumental music. The "College" and some of the early houses were built with sun-dried bricks made with sand and gravel from the cellar excavation. After almost twenty years, reported Codman, "Time, wear-and-tear and the ravages of the elements impaired its condition and about 1870 gravitation laid it low."[21] In his letter to the London *Leader*, Henry Edger described it as a "square brick building, thirty-two feet each way, containing two stories and attics. The ground floor is occupied by the time store and several workshops — a smithy, carpenter's shop and printing press. The upper part is dwellings — already in part occupied" by people whose houses were under construction.[22]

Warren understood that gravel or concrete walls were problems, mainly because "of the want of time between the rains to harden or crystalize the mortar." One solution was to let the strength of the building depend on its wooden framework, setting up the "usual studding about two feet apart . . . so that the corners only come to the weather, and filling in between these with the gravel mixture." Another was "to make mortar into brick in the common way and dry them in the sun." But because of weather damage, he doubted that this would be strong enough for "walls unaided by a frame work of wood." They needed some outside coating to keep out the rain, he concluded: "if any correspondent knows of any thing that has been tested and reliable, he will confer a service by communicating it."[23]

Modern Times, reported B. D. J., combined the raw look of a frontier town with the features of individual sovereignty:

> In that open door we see a tinsmith at work: there is a shoemaker. Outside this unfinished building is a whiskered and mustachioed mason [Bowles — spelled Boles by B. D. J.] mixing mortar; and over the way, a tolerably pretty girl with Bloomer pants is sitting in the window with her feet on the sill, trying to poke music out of a common looking banjo! The houses are each one different from its fellow: — they plaster the *outside* and leave the interior unfinished. Some of the roofs are of paper: there are a profusion of sunflowers and crimson princess' feathers. There is no shade — no shrubbery, except the natural scrub oaks — there are no barns, no big woodpiles — no stacks of hay or grain.[24]

Except for the federal census of 1860, the only roster of sovereigns is the September 1852 *Circular*, signed by "every adult citizen on the ground." The list of twenty-six adults is in order of households, with the name of a wife or cohabitant printed under that of her male housemate:

B. F. Bowles,	James D. Blacker,
M. Ellen Bowles,	Eliza S. Blacker,
J. [James] M. Hilton,	William Metcalf,
Sarah C. Hilton,	Sophia E. Hayward,
Benjamin Pierce,	Sarah Metcalf,
Mary J. Pierce,	Jane Metcalf,
Rose Anne Newberry,	John Metcalf,
Robert Gray,	Henry Russell,
Angelina Skinner,	Eliza A. Russell,
William L. Burdick,	G. [George] S. McWatters,
Harriet A. Burdick,	C. [Charlotte] McWatters,
C. [Curran] Swaim,	Jane Cran,
H. [Henry] Swaim,	Josiah Warren.[25]

The *Circular* warned prospective settlers not to rely on the blundering and inaccurate press for information about the village: "Indeed, the subject is so very new, and so immensely extensive, that we do not expect editors, nor any other persons who are absorbed in other pursuits, to study it sufficiently to do it justice . . . the common mode of opposition is in appealing to ignorance and vulgar prejudices." The signers did not want their "principles now unknown to the public" to be interpreted by uninformed, envious, and often defeated hobby-horse riders, venting their spleen on Modern Times. The proper way to obtain understanding of what was too innovative and complex for a "newspaper article or a public lecture" was to read the two basic works on the subject, Andrews's *Science of Society* and Warren's *Equitable Commerce*, available at Fowlers and Wells in New York and Boston, "Prices, 75 cents and 25 cents."[26]

When he returned to Modern Times in 1852, one year after his first visit, Henry Edger marveled at the "great progress" made at "the sturdy young village." In a new letter to the *Leader*, captioned by the editor "Hard Times at Modern Times," he wrote that "Houses of various sizes and styles of architecture from the rude log cabin to the neat and almost elegant cottage residence, were dotted here and there where a year ago I left dismal stunted pines and tough oak brushwood . . . I found gardens that seemed struggling into existence amid the piles of lumber, lime, sand, mortar, bricks . . . lying around every where." The coming cold weather will be less severe than the "Hard Times" of the first winter, which the pioneers intensified by their "horror of Fraternity-

Sentimentalism" (Edger's translation of individual sovereignty) that forced "everyone to shift for himself as best he could." Now the people were "at least better provided with habitations." The time store was open for only one hour a day—"that being the extent of the demand" by a population of "some fifty or sixty souls." At this time, when he had begun to study Comte but was not ready to proselytize for him, Edger commended the Warrenite movement for inspiring its votaries— however few—with a "confidence and zeal that cannot be surpassed, and have, perhaps, seldom been equalled."[27]

By December 1854, Warren estimated "between sixty and seventy inhabitants . . . all told—two or three families expected daily." However, several families left for want of enough employment, while others "refrain from coming," partly because of unfavorable publicity "and partly because of the conduct of professed friends." The problem of Modern Times's future expansion required serious study: "True and healthy growth will be only in proportion as capable minds can be reached, and as we counteract the first crude impressions of news-mongers, and the worshippers of mere novelty."[28]

CRANKS, FADDISTS, AND OTHER BIZARRE "PROFESSED FRIENDS"

The magnet of permissiveness attracted a fringe of cranks and faddists, the "worshippers of mere novelty" who, according to Warren, knew nothing of the principles for which the village stood. When reminiscing about Modern Times, Josiah complained that some early settlers "were full of 'crotchets,'" convinced that the world depended on his or her particular hobby. One man believed children ought not to wear clothes and "inflicted some crazy experiments on his [own] in the coldest weather." A woman picked up the idea "and kept her infant naked in the midst of winter."[29]

The delusions of fanatics mocked "sound theories based on experience." Because expulsion was inconsistent with the principles of equity, settlers whose conduct was obnoxious were given the silent treatment until they left. Stronger action was taken, however, against "a German who was wholly or partly blind and paraded himself naked in the streets, with the theory that it would help his sight. He was stopped by an appeal to the overseer of the Insane Asylum." This restrictive solution, involving the power of outside authority, seems completely contradictory to the doctrine of personal freedom; apparently, public nudity exceeded Modern Times's limit of tolerance. The same "blind" man "saw well enough to take a neighbor's coat from a fence" where its owner (not a resident of Modern Times) was working, leading outsiders to believe that "we were a nest of thieves as well as fanatics." To redeem their reputation the sovereigns distributed "handbills describing the person" and urging neighbors who were missing anything to come to Modern Times "and look for it on his premises." This object lesson, concluded Warren, "placed the responsibility upon him, *Individually,* where it belonged, and put an end to his pilfering."

In another apparent violation of individual rights, Josiah heaped scorn on a female sovereign for wearing men's clothes in public. Because she had, he noted sourly, "a bad form, the clothes a bad fit and of the worst possible color and texture," she cut "such a hideous figure" that women slammed their windows shut and men looked away as she passed. Once more, the "sensation news paper reporters" found aid and comfort within Modern Times for denigrating the village. Warren acknowledged that this woman may have been a rebel against "the tyranny of fashion," but she did not need to vindicate her right to dress as she pleased at Modern Times, the citadel of "absolute *Sovereignty* in all things (within her own sphere)." She should have respected the rights of the other sovereigns not to be "unnecessarily disgusted and offended by her" outlandish costume. It never occurred to her, declared Warren rather smugly, that "the influence of Woman is one of the greatest civilizing powers we have." The all-important Freedom to differ can come only by *"Placing Responsibility where it belongs."* Warren yielded to no one in his ardor for personal liberty, but he consistently opposed what to him were gratuitous provocations to the defenders of convention.

He remembered further examples of irrational behavior by cranks. In a strangely unsympathetic report, he recalled a young woman who had "the diet mania to such a degree that she was said to live almost wholly on beans without salt . . . tottered about a living skeleton for about a year and then sank down and died (if we can say there was enough of her left to die)." At her funeral the "poor girl's" brother, who shared her dangerous eating habit, "had the candor to acknowledge" that she died from "theoretical speculations about diet." As usual, Jo-

siah evaluated the incident by its impact on Modern Times's reputation; the next newspaper story, he wrote, announced "that 'those people' there are killing themselves with fanatical theories about their food."

Sent in to discredit Modern Times, Warren believed, these sabo-
teurs maliciously furthered the image of eccentricity fastened to the
village. They failed to deter the gathering of a small but versatile band
of "capable minds," but their antics probably hindered future growth.

THE ARRIVAL OF NEW AND STABLE SETTLERS

In contrast to the ultra-eccentrics, a contingent of settlers from Massachusetts provided a center of stability in this circle of idiosyncrasy. At
an 1852 meeting in the Music Hall of Boston, the "able presentation"
of Stephen Pearl Andrews aroused Charles Codman's interest in equity commerce. Further investigation convinced Codman "that the solution of the Social problem had been found." He soon visited Modern
Times, met all the sovereigns, and "purchased 2 Acre lots on 2nd and
3rd. Aves. From this time it was my fixed intention to join the movement." For five years Codman worked at his business of "Sign and
Decorative Painting," scrimping until he acquired a grubstake. On
1 April 1857, at the age of thirty, he became a permanent resident of
the Long Island village in which he lived until his death, fifty-four years
later. He and his fellow migrants from the Bay State "were known at
Modern Times as the 'Boston group.'" Along with his wife, Caroline
Adelaide Blaisdell Codman (known as "Ada") and his father, William P.
Codman, came William Upham Dame, Edward Linton, and Peter and
Abigail Blacker; Blacker's brother and sister-in-law, James D. and Eliza
Blacker, had lived at Modern Times for the past five years.

William Upham Dame, one of Modern Times's Yankee craftsmen,
built the well-preserved octagon house on the east side of Brentwood
Road (Modern Times's Fifth Street) between Third and Fourth Avenues. Dame, an expert carpenter and cabinetmaker, converted the second floor into an assembly room "and named it 'Archimedian Hall'
where for some years we danced and held our Meetings." Mayor William J. Gaynor of New York City visited Brentwood in 1904. When
he asked Dame why an eight-sided house, "he responded . . . economy
of space, no space being lost in acute angles." Given landmark status

by the town of Islip, this well-preserved house is a now a residence of the Sisters of Saint Joseph.[30]

The Blackers combined enthusiasm for the equity movement with deep concern for village affairs and an aptitude for business. James D. Blacker, active in school affairs, was one of the first at Modern Times–Brentwood (along with Henry Edger) to plant "a nursery of fruit trees." The Peter Blackers ran a harness shop and saddlery in the village until Peter's death in 1884. Their son, Frank E. Blacker, who came to the village when he was nine, grew up to serve in the Civil War and then become Brentwood's earliest notary public, as well as its three-time postmaster. Their daughter, Eleanor Blacker, was Modern Times's first schoolteacher; in 1855 her tragic death, at the age of eighteen, dismayed the village.[31] Little is known of William F. Codman, Charles's father, except his listing as a day laborer on the 1860 census and his death at the age of eighty in 1878. At the time the 'Boston Group' arrived, wrote Codman, "there were about a dozen families then, poorly housed for each one's capital was very limited and none to spare except for things of absolute necessity." At first they had to carry water in pails from Dr. Peck's farm, a half-mile to the east, but soon "the public well was . . . dug on the southeast corner of 3rd. Ave. and 5th. St. on the land of Mr. W. U. Dame [lot 141]." Lack of worldly goods was no bar to boundless enthusiasm. Putting their faith in the future, this congenial band of brothers and sisters in the movement was willing to skimp on material comfort, sure that its version of justice and freedom would be "a light to all the world, a beacon to show the way out from the evils of competition and tyranny which had for all time dominated in human relation . . . and the sacrifices of pioneering in the howling wilderness would be of short duration, sure to be followed by enduring peace and plenty."[32]

The Boston Group gave solidity to Modern Times as afterwards they did to Brentwood, the lifelong home of most of them after leaving their native New England. They typified the majority of civic-minded sovereigns, who came to the pine woods to build a village as well as a movement. In the long run their cause did not take root on Long Island, but they did.

In 1854 an archetypical band of pioneers made the six-week trip to Modern Times from the Western Reserve of Ohio in Isaac Gibson's covered wagon. Gibson, then in his thirty-fifth year, took his doctor's advice to move to the balsamic air of the Long Island pine woods, there possibly to postpone his death from tuberculosis. As Verne Dyson dryly observes, "Gibson fooled his doctor. He recovered completely from his malady and died of old age a half-century later. His recuperation became a famous local incident, one frequently mentioned through the years in the prospectuses of hospitals and health resorts."[33]

With Gibson came Miss Mary Jane Prantz, known as "Jenny," a seventeen-year-old who married William U. Dame and lived in Modern Times–Brentwood until her death in 1911, the only first-comer to outlive Codman, if only by six weeks.[34] Other passengers in Gibson's wagon were "Mr. and Mrs. Jenkins [Zachariah and Mary] and two little children [first names omitted] and Mr. I. [Isaac] Haines," all of whom, including Jenny, "were attracted by the Equity program."[35]

The New York State census of 1855 reported 85 residents,[36] a total reaching 126 on the Federal tally five years later.[37] The population never came close to the thousand families hoped for by Warren, the number needed to form a trading base which, in the "right proportions of the different professions, could render the current barbarian money almost useless among themselves, and place each in a state of ease and pecuniary independence by the employment of two or three hours per day."[38]

Small as Modern Times was, few model communities matched the good-natured spirit and character of its egalitarian settlers. On Memorial Day 1905, a handful of survivors and friends assembled at Brentwood Cemetery to honor the pioneers of equity commerce. Edward F. Linton, who had lived at Modern Times with his father, paid tribute to that small group of liberty-loving people who "created an oasis in a desert wilderness . . . to [found] a community . . . and establish a social order themselves, wherein the highest intellectual freedom could be attained."[39]

MAKING A LIVING

The manuscript census of 1860 recorded Modern Timers engaged in the following occupations:[40]

> harness maker—Peter I. Blacker;
> carpenter—Isaac L. Gordon, James M. Hilton, H. W. Ballard;

shoemaker—Joseph B. Crowell, Isaac Haines (Hayes on the census);

painter—James D. Blacker;

lithographer—Josiah Warren;

farmer—Myndert M. Fish, M. B. Pierson, William Simpson (Stimson on the census), Barney H. Lewis, and Stephen Taylor (a well-to-do farmer not in sympathy with Modern Times, whose property bordered the village);

farm laborer—Michael Stanley (a sixteen-year-old from Ohio who lived in the Taylor household), Dauphin White;

day laborer—Clark Orvis (who also managed the "Eating Saloon"), Justin Smith, James Wormwood, Daniel Dow (Dowd on the census), William P. Codman (Charles Codman's father), Stilman Hazelton, Barney O'Rourke (Rook on the census), and Isaac Gibson;

dentist—Edward Newberry;

physician—John Simpson (Stimson on the census, the father of William Simpson, the farmer):

nursery-man—Henry Edger (soon followed by James D. Blacker);

servant—Mary Giles (a fifty-three-year-old English woman in the household of the sisters Ann and Mary A. Gliddon, also from England, whose connection with Modern Times is unknown);

paper boxmaker—Charles A. Codman and William U. Dame (a sign-maker and a cabinetmaker, respectively; their listing as boxmakers supports the existence of the paper-boxworks discussed below);

merchant—William Metcalf (Before settling at Modern Times, Metcalf kept shop in Brooklyn, which accounts for his census designation. At Modern Times, where the time store dispensed merchandise, he was a carpenter and housebuilder. After Modern Times became Brentwood, Metcalf operated a small, conventional store from his log cabin: "It was said of him that he was so stingy that to make the scales balance, he would bite a coffee bean in half")[41]

A calling that probably petered out before the 1860 census was the sweaty trade of grubbing stumps, pursued for a fee in the early years by the brothers Swaim. An unrealized source of employment was the wooden velocipede invented by Clark Orvis, classed as a laborer on the census. Unfortunately, remarked Codman, the contraption fell apart under "the strain of the experimental tests . . . Yet it evidently had its merits, it antedated the bicycle."[42] The resourceful Orvis managed the "Dining Saloon," a prototype of the cafeteria just as the time store was a harbinger of the discount store. Opened *"on a very small scale"* in the fall of 1854, everything served was "minutely individualized,"[43] explained Warren in his *Periodical Letter.* The bill of fare showed the price of every item, even molasses, butter, and sugar, "divided into most minute quantities from half a cent to two or three cents worth of different eatables," so that diners know the cost of each thing *"before engaging it."* Because the operation was so small, Orvis "cannot . . . make use of the Labor Notes as a circulating medium," but was forced to accept only cash, with the pledge that "when the receipts exceeds [sic] the 'costs,' THE PRICES OF FARE WILL BE REDUCED." It was therefore in everyone's interest to patronize the Eating Saloon on the premise of "Cooperation for mutual benefit!" The higher the volume, the lower the prices, yet "the whole is conducted by one Individual who is the sole proprietor and manager, as any other keeper of an eating house in any of the cities." Warren hoped that someone would set up the "Lodging House . . . required to Cooperate with the Eating Saloon," which might not "secure a living to its keeper," but would be "of great service, particularly to visitors."[44] No one attempted such a venture, although rooms were set aside on the second floor of the "Mechanical College" for people with houses under construction.

There were several medically-inclined sovereigns. Edward Newberry, of Modern Times, was the only dentist in Islip on the census of 1860. Codman described him as "one of the notables born in London, England in 1811 . . . the 19th child in a family of 37 (the offspring of two mothers)." Edward came naturally to his interest in community living—his father, after suffering "disappointment in results of experiment with adopted children," decided to sire the population of his own model village. Born and brought up in communal surroundings, young Newberry's "character and activities were shaped for his whole career." After coming to the United States as a young man of twenty-six, he practiced dentistry for more than fifty years at his Manhattan (499 Third Avenue) office, while living at Modern Times–Brentwood from 1855 until his death in 1897. He devoted his altruistic life, added Codman, to putting the needs of "the other fellow first." In addition to dentistry and medicine, this most versatile of the sovereigns was at home with chemistry, botany, and geology, and was among the first to "practice Homeopathy in his N.Y. City office, [and] to recognize the truth and importance of Gall & Spurzheim's discoveries of the functions of the brain, later known as phrenology." Newberry combined his interest in the cranium with his ability as "a gifted artist": nineteen of his water-color sketches of heads grace a wall of the Brentwood Public Library. He also excelled "in portraying flowers and fruit." His wife Rose Anne Newberry painted well, too, as did their daughters Rose B. and Anna, who "followed art as a profession."[45]

Newberry advanced a theory for the improvement of the human race "by scientific cross-fertilization, otherwise known as stirpiculture," a means of producing superior offspring by encouraging "propagation of blonde with brunette, the billious [sic] with the locomotive, the blue eyes with the black eyes," and so on, much as "men have done in im-proving the domestic animals." Codman wound up his eulogy with a somewhat wry analysis of the perfectionist Dr. Newberry's "panacea for healing the antagonisms of current Society." Newberry became a "Modern Timer, hoping to find earnest and devoted persons with whom he could labor and impress his views. Yet, despite his perseverance . . . he never gained many adherents in practical communism, as his ideas took various and vague forms which were unstable and changeable."[46]

Codman evaluated his old friend's life in words that fit his own: "His unfaltering faith in his formula made him over hopeful, and his kindly nature and perennial helpfulness buoyed him . . . serene and tranquil, he lived a long life of usefulness . . . He was truly a "guide, philosopher, and friend."[47]

Dr. John Simpson, who came to Modern Times from Canada with his son William, a farmer, was one among the seven Islip physicians listed on the census. The most high-powered medico-sovereigns were Thomas Low Nichols, M.D., and his wife and colleague, Mary Sargent Gove Nichols. This inseparable pair of theorists and practitioners of hydropathic therapy—commonly called the water-cure—believed in ap-plying appropriate doses of water to treat whatever ailed their patients. The Nicholses ran schools, wrote books, and published a health and hygiene magazine, but were best known for their promotion of free love, the cause in which they vainly tried to enlist the sovereigns of Modern Times.[48]

Mary Gove was among the subjects of an 1855 *Who's Who* of dis-tinguished women "of every age." "Before her marriage [in 1848] with Dr. Nichols . . . with whom she is in profession associated," wrote the editor, Sarah J. Hale, "she conducted with great success a water cure establishment in [New York] city and was widely known as Mrs. Gove — her name by a former marriage — the physician for her own sex." The autobiographical sketch that followed outlined Mary Gove's self-taught development as a teacher, lecturer, and healer who believed in the cold-water cure in preference to what she held were the less satisfactory remedies of homeopathy and allopathy. She maintained "that nervous energy is restored, and morbid matter cast out of the system, by means of the proper application of water cure." She looked forward to the education of women as "physicians, and particularly to attend to midwifery practice." Warning the male monopoly that "if our medical colleges are not soon opened to women, others will be found where she will be educated," she ended on a ringing feminist-abolitionist note. "The spirit of the age," she declared, "will not any longer submit to bonds."[49]

The economy of Modern Times was designed to defy the profit system by enabling mutually assisting companions to ply useful trades on a basis of barter. However, the system of labor-for-labor exchange often failed to supply the settlers with the wherewithal they required. Bowles admitted to the *Sunday Dispatch* that Modern Times was too new and its ranks too thin to allow it to be self-sufficient. Ingenuously describing the need of the sovereigns to augment labor notes with legal tender, he told B. D. J. that many workmen — "mostly mechanics" — had to venture into the outside world to "earn what people call *money*, so that we may purchase our groceries, &c."[50]

Mechanics were not the only sovereigns forced to reenter the mainstream for work. In a chatty letter to Henry Edger in 1858, Codman informed his absent friend that a Mr. Markham [first name unknown] "has got a school . . . in Smithtown . . . some nine miles from here." Markham had probably depended on Linton financially, because after the latter left Modern Times, he "was thrown on his own resources and there being no alternative save to work or starve, exerted himself and obtained employment." Henry Fish, another teacher, "has a school for four months now in Comac" [today's Commack]. Codman's choice of the words "has a school" was ambiguous, obscuring whether Fish and Markham ran their own schools or were salaried teachers. Lizzie Piper, added Codman, was "in New York learning to work with a sewing machine."[51]

Doctors Edward Newberry and Thomas Low Nichols maintained

offices in New York. For a next dozen years beginning in 1858, George S. McWatters also made his living away from the village as an officer on Manhattan's Metropolitan Police Force. This most adventurous sovereign, whose dashing career included stints as a gold-rush prospector, a lawyer, a private investigator, and a member of the American Secret Service, also wrote detective stories. The author of the introduction to a collection of famous cases written up by McWatters praised him "as a detective officer and as a humanitarian," as well as a leader of an association "organized to afford support to the families of policemen who joined the Metropolitan Brigade in the war for the Union."[52]

There was never a factory or other group employer at Modern Times. William Bailie reported that Edward D. Linton set up "a paper-box manufactory . . . [but] this enterprise was checked by the disastrous financial panic of 1857." Before the effects of the "ensuing industrial depression" wore off, the country plunged into civil war "and all hope of regenerating society for the time being was dissipated."[53] Although Codman and Dame appear as paper-boxmakers on the census of 1860, no record exists of a boxworks, an idea possibly considered but never implemented. Another potential cottage industry, mentioned in Codman's memoir, was a proposed cigar-making establishment which the sovereigns, in spite of their need for income, rejected because they abhorred the "vile weed." The would-be operator was "a man fully enthused with the equity principle," but "as badly as our people wanted to earn a living they . . . scorned to assist in maintaining a habit which they thought harmful and injurious." Their willingness to live frugally rather than gain from a harmful habit was one more example of Modern Timers' predilection for what Codman described as "scant rations and high principles,—'Low Living and High Thinking.'"[54]

FEEDING THE SOVEREIGNS

It was difficult for Modern Timers to cope with the problems of food growing. Warren cheered prospective settlers with news that when prepared with "ten to forty dollars worth of manure," the soil was "excellent for garden stuff of all kinds"; not only was the atmosphere "clear, bright, fresh, and healthy [but] there was an abundance of pure *soft* water at about forty feet below the surface."[55] But Codman remembered that although there were some kitchen gardens, there were hardly five cleared acres as late as 1856, the year before his arrival. A major problem was that a great many sovereigns were city folk who knew nothing at all about farming, a handicap compounded by the soil's being "partly impoverished by Forest Fires, caused mainly by sparks from the R/R trains which consumed all vegetable matter." The problem in the spring," he added ruefully, "was how large a barn should be built, but the crops in harvest time could be carried in a wheelbarrow." For want of livestock, the settlers depended on the infrequent delivery of manure, or fertilizers that were, wrote Codman, of high cost and small results. He remembered "Mr. Justin Smith going over his patch of corn with a bag of highly extolled fertilizer . . . from which he distributed an iron spoonful of the stuff to each hill which was to produce an abundant crop on homeopathic treatment."[56]

This lasted several years, until systematic cultivation coupled with knowledge gained from experience began to produce the desired results. But at first, wind, drought, and ignorance resulted in meager pickings. Undaunted, "the pioneers planted trees along the streets and avenues as windbreaks and for shade and ornament—cherry and apple trees so that even the wayfarer could eat freely of the fruit, satisfy his hunger and slake his thirst without let or hindrance and after 50 years of usefulness many yet bear a yearly fruitage."[57]

If most sovereigns were strangers to husbandry, the pioneers from Ohio belonged to the green-thumbed minority. Isaac Gibson introduced Long Island to Sharpless strawberries, famous for their "sensational size —as large as apples."[58] Mrs. Jenkins brought with her "the ornamental evergreens, and the Arbor Vitae hedges were planted in 1865–70."[59] Others who proved the friendliness of the pine plains' soil were Henry Edger and James D. Blacker, both of whom planted nurseries of fruit trees.

The doctrine of equitable commerce and its living model, Modern Times, precluded large farms or industries. The founders discouraged sizeable agriculture by limiting contiguous holdings to no more than three acres, thus favoring the growth of a close-knit village instead of spread-out and often isolated farmhouses. The abundance of prosperous farmers in Islip did not hold for Modern Times, where only two of the five farmers listed in 1860 owned real property valued at more than the $100 required for census enumeration. Of their combined total value of $5,000, $4,000-worth belonged to Stephen Taylor, a resident but not a supporter of Modern Times. Barney Lewis, with real property valued at $1,000, was the sole Modern Times farmer of substance. The other three farmers—Myndert M. Fish, M. B. Pierson, and William Simpson, the doctor's son, possessed no real property worth $100 or declined to admit that they did on the census—no estimate of real or personal wealth follows their names. Because Fish and his wife Rebecca paid $80 in 1858 for a square block of Modern Times,[60] it seems reasonable to deduce that either the sovereigns were less than candid with the census taker, or that he, far from a stickler for detail, recorded values carelessly.

LABOR NOTES AND TIME STORES

The time store demanded payment in the cash it needed for buying replacement merchandise outside the village. Labor notes were taken only to cover the surcharge added to the price of an item to recompense the proprietor for his time in making the sale. In a handbill describing his first New Harmony time store, in 1842, Warren explained the process. He asked all who wished to exchange labor for labor, or to transact business at the store, to submit written estimates of the labor cost of their products and hand them in at a public meeting, from which "the Keeper of the time store will fix his labor prices, not to be changed till another public meeting."[61]

Except at the time store, the sovereigns wrote and accepted labor notes in return for goods and services. Printed by Warren, the labor notes were on onionskin paper the size of a modern dollar bill. Codman recalled that they "circulated as money, were received and paid as U.S. Issues are. I claim that they filled all the requirements of local trading and their circulation was only limited by the known credit of the person . . . They were essentially like the Millions of daily transactions—(Notes given and received) and differed only that instead of being paid in 'Legal Tender' they were paid in Labor or its equivalent in corn."[62] Warren chose corn with which to back labor notes because it was bulky enough so that no one would steal it and common enough for all to grow. A note written by P. [Peter] I. Blacker in 1857 promised "ONE HOURS LABOR IN SHOEMAKING OR EIGHT POUNDS OF CORN; OR with the consent of the holder, 10 CENTS." Another 1857 note issued by Charles A. Codman offered "TWO HOURS LABOR IN SIGN PAINTING OR 16 POUNDS OF CORN; OR with the consent of the holder 20 CENTS."[63]

Value of work was proportional to the repugnance of labor involved, each note inscribed with the heading that "The most disagreeable labor is entitled to the highest compensation." This was a feature borrowed from Fourier, whose blueprint for utopia provided that "work will be rewarded according to its usefulness, and the most disagreeable work will receive the highest pay."[64]

Warren credited Robert Owen with introducing the labor-for-labor note, repeating in an 1848 issue of the *Peaceful Revolutionist* what he wrote fifteen years before: "The idea of labor notes was suggested by Robert Owen in 1826 as a medium of exchange between Communities at New Harmony. I stated this in the *Peaceful Revolutionist* of 1833, page 4." Josiah inaugurated the public testing of labor notes in the time store he ran successfully in Cincinnati, sandwiched in time between the debacles of New Harmony in 1827, and Owen's English bazaars seven years later. As for who deserved credit for using them first in regular (not intramural) business, Warren reacted exactly as he did later when George Ripley challenged his authorship of individual sovereignty. Not only did it not matter, he said, but "I have a thousand times felt that if the subject had originated with some one who was dead I could have done perhaps a thousand times more for it." To the best of his knowledge, he was first, in his Cincinnati time store. He recalled running a school of instrumental music on the floor above the store at the corner of Fifth and Elm Streets. Some students paid their tuition of "ten dollars per quarter" and others "paid for the same instruction, *fourteen hours* of their own labor!" If such developments "peculiar to Equitable Commerce were made before the eighteenth of May 1827, then I was not the first to develope [sic] them, and the principal obstacle to my freedom of speech and action on the subject will be removed."[65]

Contrastingly, Owen's co-ops were organizations, with members, committees, and boards. The labor notes used were not independent of merchandise, and the stores were no more than consignment depots that foundered once they became "a dumping ground for unsalable items."[66]

Upon reading the draft of its program, Warren predicted the failure of Owen's bazaar on Gray's Inn Road, a forecast confirmed by the store's collapse. Whether in Cincinnati or London, it did not require a "prophet to foresee that twice two will make four." Warren regretted the fall of such a magnificent establishment," which excited "the highest expectations of its friends and the most terrible alarm to the moneyocracy," but he chided Owen for leading people to believe that the English Exchanges were replicas of his (Warren's) time store: "Mr. Owen thought he was doing me a piece of courteous justice when he said, at a public meeting in London, that 'he got the ideas from me'; I appreciate the intention [but the] features of that institution are no part of any movement ever conducted or proposed by me. With the best intentions, he had misconceived the Equitable Store, or 'Time Store,' then in operation, which, in 1829 I endeavored to explain to him."[67]

Warren was a genuine retailer who bought merchandise in the open market and sold it at cost for cash, plus a small markup for his time that was payable in labor notes. As a shopkeeper selling standard goods at wholesale prices, he conducted what may have been the first discount store in America. In addition to being a merchant, he was also a consciousness raiser who used his stores as catalysts, "the most feasible method of inoculating minds" with the need for change "that *must* be made in social labor and the trading relations."[68] The "equity store" also served as employment agency and clearinghouse, its walls covered with the posted offers of buyers and sellers of goods and services willing to trade their labor at cost.

COMMON SCHOOL DISTRICT 12

High on his rock of uncombined interests, Warren opposed connecting Modern Times to any branch of government. His plan for education did not depart from this principle: those who want a school for young children should pay whatever the cost may be, arrived at by swapping labor for labor. Adults and older children who wanted to learn useful trades could do so at his Mechanical College, with the price of courses at all times confined to cost. Josiah despised the old saw that a jack-of-all-trades was good at none. On the contrary, he declared in *Modern Education*, a brochure describing his equity school, that "He or she who can fill twenty useful departments may prove twenty times as valuable a citizen as he who can fill only one."[69]

Practical knowledge was obtainable in carpentry and cabinetmaking; forging and filing of iron; bricklaying, lathing, and plastering; painting, glazing, and paperhanging; cistern building; typesetting, printing, and proofreading; on and on through tailoring, sewing, dressmaking, shoemaking and bootmaking. Warren's school also offered instruction ranging from the agricultural arts through gymnastics and the three "R's" all the way to dancing, history, music, languages, public speaking, chairmanship, and literary criticism. A typically Warrenite course taught "A mode of securing individual homesteads to the homeless without waiting for legislation." The curriculum included the philosophy of governments, laws, morals, and manners, and especially "of money and its true functions, of a system of commerce and a kind of money which do not degrade human nature and ruin nations . . . A military drill with a mental discipline for the sole purpose of preventing all unnecessary violence to any persons or property . . . A mode of securing to all Labor its just reward (the great problem of the age), and of universal justice and consequent peace and prosperity." Tuition varied, course by course, but always covered the labor of teaching as well as contingent expenses of room, board, tools, and firewood, "the learners having the whole products of their labor to dispose of at will." Modern Times itself was the best university: "Perhaps nowhere else is the remark frequently heard from adults, that the town in which they live 'is the greatest school they were ever in.'"[70]

Warren opened his Mechanical College in the infancy of Modern Times, teaching "various trades by hourly lessons"[71] for ten years before publication of *Modern Education*. A prototype of both vocational school and adult education, the "College" was also Warren's antidote for apprenticeship, which he believed was the profit system's crafty device for delaying young people from learning trades and making a living. As Codman observed, "He held that the traditional seven years apprenticeships were unjust to the learner."[72]

Warren's plan for privately operated education was the first plank in Modern Times's platform to face opposition from settlers; his informal program was not enough for the residents, much less their immediate neighbors. On 19 February 1853, William Nicoll, Superintendent of Common Schools of the Town of Islip, authorized Francis Moses Asbury Wicks, the laird of Thompson's Station, to call a meeting at his house for the purpose of forming School District 12. On 28 May at a meeting launching the district, Wicks, Benjamin F. Bowles, and George S. McWatters were elected trustees for one year, and "Mr. [James D.] Blacker Liberian [sic]."[73]

After a three-year hiatus the project resumed full tilt in March 1856, with the election of Wicks, J. Milton Swain, and Joseph B. Crowell as trustees for respective three-, two-, and one-year terms, and James Blacker as clerk, collector, and librarian (correctly spelled from then on). A hand-drawn map by Codman, enclosed in the District 12 "Minute Book," shows that the district ran some four miles east from the line of the town of Huntington (in today's town of Babylon) to "Caleb's Road, or the Suffolk Station Road" (now Caleb's Path–Islip Road), and roughly three miles from the southern edge of Huntington to a line "three miles north of the South Country Road."

Three weeks later a meeting moderated by Henry Fish empowered the trustees to raise $400 to build a school. Of the ten men present, only Wicks and Charles Van Cott were not residents of Modern Times. On 28 March, with Henry Fish once more in the chair, the voters levied "a tax of $10 to purchase books for the library and $10 for a bookcase," as well as "$20 to buy school apparatus." On 8 April they allotted $50 to buy a site, "also $17.30 for contingencies." The minutes of these and other meetings contain no reference to the premise of cost the limit of price or to labor notes, suggesting that District 12 did not observe the precepts of equitable commerce.

The schoolhouse was built on lot 56, at Third Avenue and Fourth Street, half owned by Christopher Wray and half by Joseph Agate, two of the speculators who bought from Dr. Peck and now were the principal vendors of land to Modern Timers. Wray sold his half for a token dollar; Agate received $8.25.[74] The first teacher, reported Codman, was Miss Eleanor Blacker, succeeded by Miss Mary Swain—the daughter of Malinda and John Milton Swain—after Eleanor's untimely death in 1855.[75] It is unclear where teaching was done at first, but classes obviously were taught in other premises until the completion of the schoolhouse.

The problem of cost overrun led the meeting of 23 April 1857, Wicks presiding, to authorize "the trustees to hire the sum of $350 for one and one half years to finish the school house, build a fence, and clear the land." This measure passed by unanimous vote of the eleven sovereigns and two outsiders present. The schoolhouse, the second of

Modern Times's octagons, opened in 1857 and stayed in use for fifty years, when "it was sold and removed from the site" to make way for a larger building.[76] For generations an architectural heirloom stood unused and in disrepair, deep in a grove of shade trees at the corner of Second Street and Fifth Avenue. Fortunately, this museum awaiting a sponsor again belongs to the community, donated by its public-spirited owners, the family of the late Anna Olivieri of Brentwood. Perched on the eastern edge of the high school property, it waits while the Brentwood Historical Society searches for funds with which to restore it.

In the "Minute Book of District 12" the names of Modern Times stalwarts recur from meeting to meeting: Daniel Dow, Joseph Crowell, James and Peter Blacker, William Metcalf, William Dame, James Loveland, Henry Fish, Charles and William Codman, Barney Lewis, James Hilton, Joseph Owram, Levi Harris, Isaac Gibson, George Baxter, Thomas George, Clark Orvis, Thomas Ranney, Brian O'Rourke, William Simpson, and more—the roll book includes almost every male sovereign. When not serving as trustee, clerk, collector, or librarian, they took their seats as the rank and file. Even Warren, the archetype of anti-organization man, attended two meetings. At the first of these, in October 1861, Theron C. Leland ran against Hyman Seaver for clerk and lost on the second ballot, 14-11. Warren also took part in the annual meeting one year later, October 1862, the last time that his name appears on any record of Modern Times.[77]

Here are the names and ages of the fifteen Modern Times school children in the order in which they appear on the 1860 census:[78]

Name	Age
Ann Evans	13
Elizabeth Evans	9
Cornelia Evans	3
Sarah Hilton	11
George Dowd	9
Victor Allen	11
Mary C. Allen	9
Earnest Allen	5
Jenny L. Crowell	11
Carrie Crowell	9
Ada Crowell	7
Francette Dunbar	10

Name	Age
William Haines	16
(Hayes on the census)	
Louisa Haines	13
James D. Blacker	7

Outside children attending the school are more difficult to identify, but among them may have been three Wicks—Mary (14 years old), Julia (12), and Cornelia (7)—and three Clocks—Harrison (18), Everena (16), and George (13).

The census includes twenty-two Modern Times youngsters between the ages of five and sixteen not designated as schoolchildren. Among these twelve girls and ten boys are members of such studious families as the Edgers and the Newberrys. Perhaps some of the sovereigns preferred to educate their children at home, or send them to the Mechanical College—although pupils in the latter case should be on the list of schoolgoers. The sovereigns' youngsters did not go to work instead of to school; according to the census, the only employed child at Modern Times was Michael Stanley, a sixteen-year-old farm laborer. The discrepancy may be the fault of the none-too-accurate census of 1860 examined in chapter 6 below.

Warren's no-government policy did not jibe with the organization of Common School District 12. For adherents of equitable commerce, combination compared with original sin. Except for two petitions for roads, Modern Timers neither asked for the help nor took interest in the government of the town of Islip. Had they remained true to their credo, they would have made do with the casual classroom for grade-schoolers and the Mechanical College which Warren advocated for other students. But, by deciding to accept the rules laid down by an outside agency for the creation of a public school, the sovereigns signaled more than their general fondness for meetings and their particular care for education.

The affiliation of Modern Times with a system sponsored by the state and the county showed that, for all of its anarchistic façade, the village would not long endure as a bastion of untrammeled independence. It did not imply the immediate adulteration of pure individual sovereignty, but it hinted that not far under the surface lurked the desire for some connection with mainstream society.

4

Marriage and Free Love

MODERN TIMES WAS A CRACK IN THE WALL of proper behavior. Bound by the motto "Mind your own business," the villagers did not care whether people lived in or out of wedlock. If arraigned at the bar of marital format, the sovereigns could enter a plea of guilty with an explanation—that loving mating depends on neither ring nor rite.

Free love was a more comprehensive persuasion than free choice of marital status. It meant variety of sexual partners to some and the union of equal lovers to more, but to most of its champions it signified the right of women to marry, divorce, cohabit, and raise children as the legal equals of men. Beginning in 1852 and for several years thereafter, a vanguard of sexual radicals tried to make Modern Times the barricade of the free-love revolution. The double stigma of unconventional marital standards and use of the village to promulgate free love resulted in public perception of Modern Times as a den of fornication and a dagger thrust at the heart of propriety. This reputation tarnished its image, stunted its growth, and led its settlers to rename it Brentwood after Modern Times became a lurid byword. For all of its flaunting of convention, most couples were married and many of those who were not later tied the knot. Yet its willingness to experiment with sexual-marital reform became the most lasting contribution of Modern Times, affecting the future more profoundly than its chosen goal of equitable commerce.

Many nineteenth-century model communities adopted unusual methods of sexual pairing. Both Robert Owen and Charles Fourier hoped eventually to abolish marriage and let men and women find lovers to whom they were drawn by mutual attraction. The community would be mother and father to children unafflicted by the mental or physical malnutrition they often suffered in atomized households.

In the meantime, Owen and Fourier advocated the building of collectivist villages where time was saved and the work load shared by cooperative enterprise. Joiners did not intend to forsake the nuclear family but rather to benefit from the advantages of pooling the burdens of everyday life.

Millennialist groups went further. The Shakers, the Mormons, and the Oneida Community were as structured as Modern Times was loose. They were congregations of believers in codes of behavior, derived from works held sacred and with which members conformed on pain of expulsion. Shaker celibacy, Mormon polygamy, and Oneidan "omnigamy"—the system of "complex marriage" in which every man was the husband of every woman—were articles of faith maintained by the preaching of the unprovable to the unquestioning. These communities practiced what Louis J. Kern aptly terms "an ordered love." Rejecting any "doctrine of complete sexual freedom for the individual," all adopted "some form of community regulated sexual relation that differed from the monogamic."[1]

Modern Times took the opposite course of ordering nothing and cherishing everything friendly to individual freedom in sexual and other relations. It was a cluster of nuclear families, installed in their own homes on their own land, engaged in unordered love according to choice and never by rule. In place of a father figure was Josiah Warren, an anti-leader allergic to use of the pronoun "we."[2] Warren's only wielding of leadership was to defy the crusaders' effort, in the summer of 1853, to change the mating pattern of Modern Times from free choice to free love. If the effort were successful, the village would fall in step with the doctrinaires by "ordering" its style of love. After a rousing fight, Warren beat back the charge of the free-love brigade commanded by Dr. Thomas Low Nichols and his wife, the redoubtable Mary Gove Nichols. Before recreating this struggle, let us review the origin of "free love" at Oneida in the fertile mind of its founder, John Humphrey Noyes.

HOW FREE WAS LOVE AT ONEIDA?

By free love, Noyes meant the extension of sharing to the bodies as well as the goods of saints. "The Putney school [his first community], in Vermont," he explained, ". . . invented the term *Free Love* to designate the social state of the kingdom of Heaven as defined in *Bible Communism.*" After pondering Scripture minutely, Noyes held monogamy null and void. Oneida theology contended that "In the Kingdom of Heaven, the institution of marriage, which assigns the exclusive possession of one woman to one man, does not exist. Matt. 22: 23–30,"[3] in the last line of which Jesus states, "For in the resurrection they neither marry, nor are given in marriage, but are as the angels of God in heaven."

In her study of the Oneida Community, Maren L. Carden observes that Noyes did not interpret this passage to mean that resurrected people were sexless. On the contrary, "sexual relations exist in heaven as on earth," and collectively, not in exclusive pairing. Therefore the ideal state on earth is one in which all men are wed to all women in a system of "complex marriage."[4]

Taylor Stoehr, the historian of free love in America, notes that Noyes took this position as early as 1837, when, consumed with unrequited love, he wrote his famous letter declaring that "when God's will is done on earth, as it is in heaven, *there will be no marriage.* The marriage supper of the Lamb, is a feast at which *every dish is free to every guest* . . . In a pure [the original reads *holy*] community, there is no more reason why sexual intercourse should be restricted by law than why eating and drinking should be . . . I call a certain woman my wife — she is yours, she is Christ's, and in him she is the bride of all saints." From the time Noyes admitted the authorship of this stormily controversial letter, extracts of which appeared, he recalled, "surreptitiously and anonymously . . . in a periodical called *The Battle Axe* and hence got the name of the *Battle Axe* letter," he felt called upon at any cost "to defend and ultimately carry out the doctrine of Communism in love; and I accepted the commission with a good heart."[5]

In his analysis of the origins of the Oneida Community, Lawrence Foster shows how Noyes, after losing his status and reputation in the wake of the *Battle-Axe* Letter, gave up quixotically trying to "convert the whole world to his religious ideas . . . He would seek to realize his social ideas among tested followers in small-scale pilot projects, while continuing to propagate his ideas in the periodical press."[6]

First at Putney, Vermont, and then at Oneida, approval of limitless sex among loving saints, expressly sanctioned by Jesus, the apostles, and "the whole tenor of the New Testament," was the foundation of complex marriage.[7] In Noyes's exegesis the Second Coming—for which the Rappites and Shakers were getting ready—took place when the Romans sacked Jerusalem in A.D. 70. From then on perfection was attainable to all of God's children, although not yet achieved. Noyes believed in his own perfection because by acceptance of God he was pure in heart, integrated with Jesus in the service of bringing God's kingdom to earth. In this postmillennial era, all who strove could live by Jesus' command "Be ye therefore perfect, even as your Father which is in heaven is perfect." Had not Jesus told the young man whose wealth kept him from joining the first band of communal Christians that "If thou wilt be perfect, go and sell that thou hast, and give to the poor, and thou shalt have treasure in heaven: and come and follow me"?[8] Well, recommended Noyes, instead of giving what you have to the poor, endorse it to the Oneida Community and regenerate as a Bible Communist. The heart of Noyes's theology was "that mankind would approach nearer and nearer to perfection and true happiness and that eventually the kingdom would exist on earth."[9]

Perfectionism was Noyes's unique brand of millenarianism. A less demanding kind of Perfectionism was the Methodist version preached in the Second Revival by the Reverend Charles Grandison Finney. Noyes was to Finney what *Brown v. Board of Education* was to *Plessy v. Ferguson*. Finney's was a separate (but not equal) relationship between God and man, in which Christians tried to warrant His love by trying, however imperfectly, to be perfect sons and daughters of their perfect Father. But Noyes, while a Yale seminarian, boldly declared "that men can be perfect—and that he himself was perfect," a heresy for which his church revoked his license to preach in 1834.[10]

The Calvinist ministry's loss was Oneida's gain. Noyes started a sect of his own that built one of the most dynamic and solvent segments of the ideal village movement; Oneida, a brilliantly-managed communist project, turned a profit in every business it entered. Perhaps the most gifted of its organizers, Noyes was also a keen historian of the communitarian movement—his *History of American Socialisms* remains one of the masterworks on the subject.

But the libidinal quirks of its leader account for Oneida's unusual sexual habits. No longer must sexual love be "restricted to pairs," proclaimed Noyes. No one honeymoon, nor single lover, can satisfy man and woman: "On the contrary, the secret history of the human heart will bear out the assertion that it is capable of loving any number of times and any number of persons, and that the more it loves the more it can love." The Oneida Community's principle of the day of Pentecost may extend only to material goods, yet if we allow that spirit full scope we will also "abolish . . . exclusiveness in regard to women and children."[11]

Noyes assigned himself to be the "first husband" of virgins. Initiation took place between the ages of ten and eighteen, depending on when menstruation began: the average age of his "brides" was thirteen. In later years he shared this chore with a handful of senior disciples who also helped to decide the fathers and the times of impregnation of the women of Oneida. Deservedly known as "Father" Noyes, John Humphrey sired nine children (actually ten, but one was stillborn), during a single decade, in addition to his instruction of maidens.[12] Lest the gentlemen of Oneida overdraw their spermatic bank accounts, he instituted "male continence," a form of *coitus reservatus* by which "[we] hope to achieve birth control while retaining the physical pleasure of intercourse." Noyes, Thomas Low Nichols, and most sexologists of the time held that sperm was of finite quantity, too precious to spend unproductively; at Oneida, male orgasm was by official permission only. The Oneida publication, *Male Continence* (1872), explained that it was a healthy mode of intercourse: "it secures woman from the curses of involuntary and undesirable procreation; and . . . stops the drain of life on the part of men."[13]

Noyes's form of "ordered love" was possibly compensation for failure to adjust to his mother's indifference to Perfectionism and Oneida. Even after his father's bequest and his wife's fortune made him independent of her money, Noyes never stopped struggling with his mother. Yet according to Kern, he "was deeply attached to her, and her refusal to accept him on his terms generated a feeling of rejection and consequent hostility . . . expressed as . . . distrust and, on a less conscious level, an actual hostility toward women." Moreover, continues Kern, "Noyes's concern with his younger sisters and his fear of their betraying him as his mother did—in a definitely sexual way—can be seen as quite Oedipal when we realize that he recommended incestuous rela-

tionships at Oneida for better 'scientific breeding.' His sisters thus became surrogates for his mother in the originally Oedipal relationship."[14]

Clearly, sex at Oneida was custom-fit for John Humphrey Noyes.
Yet the concept of complex marriage carried with it the guarantee that
every Oneida Community child was the loved and nurtured object of
the entire group's concern. When Andrews, the Nicholses, and other
reformers preempted "free love" without his permission and changed
it into a secular movement, Noyes rued the day that he coined the
phrase. Withdrawing his imprimatur, he now denounced his concept
as a "terrible combination of two very good ideas – freedom and love –
[that] was first used by the writers of the Oneida Community . . . and
probably originated with them." Noyes disowned his brainchild because
of its corruption by outsiders. "Holiness must go before free love" to
establish the Kingdom of Heaven on earth. Faith is the prerequisite
for reform of sexual morality. Noyes made up the concept of free love
as "the social state of the Kingdom of Heaven as defined in Bible communism," not as a license for sexual indulgence in the way the term
had been "appropriated and specialized" by the likes of "Thomas Low
Nichols . . . : "Their platform is entirely different from ours and they
must answer for themselves. We are not 'Free Lovers' in any sense that
makes love less binding or responsible than it is in marriage." Chambers'
Encyclopedia should "get some intelligent American" to correct its account of Oneida as the home of "'Perfectionists or Bible Communists;
popularly known as Free Lovers or preachers of Free Love.'" At Oneida,
complex marriage resulted in collective parenthood, with every child
cared for and protected by the united family. Its mode of free love was
permanent union, not a temporary flirtation in which "love is paid for
as hired labor. In licentiousness, a man imposes on a woman the heavy
burdens of maternity, ruining perhaps her reputation, and her health,
and then goes his way without responsibility. Free Love with us does
not mean freedom to love to-day and leave to-morrow."[15]

Then what did freedom mean at Oneida? As at all of the "ordered" communities, it signified "freedom" to abide by rules ordained
by charismatic autocrats. Noyes's style of love was coercive, not free:
"Members paid for group support with their privacy. For the sake of
engaging in a range of sexual encounters, forbidden in the outside world,
they gave up the right to establish emotionally satisfying relationships,

to experience the culmination of the sex act, and to select partners of their own choosing."[16]

Kern puts it bluntly: "Love at Oneida was not 'free,' and those who confused complex marriage with free love erred gravely in their conception."[17] To take part in complex marriage, and its prescribed technique of male continence, was not a right but an obligation, offset by no right to decline. Members made love by appointment; men had orgasms by permission.

In his study of Shakers, Mormons, and Oneidans, Lawrence Foster points out that as early as 1837 Noyes declared he would join no religious group unless he were the acknowledged leader. God's kingdom to him was an "absolute monarchy" ruled, in Foster's words, by "the supreme leader, who benevolently delegated authority to loyal (male) subordinates" for implementation of his ideals.[18] When Noyes commenced the controlled breeding program called stirpiculture, the young men of Oneida proclaimed their zeal to live by "Father" Noyes's precepts: "We claim no rights. We ask no privileges . . . With . . . the grace of God . . . we are your soldiers." Outdoing the males in mindless obedience, Oneida women in their early forties or younger signed a resolution that they did not "belong to ourselves in any respect, but that we belong first to God, and second to Mr. Noyes as God's true representative." They renounced all rights or personal feelings regarding childbearing which in any way might hinder Noyes's program. Finally, they swore, "if necessary, [to] become martyrs to science, and cheerfully resign all desire to become mothers, if for any reason Mr. Noyes deem us unfit material for propagation. Above all, we offer ourselves 'living sacrifices' to God and true Communism."[19]

"BARTERED CONNUBIALITIES"

The argument over the use of Modern Times as the bastion of anti-marriage militants burst out in 1852, a year before the Nicholses arrived. That summer marked the defection of George Stearns, editor and publisher of the *Art of Living*, the organ of Modern Times during his brief term of residence. Stearns, from Lowell, Massachusetts, came to the village in May of that year to learn about equitable commerce, only to leave in August because the free-love contingent offended his morals.

"Modern Times," an article in the *Practical Christian* (the voice of the Practical Christian Republic, Adin Ballou's model village at Hopedale, Massachusetts) by its editor, William S. Heywood, described Stearns as "a man of considerable talent and Reform feeling" who came to his expected Utopia "full of enthusiasm and zeal, with his family and paper." At first, the *Art of Living* regaled readers with Stearns's delight in his newly found "prospect of the world's redemption." But imagine the *Practical Christian*'s amazement when it received the August and September issues, "hailing not from the city of 'Equitable Commerce,' but from the city of New York, where equitable commerce is a thing almost unknown." Why the sudden and unexpected change? Stearns's article revealed that his reason for secession was discovery of the "astounding" fact that "there is a lurking combination of personal influences, among the leading co-laborers for so-called 'Equitable Commerce' to do away entirely with the name and essence of marriage and to introduce instead what they term a 'Freedom of the Love-Relations,' or a free and respectful sanction of promiscuous cohabitation." Free-love conspirators based in Manhattan infiltrated Modern Times, boring from within until the day they were strong enough to "throw off the mask and defy public opinion." Meanwhile, these libertines "not only cut the bonds of legality, and set at nought the proprietisms of custom, but they also so scout the notion of constancy in love, and ridicule the sensibilities of one who refuses to barter connubialities. Wife to them is synonymous with *slave*, and *monogamy* is denounced as a vicious *monopoly of affections*." Applauding Stearns's rejection of evil and corruption, the *Practical Christian* saw nothing at Modern Times that would make it preferable to "the times as they universally are, or to some of the very ancient times."[20]

"To barter connubialities" was a sardonic phrase for equating spouse- with labor-swapping. There was no doubt in the mind of Adin Ballou that Modern Times was a pagan and debauched sinkhole. But, to his dismay, the individual sovereignty movement, "which made every man and women [sic] not only his own prophet, priest, and king, but virtually his own law-giver and law-maker—his own God in fact—captivated several of our Hopedale people and interested for a time quite a number of others."

ADIN BALLOU INTERPRETS "CHRISTIAN CHASTITY"

Under the heading "A Free Love Episode," Ballou's *History of the Hope-dale Community* related the scandal of 1853, the discovery by his wife of "Brother" Henry Fish's affair with "Sister" Seaver, their housemate, friend, and co-member of the Practical Christian Republic. Hauled before the Council for examination and discipline, the illicit lovers confessed and swore penitence, only to be charged soon again with the same sin. Brazenly, the miscreants made no attempt to "conceal their criminality, but rather justified it on the ground that it was consonant with the principles of the new philosophy touching personal liberty, sexual relations, and the conjugal bond, which they had embraced— in a word, they openly and unhesitantly avowed themselves to be *Free Lovers* from conviction and in practice also."[21]

Being without sin, the Practical Christians were free to cast stones. They forced Brother Fish and Sister Seaver to resign and flee the sanctum where "both their theory and their action were held in almost universal derision and abhorrence." Compounding their disgrace, the culprits found refuge in "the settlement of kindred *Individual Sovereigns* on Long Island—'Modern Times'—where they undoubtedly found congenial companionship, and unbridled liberty to carry their doctrines out to the farthest possible limit, with no one to question or reproach them, or say them nay."

Speaking of nay-saying, few proscribers of immorality outclassed Adin Ballou, as evidenced by the Practical Christian Republic's Constitution. To emphasize the sinister threat to the marriage covenant now spread abroad "under the specious and captivating guise of *Liberty* and *Reform*," Ballou cited George Stearns's article in the *Art of Living*. Who better qualified to expose "promiscuous cohabitation" than a "man of ability and character . . . unwittingly induced to take up his residence among that 'peculiar people'?" As for the Fish-Seaver scandal, this break in monogamy was one of the "few cases of indiscretion" at Hopedale, and "the only one in which the inculpated parties justified themselves . . . under the bewitching sophistries of 'Free Love.'"[22]

The *Practical Christian* proudly announced that although Hopedale permitted great freedom between the sexes at home, at socials, or in public, there were "few instances of excess, undue liberty, or impropriety, calling for reproof and reprehension."[23] But no sooner were

Fish and Seaver gone than the Republic safeguarded its purity by add-
ing ten resolutions on "Christian Chastity" to its imposing list of by-
laws. Tacked on to a long list of "not to" was any manifestations of
sex by other than legally married partners. "Pure Chastity" prohibited
all "adultery, fornication, self-pollution, and lasciviousness," not only
in the "external act but also in purpose and cherished desire." It out-
lawed having more than one spouse, being a mistress or paramour, di-
vorcing except for adultery, or indulging in married sex "intemperately,
or in any manner contrary to . . . divine order." Hopedale's parents must
guard their young against masturbation or lewdness. Single men and
women should be courteous and frank with each other but "abstain
from all fondling familiarities, effeminate conversations, and immodest
advances" or any other close attachment not "innocently aimed at
ultimate marriage." Of these resolves—which Ballou stated "covered the
whole ground involved in the divinely appointed distinction of sex,
so far as it applies to the human race"—the tenth, last, and most comprehensive restriction proclaimed "That, with our views of Christian
Chastity, we contemplate as utterly abhorrent the various 'Free Love'
theories and practices insidiously propagated among susceptible minds
under pretext of higher religious perfection . . . individual sovereignty,
physiological research and philosophical progress."[24] Resolution Ten
aimed partly at the Perfectionists but its principal target was Modern
Times.

The anarchist aspect of Hopedale was its determination not to
truck with established power, be it the state of Massachusetts or the
government of the United States. It was as sexually inhibited as the
mainstream culture from which it "came out." Top-heavy with by-laws
and regulations, the "free" Republic of Hopedale went out of its way
to make more rules in which to entwine itself, allowing transgressors
no other option than resignation and exile.

THE DEBATE IN THE *NEW YORK TRIBUNE*

Stephen Pearl Andrews, Horace Greeley, and Henry James, Sr., were
Yankee, Protestant-bred, happy husbands who debated the rules of
marriage in the pages of the *Tribune* from November 1852 through February the following year. All were reformers steeped in Fourierism—

Andrews, the activist linguist and sociologist; Greeley, the editor of the national organ of progress and the politician who helped elect Harrison, Taylor, and Lincoln before he sought the prize himself; and James, the philosopher who merged Fourier and Swedenborg into his own cloudy brand of harmony. The debate was a sequence of letters in which Andrews attacked Greeley's defense of "indissoluble marriage" and James's advocacy of liberalized laws of divorce. Andrews published the series of letters—the printed and the censored—in an 1853 book entitled *Love, Marriage, and Divorce, and Sovereignty of the Individual*, reprinted in 1975 with a thoughtful preface by Charles Shively, and additional material written by James and Andrews in 1872.[25]

The *Tribune* debate evolved slowly. Three years earlier, James had translated a critique of marriage that aroused the hackles of proper monogamists. *Love in the Phalansterie*, by a French Fourierist, outlined Fourier's view of civilized marriage (to Fourier current "civilization" was only the mudsill of future harmony; he blamed the institution for adultery, prostitution, venereal disease, and a host of other social problems).[26] Finding these subjects "obscene" and "abominable," the *New York Observer*, house organ of the Presbyterian Church, excoriated James's review. James hit back in his friend Greeley's *Tribune*, but the experience led him to walk a tightrope, as if to avoid another immersion in Presbyterian boiling oil.

James sparked the debate with his review in the *Tribune* of *Love vs. Marriage*, a free-love handbook with a title that gave away the plot but exposed the topic to public discussion.[27] The author, Marx Edgeworth Lazarus, M.D., cited James and other friends of the now defunct Brook Farm as sharing his opinions, "although considerations entirely personal may prevent them from taking openly the same grounds as myself."[28] One "entirely personal" reason was the reluctance of American Fourierists to expose those theories of Fourier which might shock any proper monogamist.

During this era of capital accumulation, men hoarded their sperm as if it were money and called the male orgasm "spending."[29] Americans, according to Shively, "tended to confuse 'passion' with economic self-interest. Thus, if each person pursued his own economic desires, if tariffs and other restraints on trade were dropped, the true order of society could be realized." But to Fourier love, not economic self-interest, "stands first among the passions." However, among all the passions love fares worst in civilization. "It is given no other outlet than marriage. Isn't this enough to suggest that civilization is an order contrary to the designs of God?"[30]

Love vs. Marriage brought free love out of the closet. Lazarus renounced marriage as a false institution that phalansterists should ignore so that, as Shively explains, "the doctrines of Fourier would liberate men and women, enabling them to 'separate or remain together' in work, love, or pleasure 'just as inclination prompts them.'"[31] Men and women will never secure the blessings of tender and concentrated affection, declared Lazarus, by "exclusive marriage vows . . . and the isolated household" (shades of John Humphrey Noyes).[32]

Decent folk of the 1850s could not or would not heed the contention that marriage was another word for servitude for wives in a form of legalized prostitution, and the more radical proposition that men and women could not complete their happiness by lifelong marriage to one mate. Lazarus contended in Fourierist style that "Every marriage, if virtually fulfilled, robs the two individuals who submit to it of their chances for passional affinity in love relations with a great number of others; thus rendering . . . the full harmony of their lives impossible."[33]

Lazarus's slogan could be "to each according to his or her passional affinity, from each according to his or her sexual capacity." As Freud held in Civilization and Its Discontents (a most Fourieristic title), the pursuit of pleasure is a threat that the marketplace cannot tolerate.[34] Nothing in the Tribune debate matched the posing by Dr. Lazarus of the core question of sexual happiness. Rather than deal with the nature of passion, the jousters tilted in the important but less crucial lists of marriage and divorce.

When he reviewed Love vs. Marriage in September 1852, James kept one eye cocked at his Presbyterian critics, warily threading a path between "his own beliefs, those of Lazarus, and enemies waiting to discredit Socialism" (read "Fourierism" for "Socialism").[35] The Observer was not appeased. James found himself enfiladed between the Presbyterians' fire and the wrath of Horace Greeley for having strayed beyond what the pious editor believed was the teaching of Jesus on marriage and divorce. At this point, Stephen Pearl Andrews joined the fray, wearing the colors of anti-marriage and riding under the Modern Times banner of individual sovereignty.

Although as committed to holy and indissoluble monogamy as he was adamantly against divorce, Greeley published a baker's dozen letters by Andrews, James, and himself between November 1852 and the following February. He opened the series by stating, "We are inflexibly opposed to any extension of the privileges of divorce . . . but we are *not* opposed to the discussion of the subject . . . On the contrary, we deem such discussion vitally necessary and already too long neglected. The free trade sophistry respecting marriage is already on every libertine's tongue." Greeley planned to expose and repudiate what to him was the turpitude generated by sovereignty of the individual and dilution of divorce law, by "presenting, reiterating, and enforcing the argument in favor of the sanctity, integrity, and perpetuity of marriage." He gratuitously inserted polygamy into the contest, claiming that it debased ancient Asia and Africa ages before the Mormons. As for allowing marriages to dissolve, "the liberty of divorce has been recognized by great historians as one main cause of the corruption and downfall of the Roman Empire."[36] Horace Greeley protected monogamy as he supported protective tariffs: the future proclaimer of "Free Soil, Free Land, Free Men" excluded free love from his list.

As he and Andrews debated who was the better socialist, Greeley denounced self-sovereignty as egotistical license; instead, he would subject individuals to "the highest good of the community." He informed Andrews that "Your sovereignty of the individual is in palpable collision with the purity of society and the sovereignty of God." His path and Andrews's would never meet, nor could he ever live in the pandemonium created by giving women the right to choose her child's father, which really meant

> her right to choose a dozen fathers for so many different children . . . So long as those who think as I do are the majority in this country, the practitioners of your principles will be dealt with by law like any other malefactors; and, if ever your disciples shall gain the ascendancy, we will go hence to some land where mothers are not necessarily wantons, love is not lust, and the selfish pursuit of sensual gratification is not dignified with the honors due to wisdom and virtue.[37]

The translation of free love to free lust and its attribution to Modern Times was the heaviest cross that the village bore. Recalling the tendency of detractors to label the village promiscuous, Charles Codman observed that "this 'Freedom of Affection' was misinterpreted as 'Free Love' (as if there can be any *Forced Love*) which was found to mean *in the minds of our critics* 'Free *Lust*' and we called 'Free Lovers' as a term of opprobrium."[38]

Whether deliberately or carelessly, both Greeley and James ignored Warren's "each at his or her own cost" provision. They and other opponents spread the impression that individual sovereignty was a purely solipsistic principle, overlooking the qualification that the right to do as each person pleases does not impede the right of any else to do the same.[39]

In his reply to the *Observer* that set off the *Tribune* round-robin, James swore that he yielded to none in "enlightened respect for marriage, whether . . . as a beautiful and very perfect symbol of religious or metaphysical truth, or . . . as an independent social institution." Social institutions, however good intrinsically, may be "very *badly administered, and so* produce mischief." The honor of marriage does not depend on binding two people together when they "hold the reciprocal relation of dog and cat . . . and divorce might profitably intervene . . . provided the parties guaranteed the State against the charge of their offspring." On this condition, James would let incompatible couples part by "freely legitimating divorce."[40]

Against this middle-of-the-road position, Greeley invoked not only the horrid examples of the polygamous ancient world, but also "a plague o' both your houses" in the name of Almighty God. James meant well, but his plan to liberalize divorce would underwrite fickleness and licentiousness, and Andrews's acceptance of free love would only compound the mischief of easy severance. Greeley did not object to divorce in cases of adultery, as expressly sanctioned in the New Testament, "although we *should* oppose even *that*, if it did not cease to be upheld by the personal authority of Christ. Beyond it, we are inflexible."[41]

Andrews hewed to the Mary Gove line. If the knot may be undone, he asked James, why tie it in the first place? Given Webster's meaning of "union for life," then marriage for less than that period was equal to *Hamlet* without the Prince of Denmark. Why stop at the law of divorce, which is only one of the many ways that society meddles with personal liberty? Andrews posed what he claimed was the weightiest question ever asked about human society, one that James should answer more broadly than by his single plank of divorce: "*What is the limit up to which Man, simply in virtue of being Man, is entitled, or right, to the exercise of his freedom, without the interference of society, or—which is the same thing—of other individuals?*" Acts should be free of legal constraint except those that protect one person against the use of force by another. James should face up to this question, but not with vague and "general references to humanitary sentiment."[42]

Andrews appealed to Greeley, as a man open to new ideas such as "Socialism, which you, sir, have done something to foster," to drop his opposition to "that social revolution which you recognize as existing and progressing toward individualism and the sovereignty of the individual." Distinguishing his own version of self-government from Greeley's statism, and at the same time driving a wedge between his opponents, Andrews flattered Greeley's lucidity: "Your positions are intelligible; so, I think, are mine; Mr. James's are such as we find them." But, continued Andrews for Greeley's benefit, his own polity had nothing in common with representative government. "I am a democrat," he avowed. "You, though not a despotist consciously and calling yourself a progressive, are as yet merely a republican . . . I am no sham democrat. I believe in no government of majorities . . . self-government means to me the right of every individual to govern himself, or it means nothing." Andrews pointed with pride to Modern Times, where "a mere handful of individuals, along with myself, do now, for the first time in the world, accept and announce the sovereignty of the individual, with all its consequences, as the principle of *order* as well as of liberty and happiness among men, and challenge its acceptance by mankind. The whole world is drifting to our position."[43]

Andrews outlined the Modern Times concept of "order," which actually was a plan for the absence of order, "in this, the *freest* spot . . . upon the face of the earth, There is no *lèse majesté*, because there is no institution of majesty to be insulted . . . there is no heresy because there is no instituted or established church . . . no seduction and no bigamy, and no adultery, when there is no *legal* or forceful institution of marriage to defend, when woman is recognized as belonging to herself and not to a husband." Woman's fidelity should be to herself, and, if to a man, at her own discretion, on her own terms, and not by any financial bargain. The new "principle of commercial equity" should apply to woman, who "shall be placed upon a footing of entire pecuniary independent of men."[44]

Compared with Greeley's cant and James's vapidity, Andrew's endorsement of woman's rights was forthright and unequivocal. He extended his hand to Greeley: "You do not and can not mean that the time is never to come when woman shall possess the freedom to bestow herself according to the dictates of her own affections, wholly apart from mercenary considerations . . . and to choose freely at all times the father of her child."[45]

Knights errant often wore heavy armor. As many abolitionists looked down on the slaves whose freedom they championed, so did males who debated woman's rights tend to patronize their feminine colleagues. At the height of the debate, Greeley inserted an ingenuous item between letters by himself and Andrews: "We acknowledge the receipt of Mrs. E. [Elizabeth] Oakes Smith's promised exposition of her views on the divorce question, which we shall publish soon . . . But we have one much longer on hand from Mr. S. P. Andrews, which we shall print first, though we consider its contents eminently detestable, while Mrs. Smith's conclusions are just, though her way of looking at the question differs somewhat from ours."[46]

Mrs. Smith, the wife of the mathematician and humorist Seba Smith, was a moderate feminist who had written for the *Tribune* and independently. Greeley had invited her to contribute to the series on marriage and divorce. Earlier in the debate Henry James referred to her, in typically double-standard fashion, as "a well-intentioned lady [who] is engaged in a very arduous crusade against the natural and obvious distinction of the sexes, the which distinction I meanwhile set great store by."[47]

When Smith's views finally were published, expressing concern that the issues pertaining to the female half of humanity were almost exclusively discussed by the masculine half—to the great disadvantage of women—she was "denigrated by Greeley and ignored by James and Andrews." In his transcript of the debate, Andrews did not see fit to include either her letter or that of an anonymous female correspondent, who "denounced the 'double standard' and defended woman's rights to more flexible marriage laws." Mrs. Smith noted sadly that "if the prophet be cast in the feminine . . . men are unwilling to receive her revelations, from the days of Cassandra onward."[48]

The debate kept up until early 1853, when the fastidious Greeley declined to print a letter by Mary Gove submitted by Andrews as the climactic addition to one of his own. Greeley's censorship stemmed from a general refusal to "tolerate the reiterated assumption that fornication, adultery, etc. are no crimes"[49] and a particular squeamishness about soiling his family paper with indelicate subjects and language. Mary Gove's letter appealed for the liberation of women from bearing the offspring of hateful relationships that corrupted marriage until it became the shame of "'lawful whoredom.'" Trapped in "'indissoluble monogamy' with a man she must abhor—a selfish, sensual tyrant," must women "lie prone because it is according to the law?" Mary Gove (and her husband Dr. Thomas Low Nichols) took for granted the misconceptions then prevailing in medical circles. "Intemperance, madness, murder, and all other vices are hereditary," she stated categorically. Shall the version of indissoluble marriage favored and whitewashed by Horace Greeley go on unquestioned, "producing (because of the husband's nature) so many thieves, drunkards, prostitutes, and murderers, and in pre-assignable proportions? Hundreds of women in such marriage murder their children rather than bear them." If crime be transmittable, as disease, then the greatest crime a man can commit is to reproduce himself, even though legally: "In the Medical College at Albany . . . are uterine tumors, weighing from half a pound to twenty-four pounds. A viscus that by its ordinary state weighs a few ounces is brought, by the disease caused by amative excess—in other words, licentiousness and impurity—to weigh more than twenty pounds . . . Monstrosities . . . produced in lawful and indissoluble wedlock."[50]

Although it abounds with incorrect premises, the unpublished letter is the most powerful, passionate contribution to the debate. Clearly, Andrews borrowed from Mrs. Nichols his previous *cri de coeur* for a woman's right to control her body. The issue, trumpeted Mary Gove, was not male lust alone or even the unfair double standard, but woman's right to determine by whom and when to bear her child: "The woman who is truly emancipate . . . needs no human law for the protection of her chastity . . . virtue is to her . . . as high as the sky above Mr. Greeley's lower law, and just as far removed from all license. *Such a woman has a heaven-conferred right to choose the father of her babe* [emphasis added]."[51] This passage is chapter and verse of free love.

THE NICHOLSES

Mary Gove and Thomas Low Nichols were born-and-bred New Hampshirites who met in Manhattan and married in 1848. Thomas had dropped his medical studies at Dartmouth and become a distinguished journalist, but with Mary's financial help he earned his M.D. at New York University in 1850. By the time of their marriage, Mary was a veteran campaigner for woman's rights, inspired to remedial action as the victim of an oppressive marriage that ended in divorce. Hiram Gove, her first husband, despised her opinions but pocketed, under existing law, the fees she earned from speaking and writing about them. He agreed to divorce her only because he owed money to her father, giving Mary up in exchange for cancellation of the debt.

In an 1848 article in *Godey's Magazine and Lady's Book*, Edgar Allan Poe praised Mary Gove as a writer who also was noted for her "lectures on physiology to classes of females. She is, I think, a Mesmerist, a Swedenborgian, a phrenologist, a homeopathist, and a disciple of Priessnitz [the founder of hydropathy]." As unable as the *Tribune* debaters to praise women without condescension, Poe described her writing style as "quite remarkable for its luminousness and precision — two qualities very rare with her sex." In appearance, Poe observed, she was short and thin, with dark hair and "keen, intelligent black eyes. She converses well and with enthusiasm. In many respects a very interesting woman."[52]

Mary lived with a series of male reformers between her separation from Gove and her falling in love with the dashing, red-haired T. L. Nichols. In her autobiographical novel, *Mary Lyndon, or, Revelations of a Life*, she spoke as one of the few contemporary women bold enough to challenge the marital-sexual double standard:

> I was a married woman. A man owned me and all the property
> I had or could accumulate. I had been forgiven rather widely for
> escaping from this owner, but he held me as it were in a net made
> up of the false ideas of marriage, fidelity, morality, and religion.

> I had earned this forgiveness of the community by my great use-
> fulness for separating from my husband, but who would dare for-
> give me if I should love another man until I was legally divorced.

Her "great usefulness," remarked Poe, is as one of the first women lec-
turers on hygiene, water cure, and feminism. In her fictional role as
Mary Lyndon, she describes the pledges that she and her husband exchange at their wedding, beginning with hers.

> I enter into no compact to be faithful to you. I only promise to
> be faithful to the deepest love of my heart. If that love is yours,
> it will bear fruit for you and enrich your life — our life. If my love
> leads you from me, I must go.
>
> He said "You are free. I ask only what is mine, through your love
> . . . I am content to trust."
>
> [She] I must keep my name — the name I have made for myself,
> through labor and suffering.
>
> [He] Agreed.
>
> [She] I must have my room, into which none may come, but be-
> cause I wish it.
>
> [He] Agreed.

The last line of the novel is the unconditional declaration that "Life
is to me, to us, THE HEAVEN OF LOVE."[53]
    And they lived happily ever after, with never a need to invoke
the exit clause of their marriage vows. As a team, the Nicholses col-
laborated so frequently in their health and marriage handbooks and
periodicals that they often confused "I" with "we." No more constant
a couple existed than the one that frenetically urged Modern Timers
to face martyrdom for free love.
    Mary Gove has not been awarded the place she earned in history.
As Warren gathers dust in the shadows of Emerson and Thoreau, Mill
and Spencer, so her image is blurred and her work ignored in comparison to the attention, however deserved, that is paid to Lucretia
Mott, Elizabeth Cady Stanton, Susan B. Anthony, Elizabeth Blackwell, and many other leaders in the movement for woman's rights. The
reason may be that Mary was neither respectable nor a suffragist. Her

biographer, Janet H. Noever, claims Mary Gove as a pioneer feminist
who "must be reclaimed by the historical record not only for the sake
of accuracy, but because of the importance of her challenge to society's
definition of the role of women . . . She was a passionate rebel . . . [who]
opposed authority and broke with established custom or tradition when
they restricted women."[54]

THE NICHOLSES COME TO MODERN TIMES

George Stearns the defector made no mistake about the nonresident
lobby at Modern Times. According to Taylor Stoehr, Lazarus, Andrews, and the Nicholses, "constituted the inner circle of the new [free
love] movement. It was Mary Nichols around whom the others flut-
tered. Like Fanny Wright twenty years earlier, or Victoria Woodhull
twenty years later, she knew how to turn to account her remarkable
endowment of energy and audacity."[55] Lazarus and his sister Ellen[56]
once resided at Mary Gove's Grahamite, water-cure boardinghouse in
Manhattan; in December 1852, Stephen Pearl Andrews addressed the
first class of young women to graduate from the Nicholses' American
Hydropathic Institute at Port Chester, New York.

In the early summer of 1853, a *Tribune* editorial denounced the
Institute as an ostensibly water-cure establishment that really was engaged in the "insidious inculcation and practical realization of Mr. S. P.
Andrews's remarkably free and easy notions respecting Love and Marriage." A few days later the *Tribune* printed a letter signed "Villager,"
impeaching Andrews and Dr. Nichols (the writer seemed unaware of
Mary Gove Nichols's participation) for the high crime and misdemeanor
of spreading "the doctrine of the sovereignty of the individual." Attempting the "practical application of such filthy doctrines as those in-
culcated by Messrs. Nichols and Andrews . . . the philosophy of the
brothel" had caused a stampede away from the school and resulted in
its demise.

Dr. Nichols indignantly answered that Andrews not only was
not on the staff, but was a gentleman of irreproachable conduct who,
whatever may be thought of his theories, was "happily married to a
beautiful woman, and has three children." Impugning the integrity of
"Villager"—doubtlessly not a resident of Port Chester but a promoter

of "a rival Establishment"—Dr. Nichols courted investigation of his own spotless conduct "as husband, parent, teacher, physician and man of business."[57]

In July 1853, at Andrews's invitation, the volatile couple removed to the Long Island pine woods to set up a new and grander school on a plat of one hundred acres, directly west of Modern Times.[58] An article in *Nichols' Journal* explained that the Port Chester Institute's closing was moot, because, explained the doctor, "I am now building on Long Island, a splendid edifice, one hundred and twenty-six feet long, and four stories high, as the commencement of the Institute of Desarrollo, an Educational and Industrial Institute, such as does not now exist, but such as the world needs more than any other."[59]

The Institute of Desarrollo ("pronounced Desarrolio, a word of Spanish origin"),[60] was to be a School of Life for the training of pupils paying $50, plus room, board, and laundry (at cost) for a sixteen-week course in "the principles and practices of Water Cure." The curriculum consisted of "lectures and studies in Natural Philosophy, Chemistry, Anatomy, Physiology, Pathology, Hydro-Therapeutics, Surgery, and Obstetrics." A diploma conferred no legal power, but, as the Nicholses did not recognize the right of "any legislators to prescribe to people who shall be their teachers and healers, we have asked for no chartered authority." Graduates qualified as water-cure physicians would fan out across the nation to teach how "not only to prepare to live, but to live."[61] Codman remembered Desarrollo, the projected four-storied complex with a tower of sixty feet and room for two hundred resident students, as "a project of grand conception but died still born."[62] After digging the cellar and laying one wall (Bowles was working on it at the time of his *Sunday Dispatch* interview), the Nicholses could not attract another dollar to augment the five hundred already invested.

THE NICHOLSES VS. JOSIAH WARREN

The Nicholses were fire-eating paladins of an endless series of movements ranging from water cure to Grahamism, phrenology, sex education, mesmerism, Fourierism, spiritualism, the Bloomer costume, homeopathy, and—in their short, explosive sojourn—free love at Modern Times. Beginning where Noyes left off, they focused on the right of woman, denied at Oneida, to choose when and by whom to bear her child. Contending that wives were legitimized prostitutes serving the passions of husbands to whom they were legal and social inferiors, the Nicholses demanded an end to discrimination based on gender. In need of a command post, they selected Modern Times.

Their battle with Warren erupted when, no sooner than their bags were unpacked, they tried to enlist an army of free lovers under the banner of individual sovereignty. At Modern Times, Noyes wrote waggishly, "Dr. T. L. Nichols inaugurated the system of 'Free Love' or Individual Sovereignty in sexual intercourse."[63] Charles Codman recalled how the Nicholses applied Warren's sovereignty of the individual to the marriage relationship: They advocated the "Freedom of the affections," claiming that "in freedom, Love would cure the evils of unhappy marriages, for the benefit of the race and improvement of the offspring and bring harmony in to replace Matrimonial discord."[64]

On Warren's part, sex and mating were personal matters for couples to handle as each saw fit, but never a rule to which all must conform. Twenty-five years had passed since he witnessed the collapse of New Harmony, accelerated by Robert Owen's gratuitous condemnation of ownership, marriage, and religion. In his Fourth of July address in 1826, the fiftieth anniversary of American independence, Owen proclaimed his own Declaration of Mental Independence, denouncing as hostile to "FULL FREEDOM OF THE HUMAN MIND . . . A TRINITY of . . . monstrous evils. . . . I refer to PRIVATE, OR INDIVIDUAL PROPERTY — ABSURD AND IRRATIONAL SYSTEMS OF RELIGION — AND MARRIAGE, FOUNDED ON INDIVIDUAL PROPERTY COMBINED WITH SOME OF THESE IRRATIONAL SYSTEMS OF RELIGION."[65]

Now engaged in building his own halfway house between the old and the new moral orders, Warren dreaded repeating Owen's mistake of attacking accepted institutions peripheral to the purpose. At state was the quiet growth of Modern Times as an incubator of equity: how could it survive once the polemics of rash associates brought down the wrath of the outside world?

Some disagreed with this cautious approach. In 1853, the apogee of their free-love orbit, Mary Gove and Thomas Low Nichols announced a new apocalypse. The August issue of *Nichols' Journal of Health, Water-Cure, and Human Progress* published "City of Modern Times," an article in which Dr. Nichols extolled the garden community where "there are no by-laws or regulations of any kind. There is no association. Each man is an individual and a law unto himself." The only rule recognized here is of *"The Sovereignty of the Individual, to be exercised at his own cost."* No one should come here unless determined to mind his or her own business and abide in the spirit of equity. Dr. Nichols informed his readers that he expressed "his own individual opinion, and feeling," but toward the end of the article he inserted a statement by "Mrs. Nichols, who enters with her usual enthusiasm and devotion into this movement."[66]

Mary Gove began quietly, even defensively, to preach the gospel of common sense to be realized in the free love millennium:

> We come together for freedom, in the midst of great reproach.
>
> We believe that Love alone sanctions the union of the sexes . . . this faith . . . does not only allow people to break false unions, but it allows them to form true ones; and if they make mistakes, it allows of their correction, instead of the perpetuation of discord and evil in children.

So far, so good. Abruptly, the pitch rose to paranoid levels as she called for volunteers for martyrdom in the cause of sexual freedom:

> Each person who wishes to go to Modern Times must answer readily and affirmatively such questions as the following:
>
> Am I brave and strong enough to meet all the difficulties of a new settlement?
>
> Have I the honesty and heroism to become of no reputation for the truth's sake?
>
> Am I willing to be considered licentious by the world, because of my obedience to a law, higher than worldlings can conceive of?[67]

WARREN COUNTERATTACKS

The participation of Andrews in the *Tribune* debate on marriage raised Warren's hackles but failed to provoke him to overt action. Not so with the Nicholses' free-love decree. The spectacle of Modern Times as command post of sexual liberation, proclaimed with his apparent approval by its heralds, Thomas and Mary Gove Nichols, enraged the usually mild-mannered Warren. That *all* Modern Timers *must* do anything breached the wall of self-sovereignty, as did the entire tone of an article speaking in the name of all when it was the product of only two. Furious at the suggestion that Modern Times promoted free love in the name of individual sovereignty, Josiah dashed off *Positions Defined,* a broadside against the Nicholses, which he nailed to the village bulletin board for all who agreed to sign: "An impression is abroad . . . that the "Equity movement" is necessarily characterized by an unusual latitude in the Marriage relations—I as one, protest against this idea. "The Sovereignty of every Individual" is as valid a warrant for *retaining the present relations,* as for changing them; and it is equally good for refusing to be drawn into any controversy or even conversing on the subject."[68]

Warren objected to any "sudden and unprepared change in the sexual relations," burdened with "more embarrassments and more disastrous consequences than their advocates or the public generally are aware of." In *Positions Defined* he removed himself even from entertaining the subject for controversy or conversation. Modern Timers were under no compulsion to answer questions, follow a specified order of love, or be responsible for anyone else's acts or words: "It is my right to have the making of my own reputation, and . . . no person . . . is to be understood as a representative of me, unless my sanction is specifically given, to every idea thus advanced; and that no Newspaper or Journal is to be understood as an organ for me, except so far as it may have my signature to the articles it may contain." An italicized *"NOTE"* appeared under the signature of "An 'Individual'": *"Although this is written in accordance with the INDIVIDUALITY which it asserts, it may be signed by any number of persons with equal propriety as by one."*[69]

Positions Defined set forth Warren's insistence that no combination or organization could represent the separate sovereigns. When the Nicholses broke the unwritten rule and spoke in the name of all, he followed suit by stating what "I" feel on behalf of "us." No record remains of how many signed, but the Nicholses' hasty departure suggests that most of the sovereigns sided with Warren.

Here was the Achilles' heel of individual sovereignty. It was vulnerable when threatened, forced at that moment to waive the independence of each from all and let the majority rule. Philosophical anarchism is a beautiful bird that cannot fly, a means of exposing the pretense of power but hard-pressed to cope with decision making.

When faced with a challenge to his unstated but understood role as leader, Warren took action to mobilize opinion against the Nicholses. The village he envisaged as the shining example of equitable commerce stood accused of sexual licence because of its link to the free-love crusade. His concern was to guard Modern Times against further attack once the spotlight of the *Tribune* debate exposed it to thrill seekers, scandalmongers, and prying opponents of social change. Yet compared to his economic program, which had no chance of prevailing against the surging factory-market system, the campaign to reform the law of marriage was an idea whose time was near.

Using Warrenite terminology, the Nicholses defined free love as a method for men and women to satisfy their true attraction, doing what is best for each "so long as [it] does not infringe upon the equal right of another." But Warren recoiled from their ultra–free-love gospel, as expressed by Mary Gove on another occasion. "If this is monogamy – the single and eternal union, very well – well for those who are fortunate enough to find it; or who keep trying and experimenting until they do, or do not. If it is variety – either a succession of loves, or several, various in kind and degree at the same time, it is nothing to me."[70]

Warren declined to join the Nicholses in all-out war on marriage, which to him was not the enemy. He assailed their effort to speak for the village, declaring in his newsletter that many Modern Timers "strongly object to Nichols' Journal being considered the organ for the place." The only "free paper" was one that expressed the views of "its editor or conductor; and a very small sheet will contain all I have to communicate periodically." The Nicholses had no warrant to formulate policy for the village in their paper; moreover, their book on marriage contained an "an astonishing amount of wild, undigested statements and delusive reasoning" which could lead inexperienced readers to "embarrassing and disastrous positions." Taking a far from militant stand on mating, Warren wrote that "From twenty-nine years constant contact with this subject, as one of the greatest of human interests to be ameliorated, I am entirely satisfied that no systematic or extensive changes can be suddenly made in the Marriage relations with safety."[71]

Warren struggled to shield Modern Times from its increasingly sinful reputation as pulpit of free-love fundamentalism. "Mr. Warren deprecated this phase of agitation," noted Codman, "mainly from fear that this Equity movement might be burried [sic] out of sight by that of Freedom [free love]."[72] Years later, when reminiscing about Modern Times, Warren responded to a questioner who "intimated that the odious doctrine of 'Free Love' was fastened on the village in order to set the public against the movement." The right of self-sovereignty, Warren asserted, gave free scope for "Free Love, or any ism or crotchet, however ridiculous or dangerous." Individual sovereigns had perfect freedom so long as they acted at their own cost: "Whoever tries what is vulgarly known as 'Free Love' (if I understand what the words mean) will find it more troublesome than a crown of thorns: and there is not much danger of its becoming contagious where the results of experiments are made known." Josiah's typically free-choice conclusion was that however disastrous its consequences, "to forbid it and keep people ignorant of the *effects* of it [would invite] danger of trouble inexpressible." One way to link marriage with equity might be contractual bonds between mates, renewable by mutual consent "for a definite, specified length of time, understood and agreed upon. In some countries the time agreed on is a year or two."[73] That was the limit of his willingness to change the format of wedlock.

In his biography of Warren, William Bailie reported one of Josiah's few other statements on marriage, expressed in a letter written when he was seventy-five years old. Warren's conclusions, reached after study of the subject from the time he was sixteen, were similar to what he said twenty years before in the *Periodical Letter*. The present condition was "frightfully wrong . . . [but] with the sudden and total abolition of all Marriage customs and habits, without replacing them with some definite, regulating, preserving thought and arrangement, our social condition would be worse, if possible, than it is now."[74]

THE NICHOLSES' RETREAT

Two months after *Positions Defined*, *Nichols' Journal* pleaded for correction of all that was wrong with sexual relations in general and with marriage in particular. It chided Warren for evading these vital issues. "Mr. Warren may refuse to discuss this subject: we cannot refuse. No man of science and philanthropy can refuse to speak the truth on a question so vast and important. The World wants light on this more than on all the other subjects; and it shall have what light we can give it! *Are we right or wrong?*"[75]

Hyperbolic and rhetorical as their questions usually were, the Nicholses deserved an answer to this one. When it was not forthcoming, they left Modern Times abruptly, for more reasons than lack of support for Desarrollo.

Warren won the battle but lost the war. The Nicholses' influence lingered, stirring up the village as did no other single issue. The free-love controversy fueled public perception of Modern Times as Sodom in the pine barrens, but it helped to focus attention on the need for reform of the rules of marriage. It was also the Nicholses' last hurrah for sexual radicalism. After leaving Modern Times they trimmed the lamp of free love, recommending to the small membership of their new and short-lived model village, Memnonia, in Yellow Springs, Ohio, that sex was for procreation only. Here they ran afoul of Horace Mann, who feared that the presence of sexual radicals would smear the reputation of his newly formed Antioch College. He fretted needlessly: once the Nicholses saw the light of chastity they no longer crusaded for free love.[76] The last stop on their intellectual pilgrimage was in April 1857, when they announced their conversion to Roman Catholicism:

> We have been socialists of the school of Fourier, and have earnestly labored for the establishment of a unitary or harmonious society. Our studies and efforts have brought the conviction that such social regeneration is possible only in a holy life. It has pleased God to bring us to accept his Holy Church. In that Church we see the order, the devotion, the consecration, the faith and obedience necessary for the great work of human redemption. Believing in and submitting to the Church, we look to the accomplishment of its divine mission . . . I have found already inexpressible peace.[77]

As usual, "we" and "I" are mixed. Taylor Stoehr observes that Dr. Nichols, reborn as a sexual purist after adoption of religious faith, revised his *Esoteric Anthropology* (1853), "pruning the free love from the physiology [of] the first marriage manual deserving of the name."[78] At the time of the Civil War, the Nicholses expatriated themselves to England, where they renounced free love, converted to sexual purity, and continued pressing for food reform, water cure, and hygiene for the rest of their long and useful lives.[79]

Thomas Low Nichols included a disparaging sketch of Modern Times in his book, *Forty Years of American Life,* a pungent view of antebellum society through the eyes of a Yankee Alexis de Tocqueville. Nichols strayed from objectivity to pillory his former home as the nadir of anarchistic license, where marriages dissolved at will "and free love was placed in the same category with all other freedom. A man might have one wife, or ten, or more, if he could take upon himself the proper cost . . . and the same freedom was asserted for women as men."[80]

This Greeleyesque judgment was tossed off as if the author never championed the doctrine he now professed to abhor. Published ten years after the Nicholses' failure to order the love of Modern Times, it should be taken with a grain or two of salt, if not simply labeled sour grapes, T. L. Nichols, if anyone, knew that the gist of free-love philosophy was affectionate pairing, not Mormon polygyny or Fourierist polyandry.

Polygamy among consenting sovereigns at Modern Times was conceivable, but rare. "We are not Mormons," declared Benjamin Bowles in the *Sunday Dispatch* interview of October 1853, just after the Warren-Nichols schism. Warren recalled one young man who came to the village to live in a house with three young women. In their relaxed tolerance, "The settlers, faithful to the great sacred right of Freedom even to do silly things . . . [let] them go on entirely undisturbed, though the effects of their conduct were disturbing every other settler." Not even two people, let alone four, can drive one horse at the same time, remarked Warren: "Three months trial taught them this inevitable lesson," but, he concluded ruefully, "the effects toward the place were much more enduring."[81]

In his article published in 1865, eight years after his visit, Moncure Daniel Conway portrayed Modern Times as an antebellum Peyton Place. After a long account of his enjoyment at taking part in a Sunday philosophical give-and-take, Conway proceeded to report that mating at Modern Times was an informal game of catch-as-catch-can. His version of how potential bed-partners showed whether they were spoken for makes his account stand out from any other. "The relation could be dissolved at pleasure without any formulas . . . Those who stood in the relation of husband or wife wore upon the finger a red thread; and so long as that badge was visible the person was understood to be married. If it disappeared the marriage was at an end."[82]

If accurate, this report should be corroborated by some other history, memoir, or record of Modern Times. Because no other source mentions "red threading," the thought arises that Conway the novelist may have been stringing his readers along. Or might the red thread be Conway the reformer's metaphor, calling on his Victorian compatriots to relax their austere morality?

THE SOVEREIGNS' OPINION

Warren understood much better than Andrews or the Nicholses that the people of Modern Times preferred to talk than to fight for reform. They thought of the village as home and subsistence—a model for emulation but not a fort from which to bombard the world. The sovereigns rejected the confrontational style. Talk was their surrogate for action: they were sociable rather than socialist. They engaged in a nonstop seminar in which individuals took positions, accepting the right of others to differ. Their answer to the Nicholses' question "Are we right or wrong?" was a qualified "Yes" and "No." Yes, you are right to raise the issue of free love, but no, you are wrong to expect us to join your crusade. We may experiment with it, we will surely debate it, but we will not march on your picket line. Modern Times may be your battlefield of Armageddon, but to us it is home, the first home that most of us are able to own.

To see Modern Times through the pioneers' eyes is to witness a genial, garrulous band of freethinkers, thrashing out every aspect of reform in a sort of continuous kaffeeklatsch, aiming to understand, not to judge. This easygoing sanity—so different from the rigidity of Oneida, Hopedale, and Shaker "order," or the intensity of the Nicholses, or the prudery of mainstream morality—is reflected in Charles Codman's memoir. Remembering many a talk-fest on the marriage relations and free love, his quintessentially Modern Times judgment was: "'Twas a fruitful topic for discussion." Despite what the mudslingers said, "there were very little changes among our people—the married remained in the bonds of matrimony and the unmarried did not drop into immorality." The current marriage relation was "far from ideal," so connected to women's need for financial support that it often was *"but a condition of Concubinage* tho' it may have the Sanction of Church and Law." As might be expected, "our people examined the subject" and came up with conclusions that varied "as each one's right." His version of "the truth" contradicted Mary Gove's party line. The truth was "that while many of the 'Sovereigns' upheld the Mother's choice of the Paternity of her child, yet 'twas a theory hardly ever put into practice but was a favorite text for many an argument for Freedom in all domains of thought and action."[83]

Unwilling to march with the ultras, the pioneers ambled along at their own moderate pace in reforming existing convention. They took two significant stands: to be indifferent to the marital status of settlers and to provide a haven where men and women could reshape their lives in the wake of unhappy marriages. "Do you hold to marriage?" asked B. D. J., the *Sunday Dispatch* reporter, to which question Bowles gave an interesting answer: "Oh marriage! Well, folks ask no questions in regard to *that* among us. We, or at least some of us, do not believe in life-partnerships, when the parties can not live happily . . . We don't interfere: there is no eavesdropping, or prying behind the curtains."[84]

Bowles's answer reflected not only the Modern Times motto of "Mind your own business" but also the sovereigns' reluctance to talk about marriage with strangers—testers of aberrant social theories make easy targets for muckrakers. There is no confirmation of Conway's "red-threading," just as Nichols's contention that marriages were dissolved at will may have been a disgruntled distortion. But if no one answered the Nicholses' bugle call for martyrs brave enough to sacrifice reputation and risk everything for free love, Bowles forthrightly stated the sovereigns' disdain for propriety.

Moncure Conway was not just spinning another red-thread yarn when, with Mary Chilton as his example, he showed the value of Modern Times to victims of incompatible unions. This lovely and gracious Southern woman once was trapped in a marital situation similar to Mary Gove's; after she separated from her husband, he and the law cruelly deprived her of her children. Chilton's experience "led her to sum up the chief evils of society in the one word *marriage.* Indeed, it was plain to me before I left Modern Times that nearly all who resided on that lonely shore had been cast there by the wreck of their barks."[85]

Mary Chilton and Theron C. Leland married and lived for the rest of their lives in Mrs. Nichols's ideal state of "single and eternal union." Clearly, Modern Times was one of the few places where, in the heyday of Grundy, a divorced woman with three children was welcome to settle, meet her future partner, and live with him before they married.

"NOW FOR GOSSIP"

Conway often garnished fact with fiction, but not in his judgment that Modern Times was a harbor for refugees from disastrous marriages. Josiah Warren, married but estranged from his wife, no doubt lived for a while with Mrs. Jane Cran, a woman of uncertain marital status. William Metcalf and Sophia Hayward legalized decades of cohabitation by marrying in their seventies, perhaps after the death of Sophia's English husband.[86] Henry Fish and "Sister" Seaver, when the Practical Christians of Hopedale condemned them for adultery, turned to Modern Times as naturally as fugitive slaves to the underground railway. Henry became a pillar of the community, his support for public education confirmed in the "Minute Book of District 12." The 1860 census listed him as living with his wife, Malinda, perhaps the former "Sister" Seaver. Sadly, his name appeared for the last time on the roster of Union Soldiers: "Henry Fish, Brentwood, 84th [N.Y. regiment]; m [missing in action]."[87]

Mulling over his years in the village, Codman recalled only two children born out of wedlock. On one occasion, "the Mother was later married and became a 'respectable married woman.'" The other was by intent of a "Lady who lost no credit among our people" by choosing an "intelligent, upright, and healthy man as the father of her boy and was proud that she had done so."[88]

But in his long letter to Henry Edger while the latter was in England, late in 1858, Codman gave a more candid version of the lady and her upright man. "Now for gossip," the letter began. ". . . Martha Loveland has moved to Ada's house and occupies the north room. Her appearance indicates a rapidly approaching maternity." The prospect of motherhood was not pleasing to Martha, who was "badly off" for birthing and baby supplies. When Mrs. Fisher informed the villagers of her plan to "hang up a stocking on Christmas Eve for the benefit of Martha," Emily told her that "she had conscientious scruples against furnishing any aid or comfort to Martha while [Edward] Linton, the reputed father" [now gone from Modern Times] was reported to be "earning $15 per week." Mrs. Fisher replied that "Martha was an individual and did not look to Linton for support and that probably she did not know whom to charge *it* upon, that she had been intimate with several." If so, suggested Emily, let "Martha's lovers cooperate in the matter."[89]

Linton's departure from Modern Times, wrote Codman cheerily, met with "the almost universal joy of its inhabitants." His impregnation of Martha Loveland and subsequent move away from the village apparently were taken in stride by his wife. "Mrs. Linton," continued Codman, "is quietly domesticated with Mr. Wormwood in the original Bowles cottage. They seem like two turtle doves. I think her quite a pleasant woman."[90]

In addition to shedding light on the sexual mores of Modern Times, the letter revealed that as early as 1858, five years before he and Ada divorced, Codman lived with his future wife while Ada lived in another house. It is not clear if, or when, Ada moved back to her husband's home, but she resided there in 1860, according to the census (a less than ironclad source); the Codman household consisted of Charles and Ada, Charles's father, William, and Miss Emily Studley, Charles's later and afterwards permanent wife. This design for living did not imply a three-cornered affair—Charles and Ada were legally separated—but rather a friendly solution to Ada's need for shelter.

Charles's estrangement from Ada and his relationship with Emily began before, or soon after, they all departed from Boston. The separation agreement "made this 29th day of July A.D. 1858 between Charles A. Codman of the County of Suffolk in the State of New York . . . and Caroline Adelaide Codman his wife" committed Charles to assume support for Ada for the rest of her natural life at the oddly low rate of four dollars a year—"payable quarterly." On the following 13 June, the parties canceled the first deed with a new arrangement, calling for Charles to pay Ada the lump sum of $500, in consideration of which she would "forever acquit and discharge [him] . . . from the payment of all or any part of said yearly allowance."[91]

Charles and Emily were a devoted couple who shared an abiding interest in all sorts of social activity. From the time they wed until Emily died, twenty-three years later, their home was the center where every Sunday evening the village intelligentsia met for refreshments and lively discussions.

Several other eyebrow-raising households stand out on the census of 1860. One was the *ménage à trois* of sixty-year-old Barney Lewis and his female companions, Caroline Loring, thirty-five years old, and Lizzy Piper, thirty—all Vermonters by birth—along with Warren Piper, Lizzy's year-old son. Another unusual combination was New Hampshire–born Sumner Fisher, thirty-nine, and a thirteen-year-old English lass, Mary A. Culpeck. Mrs. Fisher (the generous woman who hung up a Christmas stocking for Martha Loveland) does not appear on the census taken two years later. There are no data to determine if these households were love nests of people far apart in age, or innocent combinations arranged by families or friends. As may be said about many a Modern Times affair of the heart, *honi soit qui mal y pense*.

Although these examples reinforce the village's spicy reputation, the devotion of couples like Mary Chilton and Theron C. Leland and Charles and Emily Codman, before and after their second marriages, validates the primary role of Modern Times as a refuge for unhappy spouses.

THE EVIDENCE OF THE DEEDS

It is risky to draw conclusions from meager evidence, but the deed *Libers* more than the census suggest an answer to the puzzle of whether couples were married, cohabitants, or merely friendly roommates. For example, the 1860 manuscript census shows Rebecca Cornwall as an apparently unmarried woman living with Myndert Fish (not a known

relative of Henry Fish), but their several recorded deeds name her as
Mrs. Myndert Fish.[92] In the 1852 Circular are the paired names of Robert Gray and Angelina R. Skinner, whom the deed *Liber* shows as
man and wife—Robert and Angelina Skinner Gray.[93] Evidently, some
female cohabitants were either Lucy Stoners or wives who used their
maiden names on other than legal documents. This practice may apply to the household headed by Stilman Hazelton, forty years old, who
lived with Hannah Dunbar, thirty-nine, and her eighteen-year-old
daughter, Francetta—he from Vermont and they from New Hampshire
—or that of Stephen Taylor, thirty-six, who lived with Jane Wilson,
thirty-five—both of whom were from Connecticut.

Among Modern Times's most remarkable deed-holders was James
Arrington Clay, of Gardiner, Maine, "one of the first free lovers called
to account for his affronts to popular mores and the law of the land."[94]
Clay, forty years old and married, went to jail in Augusta on a charge
of adultery plus lewd and lascivious cohabitation with a young unmarried woman he had brought into his home. "The evidence," he wrote
in his account of the case, *A Voice from the Prison*, ". . . was that we
slept in the same bed," a charge less provocative than it seemed because when "two respectable medical men" examined his friend Lily
she proved to be a virgin.[95] Clay paid his immaculate lover's fine but
served six months in jail himself (August 1855–February 1856). While
in prison he heard the shocking news that Lily soon would marry, entering a state that Clay informed her "sounds to me like legal slavery,
legal suicide, legal murder, legal death."[96]

The Suffolk County *Liber* of deeds shows that Clay bought lots
149 and 150 at Modern Times on Christmas Eve 1855 (the date is somewhat mystifying because he was in jail at the time), and sold them in
May 1860.[97] He visited long before making his purchase, as his book
contains a "Letter to Eva [his young daughter]" written from "Modern
Times, L.I., N.Y., 1852."[98] Calling himself "a cast-off by those who love
their idols better than the truth," Clay implied in the letter that he
and his wife were separated, a situation familiar to many residents of
the village. Except for his real estate transactions, no evidence can be
found that he took part in Modern Times's activities. Perhaps the Clays
reconciled by 1860; their Modern Times holdings were sold by James
and Emily S. Clay, his wife, both of Gardiner, Maine.[99]

The rhetoric of James Arrington Clay and the other free-love activists paralleled William Lloyd Garrison's. Clay's abolitionism extended from chattel to wage and marital slavery, but "Marriage slavery, first of all." Although he was a tub-thumping Scripture citer, some of his views resembled Warren's. He protested that "any majority, or minority, exercise their laws over me, when I infringe not on the rights of other individual beings."[100] "Clay, like Warren," remarked a communitarian scholar, "accepted private enterprise while rejecting capitalism."[101]

"I ask for the complete emancipation and self-ownership of woman, simply as I ask the same for man," declared Andrews to James and Greeley.[102] "We oppose Marriage as Abolitionists oppose Slavery," thundered the blissfully married Nicholses, as they condemned Marx Edgeworth Lazarus, their former fellow scourge of wedlock, for deserting the ranks of bachelorhood in 1855.[103]

GOOD TIMES AT MODERN TIMES

The sovereigns were short on capital, long on ideas, their days and nights enlivened by talk, music, and drama. In the summer of 1854, a reporter for the *New York Weekly Leader* attended a dancing party at Modern Times. In his sprightly write-up, "D. P. W." marveled that the girls all wore the Bloomer costume and asked the men to dance, a custom that "took us down . . . This custom is not exclusive; sometimes the men ask the women . . . By the by, how these Modern Timesers do dance! We, who thought ourselves tolerably well posted up, were literally nowhere among the Bloomers."[104]

"Mrs. Bloomer's" style of female apparel "comprising short skirts and Turkish trousers" had just become popular, Codman remarked. "Many of the ladies of this Village," he continued, "adopted and wore the costume, thinking it both healthful and convenient, and as 'twas the custom of women reformers to wear short hair, the Bloomer costume gave a youthful appearance and added to their comliness [sic]. I may mention here that male reformers wore their hair long—a sort of badge— an outward sign of their affiliation with progress."[105]

D. P. W. agreed that the Bloomer costume gave its wearers a young and girlish look. During the evening, he reported, "one of the 'Individuals'–Mr. I. H. Cook" sang a popular song, "The Bloomer." One pictures the sovereigns, men with long hair and women with short, singing along to the rollicking tune of "Oh! Susanna":

1. Come, all ye daughters of the land
        And sing in joyous strain,
    For your salvation is at hand
        From fashion's filth and pain.
    Loud let the name of Bloomer sound,
        Hills, plains and valley's o'er–
    As lightly, freely, skip and bound,
        As birds unfettered soar!

O the Bloomer! that's the dress for me!
Soon may its beauty, freedom, health appreciated be!

2. "The House I live in" shall no more
        Be burdened and confined;
    With broom I'll sweep the hearth or floor,
        But not with skirt behind.
    I now can walk or run erect:
        I now can whirl or dance:
    Pass nimbly up and down the stairs,
        For now I–wear the pants!

O the Bloomer! etc.

3. I'll never mind the scoff or hiss
        Of senseless fop or belle,
    For they have sorrow, I have bliss;
        They're sick, but I am well.
    My garments e'er shall indicate
        Thought, purity of mind.
    My form shall be elastic, straight,
        Attractive and refined!

O the Bloomer! etc.[106]

Seasonal "Jollifications" planned included "a dance after theater Christmas . . . a Refreshment Party on New Year's Eve, and another on Paine's Birthday, 29th January."[107] Dances, plays, and musicals were held in "Thespian Hall" at the corner of Third Avenue and Fifth Street;

later, William U. Dame transformed the second floor of his octagon house into "Archimedian Hall," where for some years the sovereigns danced and held meetings. Henry Edgar formed a Glee Club for men, "also one for women . . . rendering mainly English [madrigals] and German compositions." There was a Shakespeare reading club: the village circulating library had "some 300 Volumes." Discussion was the favorite sport: at one time "the philosophers organized a Foot Ball game, but very soon gave it up . . . [they] were better at talking than kicking each others shins."[108]

"LOW LIVING AND HIGH THINKING"

A clique of sexual radicals tried to make Modern Times its sounding board, stretching sovereignty of the individual to fit its anti-marriage party line. Their tone, however, was too strident for the low-key majority of sovereigns. Warren and most of the settlers declined to turn the village into a combat zone for free love. Perhaps the "Peaceful Revolutionist" was wrong to dodge the sexual-marital challenge and hew to the line of equitable commerce, an arrow against exploitation that proved helpless against the onslaught of the factory-market-profit system. But rather than take an official position binding on the community, he and most Modern Timers preferred that couples make their own decisions to marry or to live in what Adin Ballou and a good many others called sin.

This enclave of happy-go-lucky eccentrics dented the facade of Victorian-American prudery. Their open-mindedness scorned drummers of misinformation who peddled the doctrine that masturbation, nocturnal emission, sex before marriage, sex during marriage except for propagation, and sex after the age of fifty were either sinful or physically dangerous (probably both). The sexually heretical sovereigns defied the "spermatic economy," the theory that semen was a nonrenewable asset for which there was no depletion allowance.[109] They thought of their somewhat immoral, luxury-free, and mentally stimulating life-style as one of "Low Living and High Thinking,"[110] the Brook Farm slogan picked up by the sovereigns with "plain" replaced by the double-edged "low."

The appropriate pivot of Modern Times was the issue of woman's rights, a focus of national attention long after equitable commerce faded into memory. Mary Gove and Thomas Low Nichols, Stephen Pearl Andrews, and Marx Edgeworth Lazarus — the men often patronizing the women they sought to liberate — were victors in the long run over moralists even more heavily burdened with myths of the double standard.

Josiah Warren. This picture, labeled "From a Photograph by Frank Rowell," was used as the frontispiece for William Bailie's biography, *Josiah Warren, the First American Anarchist: A Sociological Study* (Boston: Small, Maynard & Co., 1906). Courtesy of the Warren MSS, Workingmen's Institute Library, New Harmony, Ind.

The Pine Barrens, the Metcalf-Hayward House, and Josiah Warren's "Mechanical College." Pencil sketch by A. J. Macdonald, June 1852, in his "Materials for a History of Ideal Communities" (The Yale University Collection of American Literature, Beinecke Rare Book and Manuscript Library, Yale University). Photograph of the drawing, courtesy of the Modern Times Collection, Brentwood Public Library, Brentwood, N.Y.

Stephen Pearl Andrews. Courtesy of the Modern Times Collection, Brentwood Public Library, Brentwood, N.Y.

Edgar Fenn Peck, M.D. Courtesy of the Modern Times Collection, Brentwood Public Library, Brentwood, N.Y.

Thompson's Station. Courtesy of the Modern Times Collection, Brentwood Public Library, Brentwood, N.Y.

Labor notes used at Modern Times. Courtesy of the Modern Times Collection, Suffolk County Historical Society, Riverhead, N.Y.

Charles A. Codman. Courtesy of the Modern Times Collection, Brentwood
Public Library, Brentwood, N.Y.

Emily Studley Codman. The second wife of Charles A. Codman. Courtesy of the Modern Times Collection, Brentwood Public Library, Brentwood, N.Y.

Henry Edger in early life and in later years. (Brentwood, N.Y.: Brentwood Village Press, 1950. Courtesy of the Modern Times Collection, Brentwood Public Library, Brentwood, N.Y.

Schoolhouse at Modern Times. The octagonal, one-room building used from 1857 until 1907, moved in 1989 to the grounds of Brentwood High School, where it awaits the raising of funds to restore it. Courtesy of the Modern Times Collection, Brentwood Public Library, Brentwood, N.Y.

5

Equitable Commerce

JUST AS MODERN TIMERS DID NOT CARE if couples lived out of wedlock, so were they indifferent to whether people believed in any religion or none. To most sovereigns the right to believe was more important than what was believed; they renounced the practice of formal religion in favor of nondenominational humanism. "'True religion,'" defined by Warren, "is *my* individual religion, and so with every one else's. No two have precisely the same conception of it! The recognition of the inherent right of individuality is the only harmonizer."[1]

The acceptors of the village's truths, wrote Andrews soon after the founding, include "clergymen . . . christians, infidels, and atheists."[2] Charles Codman's list of faiths represented ranged from Universalists, Swedenborgians, Shakers, and Quakers to Spiritualists and freethinkers, "and between them all shades of belief."[3] These unnamed "shades" included "Come-Outers," Fourierists, Episcopalians, and Henry Edger's converts to the Religion of Humanity.[4] A few Irish Roman Catholics augmented this libertarian potpourri, which tolerated all beliefs and debated them on Sundays in place of sectarian worship.

Warren, Andrews, and most of the sovereigns were rationalists with low-church Protestant backgrounds. Of the four signers of "A Card—To the Public," the 1853 *Tribune* advertisement for Modern Times, two were former ministers: Robert Gray, "late Congregational Pastor, Boonton, N.J.," and Benjamin Franklin Bowles, "late Universalist Pastor, Southbridge, Mass."[5] Another signer, Theron C. Leland, was a graduate of Wesleyan Seminary at Lima, New York, who went on from Modern Times to take a leading role in the free-thought Liberal League.[6] An exception to the nonsectarian rule was the fourth signer, William Metcalf, a charter buyer at Modern Times but never a full-fledged supporter. One year after Modern Times's change of name, Metcalf was one of seven incorporators of Christ Episcopal Church of Brentwood.[7]

The concept of individual sovereignty does not encourage formation of sects with two or more members. Whatever their personal lean-
ings, the villagers met on Sunday and often during the week as a secular
congregation concerned with discussion of ideas and issues. At these
frequent and free-flowing sessions, recalled Codman, "it was each one's
right to think and speak; and they who differed had equal right to
think and speak or decline to be listeners . . . for 'twas recognized that
those who believed in the torments of an ever-flaming hell had as much
right to Hell as did the Agnostics who disbelieved, and so concord
reigned supreme, and none looked crosseyed at the other."[8]

SUNDAY AT MODERN TIMES

Moncure Daniel Conway, a minister and reformer, wrote an almost
verbatim report of one of these meetings in an article, "Modern Times,
New York," published in the *Fortnightly Review* eight years after his 1857
visit.[9] Conway, dismissed from the Washington Unitarian Church for
his opposition to slavery, was the pastor of the First Congregational
Church of Cincinnati at the time of his weekend at Modern Times.

Conway expected to preach at a service, but when he rose that
morning and observed the sovereigns tending their gardens, he began
"to question whether they had any Sunday at Modern Times. An invitation to 'go to church' soon settled that question."[10] Conway wrote
"church" from force of habit, on the presumption that such was the
function of the building which, however, he soon discovered, "was used
for every kind of gathering. It was a plain room with a stage, and served
for religious lectures, discussions, theatricals, concerts, and indeed, what
ever meetings the villagers needed for amusement."[11]

More of interest to him than his sermon were the Modern Timers
themselves, "especially the ladies and their clothes." The women more
than made up for the men's lack of sartorial inventiveness, expressing
individual taste in a truly Modern Times manner. Only two or three
wore dresses "at all resembling the common one, [yet] the short skirt
and plain white stocking predominated." The wide-brimmed hats bore
few decorations, "and the colours and shades worn [indicated] a certain degree of taste among these ladies."[12]

The people took their seats with their children beside them, remaining silent for some time, until "a gentleman and a lady began to sing, 'There's a good time coming,'" in which the entire company joined. Conway read from the Bible and from Emerson's essays, and offered a prayer to "The Great Spirit," after which the people sang a hymn "concerning an expected day 'When the Might with the Right / And the Truth shall be,'" and the minister delivered his talk.[13]

In his sermon Conway praised the human mind as the sheath of whatever revelation exists. He called for the enthronement of Science, with a capital "S," and for the dispersal of dogma by focusing intellectual light upon the "great problems of the Universe." To the true worshiper of today, he noted, religion was synonymous with culture of the intellect.[14] If he mentioned God, prayer, or sin in his talk, Conway failed to record it. The sermon, delivered to an audience of skeptics by the future biographer of Thomas Paine, was a harbinger of what is now called secular humanism, divesting religion of mystery and dispensing with clerical guidance of conduct.

The morning service was only the prelude to a long afternoon of discussion in which, in place of an assigned subject, the topic of "the improvement of man and society sprang up, to become speedily a banyan-growth, reproducing itself from each individual's particular point of view." Unsullied by cant or acrimony, the conversation spun a seamless web of edification. Conway admired "the easy, cordial relation of one with another at Modern Times, a frankness and simplicity of intercourse which gave assurance that they were held together by a genuine attraction, and sustained by mutual sympathy."[15]

His "meager account" of a session in which every speaker said his or her piece in the same flowing, elegant style suggests that Conway's fluency as a writer took precedence over his devotion to a literal transcription. The lead-off speaker, a man identified only as "A," defines the motives of the communitarian movement in general, and of Modern Times in particular. Having tried the political route to reform, "A" is convinced that piecemeal change will never erase what was wrong, but merely alter its form.

> I learned that the laws which oppressed the negro or woman were part of the general condition of the social system. The political reformers were like men sweeping snow from the streets and gardens whilst winter was yet in the sky, and would tomorrow cover all

over with another snowfall. No fear of snow, thought I, where summer reigns. *And if those hearts which love justice and trust truth should gather together somewhere and form a society of their own, there would be a perennial social springtide* [emphasis added]. Such a society might consist of two or three only, but the Highest would be among them if they were gathered in the name of the Highest. This would not be running away from general duties in the world; if true, it would be a pattern from the Mount shown to the calf-worshippers below; it would be a still small voice of protest against the evil fashion of the world; and it might and must become something cosmic in the end. *For this reason I came to Modern Times, which, more than any community that I have seen, represents the idea I have stated* [emphasis added].[16]

Although probably enhanced by Conway, "A's" statement summarizes the purpose of the communitarian movement, in language combining religious with secular images and laced with sentiments partial to reform, abolition, and woman's rights. Reform by itself will not remake the world, only clumsily patch it up; but one righteous village, however small, can show how the good society could and should function. On the surface "A" is a nontheist, muffling God behind "the Highest," but clearly the Bible shapes his thinking. His saving remnant who "love justice and trust truth" can by its example divert the world from the path of evil, with the sovereigns of Modern Times assuming the role of Moses campaigning against idolaters.

Speaker "D" agrees on the futility of wasting our strength sweeping snow in the winter when, if we know where to look for it, spring is close at hand. Moving the frame of reference from Exodus to Revelation, "D" is sure that "In man there is an earth beneath and a heaven above. If the soul should be filled with a higher faith, that new heaven would be followed by the new earth." Mankind welcomes inventors, but he who discovers a spiritual truth as grand as, say, telegraphy, "is crucified—decorously in these later years—but still crucified." The stoning of prophets must cease. The world needs a parliament of thinkers for the advancement of truth and faith. The dawn of the new heaven is now in its first faint flush, "and may not the little group in this room, harmoniously seeking to gain a higher standpoint for each through the help of all, be a first response—like the first violet which answers to the earliest advance of spring?"[17]

Following "D" speaks a woman who believes that "the first need of the world [is] a moral and social Protestantism." Americans may have broken the external fetters linking thought to "the Romish or to the dark ages," but the inward chains are far from shattered. To support her thesis that society still is oppressed by ancient creeds, she marshals a list of grievances: "Dress is still ascetic, Marriage is yet medieval — (A Voice: 'Especially evil')—and the codes concerning Woman belong to an age which debated whether women had souls. Theological freedom is but an embodied ghost until it can *legitimate* its own institutions and its own morality. The world talks indeed of progress; but how is it to go forward upon legs that have been withered these three or four centuries at the last?"[18]

"WE ARE PROTESTANTS—WE ARE LIBERALS"

The speeches recorded by Conway are probably accurate connotatively but polished with editorial gloss. A more literal interpretation of what "Protestant" meant to the sovereigns is rendered by "B. D. J.," the reporter who wrote the feature article on Modern Times in the New York *Sunday Dispatch*. Because the printed remarks flow too smoothly for the rhythm of informal speech, it is likely that B. D. J., as Conway, embellished the words of his subjects. Besides, journalists seeking to build circulation were not above shocking their readers by garnishing statements of Modern Timers.

With these caveats in mind, here is how Benjamin Franklin Bowles, stonemason and former Universalist pastor, defines *Protestant*: one who protests against any law that interferes with individual rights, as distinguished from one who belongs to a particular order of Christians. At the time of the interview, Bowles was building the concrete foundation of the Nicholses' projected School of Life, the Institute of Desarrollo, which neither he nor B. D. J. knew would never be completed. Some thirty-eight years of age, Bowles impresses B. D. J. as a well-informed man of intelligence, who responds frankly but briefly to queries. He begins by explaining what Modern Timers are not: "No, we are not Fourierists. We do not believe in Association. Association will have to answer for very many of the evils with which mankind are now afflicted."[19]

Association was Fourier's word for his plan for social reorganization, made popular in the United States by Albert Brisbane, its chief
propagandist. François Marie Charles Fourier was a system builder who
gave priority to society's needs over those of the separate people. His
bold design for living, although it appreciated "the need to establish
social institutions that were psychologically gratifying," considered people
not as "individuals but interdependent parts of a social whole."[20] Not
so, declared Josiah Warren: "It is in *Combination* or close connection,
only, that compromise and conformity are required—Peace, harmony,
ease, security, happiness will be found only in INDIVIDUALITY."[21]

By his denial of Fourierism, Bowles means that Modern Times
is neither a joint-stock venture nor a phalanstery where residents live
under a single roof. "We are not Communists," he avers, removing
Modern Times from equation with the Shakers, Rappites, Oneidans,
Icarians, or other collectivist models. "We are not Mormons," he adds,
refuting rumors of polygamy, and "We are not Non-Resistants," he concludes. "If a man steals my property or injures me I will take good care
to make myself square with him."[22] In his final disclaimer, Bowles skews
the meaning of Non-Resistance, a movement concerned more with institutions than individuals. In his study of *Radical Abolitionism*, Lewis
Perry defines Non-Resistance as a movement inspired by Garrisonians,
who "took Christ's opposition to violence, even in response to injury,
and extended it to oppose all institutions based on force. Armies were
one such system and so were slavery and human government."[23]

Unlike the Non-Resistants of Hopedale, Massachusetts, the citadel of "Practical Christian Socialism" founded by Adin Ballou, the people
of Modern Times never took the pledge of pacifism. They opposed the
concept of centralized government, as well as the use of armed force
to protect it, yet, during the crisis of civil war, fifteen men of Modern
Times marched off to defend the Union.[24] This reversal took place long
after the interview in the *Sunday Dispatch*: Bowles scorns Non-Resistance because it promised impunity to an aggressor against another
person's liberty. Perhaps he thinks of self-sovereignty as an updated version of "Don't tread on me," a warning that he will retaliate against
anyone threatening his independence. This stance is more rhetorical
than practical; crime and violence are foreign to Modern Times, where
settlers voluntarily keep the peace in accord with the precepts of equitable commerce.

In contrast to the woman at Conway's meeting who calls for a moral and social Protestantism as the first need of the world, Bowles is more explicit. "We are *Protestants* — we are *Liberals*," he contends. "We believe in the SOVEREIGNTY OF THE INDIVIDUAL. We protest against all laws which interfere with INDIVIDUAL RIGHTS — hence we are *Protestants*. We believe in perfect liberty of will and action — hence we are *Liberals*."[25]

Here is *protestantism*, lower case, the priesthood of all believers become the sovereignty of each individual. The Modern Times of Warren and Bowles resembles Locke's state of nature before the adoption of civil government, defined in the *Second Treatise of Government* as "the state all men are naturally in, and that is, *a state of perfect freedom* to order their actions, and dispose of their possessions and persons, as they think fit, within the bounds of the law of nature, without asking leave or depending upon the will of any other man."[26]

Although not explicitly stated by its philosophers, if Modern Times had a religion it could have been belief in Locke's "state of perfect freedom," a condition that, by their example, the sovereigns hoped to convey to the nation. Bowles cites the gospel of equitable commerce to B. D. J.: "We have no compact with each other, save the compact of individual happiness, and we hold that every man and every woman has a perfect, an inalienable right to do and perform . . . just exactly as he or she may choose . . . But . . . this liberty to act must only be exercised at the *entire cost* of the individual so acting. Neither he or [*sic*] she has a right to tax the community for the consequence of their [*sic*] deeds."[27]

When asked if he acknowledges the need for any controlling power beyond that of individual will, he replies, "Not much, not much." Instead of responding to whether a power higher than self was required to regulate human affairs, Bowles urges B. D. J. to read the *Science of Society*, the book by Stephen Pearl Andrews presenting the ideological foundation on which the village was built.

THE SCIENCE OF SOCIETY

Published in two parts in 1851, and combined in one volume the following year, *The Science of Society* is the *Summa Theologica* of equitable commerce, expounding with erudition and eloquence Warren's remedy for the social problem. Part 1, "The True Constitution of Government," the text of an 1850 lecture by Andrews before the New York Mechanics' Institute, construes the political, religious, and social applications of sovereignty of the individual. Part 2, on "Cost the Limit of Price," examines the economic system of ownership shorn of exploitation, which Warren and Andrews put forth to be tested and proven at Modern Times for universal adoption. Benjamin R. Tucker, Warren's heir as apostle of philosophical anarchism, republished *The Science of Society* in 1888, when it had fallen out of print. His "Explanatory" noted that Warren, with whom he became acquainted during the last years of Warren's life, "was never tired of praising Mr. Andrews's work as in his opinion the soundest exposition that ever had been made or ever could be made of the two principles which he (Mr. Warren) had introduced to the world in his less pretentious work, 'True Civilization.'"[28]

A careful look at the text, however, reveals that it is as much a strained attempt to reconcile Warren with Fourier as it is a detailed exposition of equitable commerce. "The True Constitution of Government" specifies Protestantism, Democracy, and Socialism as the trio of major developments that characterize the current epoch. Far from being separate principles, they are branches of a single tree, three partial announcements of one essential principle. To Andrews, "Every manifestation of that universal unrest and revolution . . . known technically in this age as 'Progress,' is nothing more nor less than '*THE SOVEREIGNTY OF THE INDIVIDUAL.*' It is that which is the central idea and vital principle of Protestantism; it is that which is the central idea and vital principle of Democracy; and it is that which is the central idea and vital principle of Socialism."[29]

Protestantism, democracy, and socialism are identical, claims Andrews, in that they assert supremacy of the individual and so reverse the age-old practice of subordinating and subjecting the person to the "Church, State, and . . . Society respectively." Sovereignty of the individual is not only common to all three movements, it was the engine driving each: "it is not merely a feature . . . but the living soul itself, the vital energy, the integral essence or being of them all."[30]

The new era dawned, continued Andrews, as soon as Martin Luther declared the right of private judgment in matters of conscience, "the first streak of light that streamed through the dense darkness of the old *regime*." Next was the English Revolution, when Hampden,

Sidney, Cromwell, and others denied the divine right of kings and terrified the "old world [by] assertion of inherent political rights in the people themselves." The flower of liberty planted in England blossomed in America, where the Declaration of Independence gave rise to the West's first democratic republic, followed by revolution in France and, in rapid succession, Thermidor and the return of reaction to Europe. "Finally, in our own days," the red glare of French socialism illumines a world unsure if this new phenomenon would be "the omen of fearful events [or] the solution of the social problem."[31]

Protestants and their churches may differ in doctrine as long as they maintain supremacy of "private or individual judgment in matters of conscience." That is what makes them Protestants, as distinguished from Roman Catholics, who vest supreme authority in the church, pope, priesthood, or institution "other than the Individual." Democracy and its institutions may differ in every respect except the essential condition that powers of state "reside in, are only delegated by, and can be, at any moment, resumed by the people." The expression "the people" is only a symbol for an aggregate of individuals, whose combined delegation of power to government turns them into an entity. Passion for popular sovereignty separates democrats from the "Despotists" who defend the divine right of kings. Throw open the polls, urges Andrews, "make the pulpit, the schoolroom, the workshop, the manufactory, the shipyard, and the storehouse the universal ballot-boxes of the people. Make every day an election day, and every human being both a candidate and a voter, exercising each day and hour his full and unlimited franchise."[32]

As for socialism, third link of the chain reaction resulting in individual sovereignty, its outward forms are only "the mere shell of the doctrine." Whatever their means, alleges Andrews, all socialists pursue the same end of securing the paramount rights of the individual over social institutions. This definition will surprise those who do not know they are socialists and others who think they are but are not. It excludes the Shaker, Rappite, Oneida, Amana and other model communities ruled by religious concepts, submissive to laws and leaders, and based on "the readoption of popish or conservative principles." Such sectarian and controlled societies appear to lead the socialist life but do not, in Andrews's estimation, because they are "neither Protestants nor Democrats, and, consequently, not Socialists."[33] Fourier's system qualifies because its formulator's "celebrated formula that 'destinies are proportional to attractions'" means in plain language that society must be reorganized so that everyone "be a law unto himself," the sole judge of his needs.[34] This anarchistic twist is a loose interpretation of Fourier, to whom society's interests took precedence over those of the individual. Andrews, in spite of his endorsement of equitable commerce, never fully revokes his support of Fourier, whom he ranked as "really about the most remarkable genius who has yet lived."[35] Fourier's system of combined interests and responsibilities might be hostile to self-sovereignty, but that is "merely incidental," affecting the surface and not the substance. "Socialism demands . . . the emancipation of the Individual from social bondage, by whatsoever means . . . in the same manner as Protestantism demands the emancipation of the Individual from ecclesiastical bondage, and Democracy from political." All who work for this goal are socialists, whose factions vary from one other by "mere specific differences, like those which divide the Protestant sects of Christendom."[36]

Socialism and democracy cannot flourish independently. The core of socialism is the proper and just reward of labor, to achieve which the socialists join in association. The democrat, however, sees in "connected interests a fatal blow at his personal liberty—the unlimited sovereignty over his conduct." Both are right; both are wrong. Socialists, believing that social control of wealth and power must precede fruition of personal selfhood, mistakenly propose the surrender of individual liberty for the attainment of this desired condition. The democrat, seeking the "safe and legitimate exercise of those rights which he declares to be inalienable," errs by omitting from his program the need for "harmonic social relations." Democracy without socialism is as incomplete as socialism without democracy, hence their natural affinity, as in France where the "ears of terrified Europe" ring with the "ominous cry, *Vive la République Démocratique et Sociale.*"[37]

The premise that socialism and democracy are opposite sides of the same coin is the device conceived by Andrews to reconcile Fourier with Warren. Fourier wanted to rebuild the world to secure individual freedom, replacing "the absurd mechanism" of civilization (his term for the current social order) with "combined order, in which interests are associated, and in which every one desires the good of the whole as the only guarantee of the good of the individual."[38] Warren, to the contrary, holds that sovereignty of the individual is incompatible with "national, State, Church, or reform combinations; and that combination is, therefore, exactly the wrong condition for the security, peace, and liberty of mankind." The method of reaching these ends is for each individual to "disconnect his person and all his interests from combinations of every description, with the purpose of gaining control over his own and nobody else's affairs." To restore legitimate liberty, first individualize interests and responsibilities: *"Liberty defined and limited by others is slavery."*[39]

As he weighed Fourier against Warren, Andrews tipped the scale in Josiah's favor. Because it inhibits liberty, combination of interest is "antagonistic to the very objects which Socialism proposes to attain." It prevents harmony, even in France, between democracy and socialism, resulting in the disruption and often despotic denouement of every attempt at social organization. Nature's essential law is inexhaustible variety, driving it irresistibly toward individuality. Wistfully, Andrews advised the leopard to change its spots: "Let that feature of the Socialist movement be retrenched, and a method of securing its great ends discovered which shall not be self-defeating in its operation, and from that point Socialism and Democracy will blend into one, and, uniting with Protestantism, lose their distinctive appellations in the generic term of Individual Sovereignty."[40]

To Andrews, this was the rock on which Modern Times stood. The cooperation and abundance sought by socialism by means of "the combination or amalgamation of interests" may now be found by "adoption of a simple change in the commercial system of the world, by which *cost* and not *value* shall be recognized as the limit of *price.*" This principle, which Warren discovered and Andrews set forth, will realize the benefits that socialism pursues through joint action, while simultaneously respecting and raising to heights never dreamed of "the individualities of existing society."[41]

To those brought up on Jefferson, the best of governments govern least, relinquishing most decisions to disposition by separate and sovereign individuals. Democracy's claim that all men are born free and equal means that no one is subject to rule by another, a right so fundamental that it can neither be given up nor given over to any person or group. Thus, reasons Andrews, majority rule is foreign to democracy because it transfers decision making from the individual to a surrogate. Finally, real freedom cannot be attained under present economic conditions because, in order to be applied meaningfully, its attainment presupposes the shared plenty of socialism. Therefore, the rule of majorities is a "compromise enforced by temporary expediency— a sort of half-way station-house between Despotism, which is Individuality in the concrete, and the Sovereignty of every Individual, which is Individuality in the discrete form."

Andrews did not sanction the use of force for the seizure of power, because coercion nullified personal liberty. The dismantling of combined interests must be accomplished with harmony and cooperation. As long as people stay in a state of connection, there is "no alternative but compromise and mutual concession short of absolute surrender by one side or the other." Individuality is "the most ultra-radical theory and final purpose ever promulgated," but as for immediate practice it is "eminently conservative." It follows the path of expediency by enduring the evils around us while we work to remove them. If to sanction existing government serves our long-term design, so be it. Our cause "has no sympathies with aimless and fruitless struggles, the recriminations of different classes in society, nor with merely anarchical and destructive onslaughts upon existing institutions. It proposes no abrupt and sudden shock to existing society. It points to a scientific, gradual, and perfectly peaceable substitution of new and harmonious relations for those which are confessedly beset . . . by the most distressing embarrassments."[42]

Many seekers of cooperative brotherhood complain that individual sovereignty is its antithesis, sealing individuals off from others. Not so, claimed Andrews. The concept of individuality "has nothing in common with isolation, or the severance of all personal relations with one's fellow-men." Far from being a barrier, the "creation of distinct and independent personalities" is the precondition needed for "harmonic cooperation and universal brotherhood." One may have personal contact and still be as individualized as "lodgers at an hotel," or have amalgamated interests and be as remote from each other as "partners residing in different countries."

Andrews's bent for decisions made in the marketplace rather than inside the halls of government gives his thesis an entrepreneurial spin not always in line with the cost principle. His "genuine example of true Government" is the selection by a consumer of one style of hat instead of another. By creating and manufacturing a fashion that pleases buyers, a particular hatter is self-elected to his function. By preferring one hat to those made by others, "I vote for him. I give him my suffrage. I confirm his election."[43]

"The True Constitution of Government" begins with the grand exegesis of equitable commerce as the answer to the world's problems and the heir of protestant, democratic, and socialist progress. It ends almost trivially by equating personal sovereignty with selection of hats by consumers. Individual sovereignty, the *sine qua non* for deliverance from economic oppression, is likened to hotel life or an arrangement between business partners in different countries. In another almost incongruous passage, Andrews claims that "The highest type of human society in the existing social order is found in the parlor." What legislators and statesmen dread as leading to anarchy and confusion is the free and untrammeled intercourse engaged in at "elegant and refined reunions of the aristocratic classes." Suppose that under the guise of preventing disorder such meetings were subject to laws directing which gentlemen might converse with which lady, on what subject, in what tone of voice, and with what gestures. Such laws would be comparable to the interference with organizations now undertaken by regulation. In trying to escape from confusion, "mankind legislate themselves into it."[44]

Andrews addresses the question raised by reporter B. D. J. in his interview with Bowles: to what extent is government needed? There may be, concedes Andrews, "a few comparatively unimportant interests of mankind which are so essentially combined in their nature that some species of artificial organization will always be necessary for their management."[45] A public highway cannot be laid out and administered by a private individual. In a low state of society, even parlor conversations might need supervision by codes of conduct and the presence of bailiffs. The only excuse for authority is to protect the individual from infringement of his or her own freedom. The true function of government is not to prescribe opinion, meddle with manufactures or importations, order citizens how to cut their hair, employ their time, or dispose of their lives and property, but, rather, simply and solely to protect them "against such impertinences."[46]

Government, insists Andrews, cannot be trusted to guard the people's liberty until it is stripped of arbitrary power. It must be shrunk to its narrowest dimension "into a mere commission – a board of over-seers of roads and canals, and such other unimportant interests as ex-perience shall prove can not be so readily managed by irresponsible individual action."[47]

For Andrews, "The no-government men of our day are . . . the genuine Democrats. It is they who are fairly entitled to the sobriquet of 'The Unterrified Democracy.'" The spirit of the age, "or, more prop-erly, of *modern times* [emphasis added]," is the core of protestantism, democracy, and socialism, synthesized in the concept of the supremacy of the individual over all human institutions. Because Andrews delivered the "True Constitution of Government" lectures shortly before the for-mation of the village, his lowercase reference to "modern times" may reflect the choosing of its name.[48]

Slipping into the millennialist terminology that was second na-ture to secular as well as religious designers of model communities, An-drews dwells on the harmony of the individualist dispensation whose glory transcends the forced creeds of organized churches "as the new heaven and new earth will excel the old." He stretches the premise of every man his own priest to that of every man his own sect, "the sim-ple meaning of Protestantism, interpreted in the light of its own principles."[49]

Government will "pass away" all over the world, to be looked back on in the future the way that "we in America now look back upon the maintenance of a religious establishment." Is it possible that the time will come when "every man shall be, in fine, his own nation as well as his own sect?"[50]

Bursting with optimism, Andrews foresees a future in which the government of the United States removes its hands from commerce, dispenses with the Land Office, and donates the public domain to the people. No more will war be studied, as our fighting forces disband and the State Department assumes the work of the obsolete Navy and War Departments, only in turn to fade away when "with the cessation of war there will be no foreign nations." The inventions of steamship, railroad, and telegraph will, with other technological breakthroughs, obliterate national boundaries and blend mankind into one family. In the next hundred years or two it is probable that a united human race will speak a universal language (no doubt "Alwato," invented by the linguist-philologist Andrews).[51]

Without a government to administer, predicts Andrews, there will be more need for the Treasury Office, just as cessation of executive power will end the work of the judicial branch, which will have nothing to do once crime and aggression no longer exist. "The Legislature enacts what the Executive and Judiciary execute. If the execution itself is unnecessary, the enactment of course is no less so." Bit by bit, the fabric of state will disappear and the "blessed light of day" will illumine minds now open to individual freedom. In the flowering of equitable commerce, "Patriotism will expand into philanthropy. Nations, like sects, will dissolve into the individuals who compose them. Every man will be his own nation, and, preserving his own sovereignty and respecting the sovereignty of others, he will be a nation at peace with all others."[52]

Well over one hundred years have passed, but this forecast has not come true. Yet Modern Times proves, if only at the village level, that willing people can govern themselves in harmony without the force of law or the rule of power.

The prediction of the "great day coming" is vintage Warren-Andrews, laced with the hope and passion of prophets, poets, and rebels that the age of peace and freedom is near. It bears a likeness to the vision of Micah: "nation shall not lift up a sword against nation, neither shall they learn war any more. But they shall sit every man under his vine and under his fig tree; and none shall make them afraid."[53] It also resembles Shelley's forecast of universal liberation from tyranny:

> The world's great age begins anew
>   The golden years return,
> The earth doth like a snake renew
>   Her winter weeds outworn:
> Heaven smiles, and faiths and empires
>   gleam,
> Like wrecks of a dissolving dream.[54]

Anticipation of a new Eden, reclaimed by their program for regeneration, is common to architects of an earthly heaven no matter how they disagree over the blueprints. One system builder, Charles Fourier, delineates a cycle of epochs through which the world will pass en route from losing to regaining paradise. After the fall from primitive Eden come the four "false or subversive periods" of savagism, patriarchalism, barbarism, and civilization (Fourier's sardonic term for his own time), all unhappy "labyrinths in which the human race gropes its way toward its own destiny." Four happy stages will follow in turn, from "Guarantism, or semiassociation," to the jaw-breaking zenith of "compound convergent association," in which "every one desires the good of the whole as the only guarantee of the good of the individual."[55]

One man's heaven on earth is another's "compound convergent association." Fourier designed redemption to rescue humanity from a "civilization" that wastes potentials, changes workers into wage slaves, and suppresses normal urges for pleasure. His proposed phalansteries are palaces for common folk to enjoy life in comfort, unconfined by prim morality. If not every man his own priest, than every man his own prince. And, as Mark Poster shows, Fourier's perception that human passions are irrepressible needs that, when repressed, are "distorted . . . was a clear anticipation of Freud . . . His attack on bourgeois forms of moral theory and psychology began with an appreciation of the need to establish social institutions that were psychologically gratifying."[56]

Fourier's American followers, loath to offend current prudery and bent on testing collective enterprise, soft-pedaled his hedonism. Concerning sex and mating, the relaxed community of Modern Times enacted his plan more closely than did Brook Farm, the North American Phalanx, or the other Associationist villages that came and went in the 1840s and 1850s. But what is relevant to this discussion is that Fourierists couched their panacea for solving the problems of mankind in the rhetoric of secular millennialism.

"O YE THAT LOVE MANKIND!"

Stephen Pearl Andrews was influenced not only by Fourier-followed-by-Warren, but also by Thomas Paine, the patron saint of American libertarians. Andrews's call for each person to be his or her own sect reflects the profession of faith with which Paine begins *The Age of Reason:* "I do not believe in the creed professed by the Jewish church, by the Roman church, by the Turkish church, by the Protestant church, nor by any church that I know of. *My own mind is my own church* [emphasis added]."[57] Their targets, however, are not identical. Paine fires at organized religion, whereas Andrews and Warren blaze away at organization itself. Paine bombards the wall of absurdity built by the "Christian Mythologists," attacks the superstition embedded in the Old and New Testaments, and fights to separate Jesus, "this virtuous reformer and revolutionist," from the fable who is "at once both God and Man, and also the Son of God."[58] Andrews's sights are not set, like Paine's, on confirming the merit of deism while exposing Scriptural fallacies. His concern is for freedom of individual conscience, his emphasis not on what to believe but on each person's right to decide how—or whether—to believe. Andrews praises protestantism for its generic, not its sectarian role: he sees it as the first of the great new movements that, together with democracy and socialism, lead to equitable commerce.

In the August 1854 issue of his monthly letter from Modern Times, Warren, the Yankee inventor, avows that "my neighbors have just as good right to be mistaken in religion as I have to make a blunder in some matter of mechanics; and I wish them to understand this as the basis of good neighborship." Should he offend their sense of propriety, he does so not wantonly to disregard them, but for "some good and substantial reason" which he "would gladly explain to their satisfaction."[59]

Nine years later Warren reiterates his attitude toward religion. Suppose an old-line Presbyterian neighbor "goes every Sunday to hear what I consider destructive theories . . . [and] holding his sovereignty as sacred, I offer no obstacle other than *acceptable* counsel." This judgment applies to political creeds and theories, because freedom to differ is paramount. All viewpoints are "entitled to forbearance till some attempt is made to enforce them on the unwilling." The grand idea of the Reformation is freedom to do at one's own cost what another holds to be wrong, foolish, or inexpedient. This liberty is the heart of peace and progress, because, in time, the dissenter may be proven right. "In present civilization [a Fourierist designation] institutions are above men: in true civilization man will be not *under* but *within* institutions."[60]

Warren and Andrews pick up where Paine left off. Paine thinks of government as at best an evil, needed not to rule over subjects but only to guard the natural rights of man to liberty, property, security, and resistance of oppression. The least and best government is a republic typified by the United States, which to Paine is "a representation ingrafted upon Democracy . . . What Athens was in miniature,

America will be in magnitude."[61] Warren and Andrews agree that government is evil, but not that it is necessary; they founded Modern Times as a model for proving that no compact is needed except the unwritten agreement of each to respect the rights of all.

Paine's *Rights of Man* contains the text of the "Declaration of the Rights of Man and of Citizens" by the National Assembly of France, promulgated in 1789 and attributed to him. Article III rests the source of all sovereignty essentially with the Nation, "nor can any individual, or any body of men, be entitled to any authority which is not expressly derived from it." Although vesting sovereignty in the people instead of the person, Article IV advances a definition of sovereignty of the individual, defining political liberty as "the power of doing whatever does not injure another. The exercise of the natural rights of every man, has no limits than those which are necessary to secure to every *other* man the free exercise of the same rights; and these limits are determinable by law."[62] This statement could serve as the charter for Modern Times; Warren would balk at the need for law but agree that any law required will be for the purpose defined.

Paine the deist opposes the union of church and state and believes that the victory of democracy will puncture the balloon of idolatrous priestcraft. The final lines of *The Age of Reason* read like a message to Warren and Andrews: "Adam, if ever there was such a man, was a Deist: let every man follow, as he has a right to do so, the religion and the worship he prefers."[63] Deism is an eighteenth-century compromise between some religion and none. The only tenets of this theology for thinking people are acceptance of Nature's God and the Golden Rule—plus the belief in life hereafter, its one concession to orthodoxy. It is monotheism without a church, a form of ethical humanism endorsed by Paine, Franklin, Jefferson, and other intellectual grandfathers of the framers of equitable commerce. Warren and Andrews adopt deist respect for tolerance and push it to the outer limits of individual choice. They recommend not only the priesthood of believers, and the mitosis of sects into smaller sects, but the ability of every person to deal directly in matters of faith in whatever mode of worship or nonworship chosen. Paine's admonition to follow one's own religious preference comes close to the ultimate step of becoming a sect with one member.

Deism, never the actual belief of more than a gifted minority, was a phenomenon of the American and French Revolutionary generation.

By the 1800s the "revealed" religion of the Great Awakening and other revivalist movement had all but supplanted the "natural" religion of the deists. The nonsectarian services held at Modern Times were exceptions to the prevailing custom of Sunday-to-to-meeting worship but did not mark a break with collective Sabbath fellowship. Andrews's call for congregations of one is more rhetorical than practical, spurring defiance for conformity but not an end to Sunday meetings, even if their purpose was the exchange of ideas among equals.

Tom Paine's is more than the voice of independence, tolerance, and republican democracy. His hatred of arbitrary power and his coincident passion for freedom descend undiluted to his spiritual heirs at Modern Times. The exciting message of *Common Sense* is couched in language they understood, from "Government, like dress, is the badge of lost innocence," to "We have it in our power to begin the world over again." No patron of equitable commerce failed to be moved by the stirring lines: "O ye that love mankind! Ye that oppose not only the tyranny but the tyrant, stand forth . . . O! receive the fugitive, and prepare in time an asylum for mankind."[64]

The sovereigns of Modern Times were busy preparing that asylum, for which the United States was the rightful but not yet ready site. No one looked for a rapid conversion. For Andrews, the projected blending of protestantism, democracy, and socialism into the higher form of equitable commerce will be a peaceful and gradual process: "The most ultra-radical doctrine in theory and final purpose ever promulgated in the world . . . far from quarreling with existing Government . . . sanctions and confirms it." The founders and settlers of Modern Times were neither fomenters of class struggle nor provokers of "anarchical and destructive onslaughts upon existing institutions." They upheld individual sovereignty, convinced that it "will endure the ordeal of the most searching investigation" and eventually win adoption because of its scientific validity.[65]

6

The Long Island Milieu

POCKETED BETWEEN THE PINE BELT and Great South Bay, Islip alone of the nine towns of Suffolk had no coastal frontage with New England. Hemmed in on the north, east, and west by larger and older towns, "its only water route to New York . . . [was] via a treacherous inlet through which only a few dared to venture."[1] When explaining the seal he designed for the town, Dr. Abraham G. Thompson quipped that the Eye—the mark of vigilance—was an "Eye Slip by Brookhaven and Huntington in not including in their patents the territory now called Islip."[2]

On the south side of Long Island, at an average distance of forty-five miles from Manhattan, Islip extends sixteen miles from west to east and eight in medial breadth. At the time of Modern Times's formation, the twenty-six hundred people of Islip engaged in only two main occupations—farming and "following the bay."[3] Sixteen brooks, creeks, and riverlets flowing into the bay could have furnished power for some machinery, but "the flatness of the country forbids their being utilized to much extent in this direction."[4] As late as 1883, "manufacturies [sic] except for the supply of the immediate wants of the inhabitants have never come into existence."[5]

Beginning in 1640 with the settling of Southold and Southampton, the early towns of Suffolk were formed by associations of English Puritans, who crossed the Sound to eastern Long Island after brief stays in Connecticut or Massachusetts. These seceders from New England churches with whose doctrines they differed, however slightly, found themselves beyond the orbit of Dutch or English domination, so distant were they from centers of power during the middle years of the seventeenth century. They prized their independence; their alliance with Connecticut before the creation of New York Province, in 1664,

110

was more for defense against Dutch aggression than for their own lack of ability to run their internal affairs.[6]

In their passion for autonomy, the sovereigns of Modern Times were legitimate, if less godly, heirs of the Puritan settlers. Both groups were bands of "brothers" and "sisters," determined to live free and clear of higher jurisdiction. Prime's Lockean description of the first communities might have been written of Modern Times; the early settlers were "absolutely in a state of nature, possessing all the personal rights and privileges which the God of nature gave them, but without the semblance of authority one over another."[7]

Islip was different. Title to land in this precinct (as it first was called) was acquired by neither Calvinists nor freethinkers, but by a handful of Anglican royalists who looked upon their holdings as feudal lords regarded their manors. "The whole town," wrote the nineteenth-century Long Island historian Benjamin F. Thompson, "was at one time the property of a very few wealthy individuals."[8] It began in 1684, when Governor Thomas Dongan granted more than 60 of Islip's 112 square miles to William Nicoll, for which the patentee paid a yearly quitrent of "five bushels of good winter wheat or twenty-five shillings in money."[9] The governor's grant confirmed Nicoll's purchase of these lands in 1683, from Winnequaheagh, the sachem of the Connetquot branch of the Secatogue Indians. Augmented by three more patents, the Nicoll estate accounted for most of Islip for more than one hundred years, the land held in entail and tended by tenant farmers and slaves. The Nicoll tracts ran from Great South Bay to Lake Ronkonkoma, and from the border of the town of Brookhaven to the present line between the hamlets of Islip and East Islip. Four other grantees owned Islip lands, all of them west of the Nicoll patents. Sagtikos Manor, the best-known tract, first owned by Stephanus Van Cortlandt, became the property of Jonathan Thompson, of Setauket, in 1758. He paid "1200 pounds for the 1,200 acres that extended from the Great South Bay to the middle of the Island."[10]

Because of its manorial tenure of land, the town was settled slowly. Legally authorized in 1710, the precinct of Islip transacted no business until the first recorded town meeting ten years later: "As the number of inhabitants was quite inconsiderable, and more than half the soil was claimed by one individual [Nicoll], there was no great necessity for troubling the people with the expense and responsibilities of office, where there was little or no duty to be performed."[11]

There were no more than thirty-one freeholders at the time of the 1720 meeting, nor "does it appear from these records [of town meetings] that the people of the town made a free use of their legislative powers during the first century of its existence."[12] The early town fathers' main concern was regulating the movements of swine, which they did far more accurately than they spelled, according to these representative excerpts from the town of Islip's "Minute Book":

> 1753: It shall be lawful for hoggs that are well yoked to run freely on the Common.

> 1757: No Boar shall Run on the Commons in Months of May, June, July, August, September, October & November and without any man having free Leave to held the said Boar and if the said Boar shall die within the cuting the shall Recover no satisfaction by Law.

> 1758: The townd act concerning hoodge runing on the commond continued for this year also the act concerning bores runing is continued for this year also.

> 1766: The town act concerning yoaked hogs runing on the commons and cutting boars is also continued that was made in 1757.[13]

Another important issue was the protection of Islip's share of the Bay from incursions by out-of-town poachers, as in 1765, when the town meeting minutes record that "It is also concluded upon by the majority of Voats that if any one of the Inhabitants of the precinct of Islip Shall Give Leave to any furniener to fish in the bay or also in the Creek that He Shall forfitthe Sum of forty shillings to the overseers of the poor for the use of the poor of the Said town."[14]

From the beginning, the business of the annual meeting included electing two or more overseers "to take care of ye Pore for ye yere." John Moubray received thirteen shillings in 1749 for "his Mother's nursing Old Joseph in his sickness." In 1787, Garet Monfort's reward for "findin grain for Indian hannah" was "two Pounds of the towns money."[15]

The British occupied Islip throughout the Revolution. As late as 1783, the town dated its annual meeting "in the three and twentieth year of the Reign of his Majesty King George the third King of great Britain & c." The next year marked the first "town meting of the precenct held the first tuesday in April by the authority of the good People of the State of new york and in the Eighth year of the American Independence."[16]

As if by hereditary right, William Nicoll (spelled "Nicol" or "Nicolls" by careless clerks) had been elected town supervisor since 1748. But at last democracy opened the door in 1776, when a patriot, Isaac Thompson of Sagtikos Manor, replaced him, Judge Thompson, a staunch supporter of independence and a sponsor of an organized militia, was the chairman of the Islip committee and a correspondent of the Continental Congress.[17] In 1777 he narrowly escaped being hung by a gang of marauding British sailors. Conversely, William (known as "Lawyer" or "Clerk") Nicoll, the grandson of the patentee, was at best a lukewarm patriot, who, as Suffolk's representative in the crucial New York Assembly session of early 1775, voted against a firm stand toward Great Britain. Although "not attainted of high treason," Nicoll was one of those whom a pro-Tory author "includes on a list of loyalists plundered, or imprisoned, etc." During the War of Independence, a Loyalist newspaper reported four separate raids by armed rebels on Nicoll's estates in Islip and Shelter Island. In his defense, his grandson informed the historian Thompson, in 1845, that Nicoll was "enervated by a paralysis that rendered him unfit and unable to take an active part in the scenes of the Revolution."[18]

Nicoll lands remained entailed for one hundred years, until, in 1786, an act of the New York State Legislature opened half of them for sale to the public to reimburse the family's creditors for debts incurred in the Revolution. The hamlets along the bay began to attract a new breed of settlers, holders of land in fee simple instead of servants and tenant farmers. Coming as families rather than as groups, these grantees led the outdoor life as farmers, fishers, and hunters, unbeholden to lords of manors.

In April 1790, in the second year of his presidency, George Washington toured Suffolk, his perceptive farmer's eyes taking note of the "low, scrubby oak, not more than two feet high, intermixed with small and ill-thriving pines" that were features of the landscape through Islip to Brookhaven. When Washington slept at Sagtikos Manor, he was not—contrary to Long Island legend—the houseguest of Isaac Thompson, for all of the Judge's proven patriotism. On 21 April, wrote the President, "We dined at Captain Zebulon Ketcham's, Huntington, South . . . After dinner we proceeded to a Squire Thompson's, such a house as the last; that is, one that is not public, but will receive pay for everything it furnishes in the same manner as if it was."[19]

THE FEDERAL CENSUS OF 1860

Although summary reports survive, the 1911 Albany fire destroyed the New York State manuscript census of 1855 for the entire county of Suffolk. The only way to compare Modern Times with Islip is the federal census of 1860, the one year of the village's life for which household records exist. The taker of all three tallies—population, agriculture, and industry—was Walter Scudder, of West Islip, a prosperous, middle-aged farmer and public servant.

Like those of the Nicolls, Moubrays, Ludlows and Doxsees, the names of office-holding Scudders appear in the town of Islip's records from 1729 on, in positions ranging from supervisor or town clerk to assessor, overseer of the poor, inspector of elections, and commissioner of highways.

As a census taker, Walter Scudder was inconsiderate to future historians. Although his colleague in the town of Brookhaven listed the people he counted as residents of Setauket, Stony Brook, Port Jefferson, and so on, Scudder's census of households lumped 3,845 men, women, and children under the single address of "Islip." To isolate Modern Times from its fellow hamlets of Sayville, Penataquit (Bay Shore), Midroadville (Bayport), Lakeland (Ronkonkoma), Holbrook, Islip and Islips East, West, North, and Central, and a sliver of Hauppauge, the census detective must make two assumptions. First, the *Map of Suffolk County* made in 1858 by J. Chace, Jr. prints the names of selected residents in the communities where they lived; thus, some names on the census pages can be matched with places where their possessors lived, confirming the hypothesis that Scudder made his rounds systematically, house by house and street by street. Therefore, it may be assumed that everyone listed between the first and last recognizable names of Modern Timers lived within the village. Accordingly, there were 126 Modern Timers on the census of 1860, consisting of the thirty-three households from Henry Fish, number 544 on Scudder's list, to Josiah Warren, number 576.[20]

Walter Scudder was careless. He listed his own place of birth as Ireland in spite of his Long Island heritage. By absentmindedly extending the ditto marks he made for the three families counted before his own, he negated the fact that he, his wife, and four children were as American as the subjects for dittoes were Irish. He reported that Josiah Warren came from New York and was forty-five years old: Warren, born in Massachusetts, was sixty-two at the time of the census. The final household recorded was that of Francis Moses Asbury Wicks, whose age was stated as fifty-four when he was actually forty-two. Wicks's wife Angeline, age thirty-seven, was named as Mary, age forty-five. No doubt Scudder improvised this entry, tacking it on some time after his field work was completed.

Walter spelled names phonetically, as if he never bothered to ask. Modern Timers include "Matcalf" for Metcalf, "Dowd" for Dow, "Stow" for Stone, "Stimson" for Simpson, "Hayes" for Haines, "Rook" for O'Rourke, and "Dorphius" White for Dauphin White. But no matter how slipshod, his is the only census of Islip in 1860: there is no other choice than to use it, in hopes of its general validity.

A striking difference between the 126 Modern Timers and the other 3,719 Islipians was the relative mix of ethnicity and place of birth. Islip was overwhelmingly inhabited by natives of New York State, with a scattering from other states, and 15 percent from abroad: Modern Times contained more New Englanders (42) than New Yorkers (35); 20 people (15 percent of the total) from other states; and 26 people (21 percent) from other countries. The preponderance of Yankees was exceptional for an era in which the fraction of New Englanders living in New York State averaged only 6 percent.[21]

Another anomaly was the distribution of nationalities and races. In Islip, there were more of Irish birth (253) than English (148), as well as several hundred Dutch, German, and Bohemian immigrants. At Modern Times, the 26 people of foreign birth consisted of 18 English, 6 Irish, a father and son from Canada, and none from the mainland of Europe. The Census of 1860, one of the few that record color, reports 84 black, 43 mulatto, and 9 Indian residents of Islip, contrasted to no one from these three groups at Modern Times.

It is difficult to assay the reaction of Modern Timers to slavery.

Except for signing a few published calls for settlement, the sovereigns did not go on record collectively. Clearly, many were sympathetic to abolition, the first cause named on Codman's list of reforms espoused at the village. Andrews, James Arrington Clay, and others were outspoken antislavery folk. Yet the 1860 census shows a glaring racial imbalance: not one of Islip's recorded 167 blacks, mulattos, and Indians lived at Modern Times. Most of Islip's people of color were former slaves, or descendants of slaves, whose families continued living where they did when New York State abolished slavery in 1827. Deliberate exclusion was inconsistent with Modern Times's open policy; however, most white Americans in the North—even those in the antislavery movement—were reluctant to socialize with African Americans. And it is doubtful that freed black folk, whose status was less than first-class, would have chosen to add to existing prejudice by casting their lot with a village as controversial as Modern Times.

Although the population of Islip far exceeded that of Modern Times, the number of males was equal to the number of females in both, just as each had a 45 percent ratio of children to adults. The proportion of teen-agers to children was slightly higher at Modern Times, and the mean age there was twenty-six and one-half compared with Islip's twenty-five; but neither of these differences was significant.

The town of Islip was one of the last stands of the era of homespun. If Modern Times avoided industrialism by choice, Islip did so because it was too unendowed and out-of-the-way to help it. The 1860 manuscript census of products of industries shows none for Modern Times, and only fourteen for the entire town of Islip, with a meager capital of $21,000.[22] There were three boot- and shoemakers, two each of gristmills, butchers, and wagon-maker–blacksmith shops, and single paperboard, sash and blind, harness maker, fish, and tin and copper establishments.

These fourteen businesses employed a total of twenty-four workers, exclusively male, paid $50 a month on average, a fair wage for the period. Reliant on hand- or waterpower, not steam, the annual product of Islip's reported industry reached the not exactly grand total of $31,360.[23] In 1845, Thompson took note of abundant available waterpower, the use of which would greatly add to "the wealth and importance of this portion of the country . . . Yet the natural advantages of this . . . do not seem to have attracted that attention which Yankee enterprise alone would properly appreciate."[27]

In the town of Islip in 1860, most people farmed, followed the bay, or did both. During the 1850s there were approximately eight thousand acres of improved land, about one-ninth of the total, most of them tilled by farmers, raising food for themselves and hay and grain for their horses and cattle.

Twenty-eight of every hundred men and women who stated an occupation were baymen (197) or mariners (123). The baymen, who from 1849 on tended increasingly to be immigrants from the maritime province of Zeeland, Holland, created the Long Island hamlet of Tuckertown (now West Sayville). From here they plied the shallow waters between the shore and the barrier beach of Fire Island, dealing in clams and especially oysters, with which they seeded the floor of Great South Bay, staking it out in one, two, and four-acre plots. "The bayman," a modern writer observes, "cultivates the bottom like a farmer does his land. He expects spawning time, knows how to harvest the crop. The bayman cares for his clams like potatoes: he digs them up, turns them over and they grow."[25]

The Bay was thirty miles long and from two to five miles wide, its depth an average of six feet. Those inclined to rove the deeper waters beyond were mariners, men who roved the open sea for finfish or worked the coastline as cargo shippers. Mariners also carried cordwood for the fireplaces and salt hay for lining the horse and cattle stalls of the metropolitan area. On return trips they often brought loads of manure for the farms of Long Island.

In his study of Islip's oystermen, *Dutchmen on the Bay*, Lawrence J. Taylor describes the frequently blurred distinction between the bayman and the mariner: "But the oysters [and clams] still had to be carried to market . . . the job of coast-wise trading vessels until a southern railroad line was completed in 1867 — and to a degree for several decades thereafter . . . Such mariners were typically oystermen as well, for a man could tong (scoop) from a sloop as easily as from a smaller craft."[26]

The better part of the bay that faces the town of Islip, from Nicoll Point to Patchogue, belonged to the town of Brookhaven, creating a source of intramural bickering that was amicably resolved. By the end of the Civil War, the trade in oysters and other bivalves grew into an industry, but in 1860 it was still conducted by independent baymen, to whom it was art, sport, and vocation—a complete way of life.

The occupations of bayman, mariner, and farmer blended, with many a seafaring family tending a garden, poultry, and a few head of livestock. But the census of population lists 156 farmers, whose $1,100,000 aggregate of real property accounts for two-thirds of the town's total. Add 144 farm laborers and the total of those engaged in agriculture reaches 300, compared with the 312 baymen and mariners. Scudder's manuscript census of agriculture, which omits small holders, shows only 127 farmers, owning an average of 184 acres, of which 53 were improved; these farms had a mean reported value of $8,300.[27] The number of baymen and mariners slightly exceeds that of farmers, but farmers surpass all the other pursuits in real and personal wealth.

Some of the many occupations might be classed as industrial but are not, because of the modest scale of their operations. There were 24 self-styled merchants (including William Metcalf, but not Josiah Warren), with 11 clerks, all male, of whom 7 lived in their employers' houses. Thirteen hotel keepers and helpers served the growing function of Islip as a vacation resort, a trend that Parson Prime found distressing. The list includes 25 harness-makers, 16 shoemakers, and 9 schoolteachers to instruct the 772 children between the ages of three and nineteen whom Scudder recorded as going to school, and an assortment of tailors, dressmaker-seamstresses, carpenters, masons, butchers, shipwrights, gardeners, coachmen, painters, blacksmiths, and one whitesmith. As for laborers other than farm, 111 of them presumably hired out by the day for whatever work was available.

The 99 servants in Islip (only one at Modern Times)[28] were overwhelmingly female (93), predominantly Irish (47), black, (10), or mulatto (6). Eighteen servants were illiterate, a proportion two and one-half times the overall rate for the town. Of 267 Islipians unable to read or write, not one lived at Modern Times. When servants, merchants and clerks, shoemakers, painters, blacksmiths, innkeepers, teachers, and other workers are added to farmers and agricultural laborers, the sum suggests that two out of every three gainfully employed were in jobs not directly connected with fishing or boating. Perhaps Islip's town historian was wrong when claiming, without citing a source, that during the 1850s, "About two-thirds of the male population were fishermen, seamen or skippers."[29]

The purchase of four acres by Myndert and Rebecca Fish was a sign that now that the five-year term of payment was up, neither grantors nor grantees felt constrained by the pledge not to sell or buy more than three acres. Its policy of limiting settlers to three-acre holdings was one of the sharpest distinctions between Modern Times and the town of Islip. Intended to prevent ruralization and ensure a compact community, the restriction was acceptable during the early years of Modern Times, but once the land was cleared and homesteads built, the sovereigns no longer observed it. Many wanted to add a fourth acre in order to round out a square block, or simply to exercise, as they saw fit, their sovereign right to trade in real estate, incompatible as it might be with the premise of equitable commerce.

The town of Islip was far from egalitarian. At the top of the social pyramid were John D. Johnson, of Islip village, a farmer, land dealer, and owner of steamboats, whose real estate holdings are valued on the census at $100,000; William H. Ludlow of Oakdale, the Nicolls' son-in-law and the lord of 3,400 acres from the Bay to Lake Ronkonkoma; and Dr. Alfred Wagstaff, a West Islip patrician with real estate worth $150,000 and personal property valued at $50,000. At the bottom were thirty-nine paupers, let out for support to the lowest bidder at town expense. Between these extremes fell the bulk of the townsfolk, more than half of them in houses they owned, who lived (as did the sovereigns) on the fruit of their own labor.

Most farmers with real and personal property were native-born New Yorkers, their average age of forty-eight almost twice the town's twenty-five; many were in possession of inherited estates on the Necks or the South Country Road (Montauk Highway). Of 156 farmers, 108 owned real estate worth the $100 required for listing on the census. None of the 144 farm laborers was wealthy, yet 117 were homeowners. To an optimist it would appear that more than half (434) of Islip's 792 households had more than $100 real property; a pessimist could comment that an almost equal number (423) had less. In contrast with the large number of farmers in Islip, Modern Times had only five.

RELIGION IN ISLIP

The yeomen of Islip were less devout than the congregations of Calvinist towns. In 1845, when searching the precinct for churches to report in his Long Island history, the Reverend Nathaniel Prime spotted
only two, both small—he did not count Sayville, where "the Protestant Methodists maintain preaching, but no church has yet been
erected." One, the Episcopal church of St. John's, was the Nicoll family's personal house of worship, with only fourteen communicants. The
other was the Methodist church of Mechanicsville (first called Sodom,
later Penataquit, and now Bay Shore).

The central and northern region was an almost continuous wilderness "with scarcely any inhabitants and bids fair to remain so"; except for Modern Times and a few other hamlets, it did for many decades.
The straightlaced Prime was appalled by a town so poorly provided
with churches, where "the greater part of the population must be living in utter destitution of the means of grace. From this fact, and the
additional consideration that this town is a great resort for sportsmen
and men of pleasure, the state of morals may be inferred." Islip, depraved in the eyes of the Calvinist parson from Huntington, abounded
with hotels equipped with such tools of the devil as "billiard tables,
nine-pin alleys, and other means of amusement and dissipation." Prime's
verdict was that to a man of religion and morals "this town presents
the most undesirable residence of any town in the county."[30]

Of the town's ten churches in 1860, three were Methodist, two
Episcopal, two African Methodist, and one each Congregational,
Congregational Methodist, and Presbyterian.[31] Yet that year's census
recorded that only four ministers resided among the thirty-eight hundred souls in the town.[32] Circuit riders and lay preachers helped pick
up the slack. The style of one itinerant minister, the Reverend Benjamin Abbott, reveals the typical informality of a Methodist circuit
rider. He once "preached on the text 'Thou are an austere man', pro-
nouncing the word 'austere' as though it were 'oyster'—a very appropriate text indeed for the South Shore. When his attention was called
to this, he remarked 'Never mind that, we raked in seven, didn't we?'"[33]

Islip, the only town of Suffolk County not created by Puritans,
was less preoccupied with religion than were the saintlier towns to the
north and east. But if churches were in short supply, friendliness was

not. Most farmers and bay folk of Islip took life as it came, with an easygoing respect for each other. Except for a scattering of "splendid country seats" on the necks facing Great South Bay, the standard of living was moderate. Most villages along the South road were "made up partly of permanent and partly of summer residents . . . [who enjoyed] the freedom of rural life and the healthful and pleasant surroundings of a seaside residence."[34] When the maverick village of Modern Times, deep in the northern woods of Islip, changed its name to Brentwood in 1864, it cast its lot with a larger community marked by a tolerant attitude very similar to its own.

7

Criticism and Defense

W HEN DESCRIBING HIS BOYHOOD at Brook Farm from the vantage point of 1912, John Van Der Zee Sears reminds his readers that, "in the language of the time, the Farmers were Socialists, but the Socialism of 1840–1850 was a very different proposition from the Socialism of today."[1] *Socialism* had more than one meaning. It was, writes Raymond Williams in his study of cultural vocabulary, "until 1850 [a] word too new and general to have any predominate use."[2] Williams, Arthur E. Bestor, and John F. C. Harrison agree that its first English use is by Robert Owen and his associates, as early as 1827. In *Quest for the New Moral World*, his study of Owen and Owenism on both sides of the ocean, Harrison finds that this movement welcomed the label "socialist" because it was more accurate than the older terms "radical" and "agrarian." Socialists were those who emphasized a social, as opposed to an individual, approach—including, but not limited to, economic organization. "Owenite socialism was 'the true social or cooperative and communal system,' a blend of communitarian theory, anti-capitalist economics, and a science of society."[3]

Because socialism came into the world as a near relation to communism, the words often were used interchangeably. Residents of model villages did not invoke the Fifth Amendment when asked if they were communists. The source of the "Bible communism" practiced by Shaker, Rappite, Oneida, Amana, Icarian and other religious collectives was not the *Communist Manifesto* but the book of Acts:

And all that believed were together and had all things common;

And sold their possessions and goods, and parted them to all *men*, as every man had need . . .

And the multitude of them that believed were of one heart and of one soul; neither said any *of them* that ought of the things which he possessed was his own; but they had all things common.[4]

The historian Richard T. Ely observes that the Shakers professed Christian Communism in 1776, two years after reaching the New World, so that "Pure communism in America is of the same age as American independence." He cites George Rapp's Harmonists as "another body of communists," along with Amana, "the largest of American communistic societies."[5]

One of the first to label his doctrine "communism" was Etienne Cabet, the Frenchman whose novel, *Voyage en Icarie,* glorified life on a communal island. Cabet came to the United States in 1849 to found a real-life Icaria at the abandoned Mormon city of Nauvoo, Illinois. In a letter to the publisher of *The Practical Christian,* organ of the Hopedale community, Cabet proudly announced, "Like you, I am a Communist. My doctrine is the same as that of Christianity in its primitive purity." From his more than forty works on how to bring heaven to earth, he called special attention to *True Christianity,* written "to prove that our Communism is the same thing as Christianity at its origin."[6]

Communism according to Scripture did not raise the hackles of mainstream America the way it would when presented by Marx and Engels. Indeed, the legal establishment recognized and protected the rights of communistic societies. Carol Weisbrod, the historian of communitarian litigation, points out that in nine reported lawsuits brought by disgruntled former members against a communal association, the state and federal courts sustained the defendants.[7] In a case involving a former Rappite's claim for return of his assets, the Pennsylvania Supreme Court upheld the communist sect. The decision, written by Chief Justice John Bannister Gibson, ruled that "It may be true [that] the business and pursuits of the present day are incompatible with the customs of the primitive Christians; but that is a matter for the consideration of those who propose to live in conformity with them."[8]

The Harmonists—called Rappites after their charismatic leader, George Rapp—were believers in the Second Coming who patterned themselves on the early Christians by pooling their assets and living communally, taking their wages in sustenance and the certainty of salvation. Oddly, or perhaps logically, this band of pietists from Württemberg turned a tidy profit while waiting for the Apocalypse; although far from the centers of traffic, they were skilled and successful players in every market they entered. Judge Gibson was under no illusion about the group's authoritarian cast. However, in a grudging compliment to the defendant, "Father" George Rapp, he remarked that a man "who conscientiously declares an indifferent or absurd theory to be essential to salvation, may be a fanatic, but he is not a cheat."[9]

In short, although communism did not appeal to most Americans, it was well within the limits of legal, Christian conduct. To Judge Gibson, "The sum of the matter is, that a member of a religious society may not avoid a contract . . . on the basis of its peculiar faith, by setting up the supposed extravagance of its doctrines as proof that he was entrapped."[10]

In one of a series of articles analyzing communal contract cases, a sympathetic lawyer wrote that in addition to Judge Gibson, Supreme Court Justice John McLean supported the opinion "That in adopting community of property persons are but following the example of the Apostles and adopting a rule ordained by them." The attorney, James W. Towner, declared that "Communism conserves contract," just as "contract supports Communism."[11]

The ideal village movement made little distinction between communism and socialism. One of the nineteenth-century masterworks on these communities is Charles Nordhoff's *The Communistic Societies of the United States*; another, by John Humphrey Noyes, is the *History of American Socialism*.[12] Concerning the origin of his Oneida Community, Noyes wrote that "the socialist book, called Bible Communism," put out in the settlement's first few months, was "the frankest possible disclosure of the theory of entire Communism."[13]

Noyes was not only a founder and leader but also a brilliant theoretician of the communitarian movement. His perspective widened when he acquired the manuscript of A. J. Macdonald, the wandering Scot who collected a storehouse of information by visiting one model village after another. In 1854, before he was ready to publish his findings, Macdonald died of cholera: Noyes made Macdonald's manuscript the foundation for his own perceptive work, after which he gave it to the library of his alma mater, Yale University. Both Noyes and Macdonald blurred the line between socialism and communism. In Macdonald's findings were "notices of leading Socialists, such as [Robert]

Owen, Fourier, Frances Wright, &c." Ten pages further, Noyes reported
that "Robert Owen came to this country and commenced his experiments in Communism in 1824."[14]

"Socialism" was the antebellum catchword applied to any ideal
community bent on replacing the greed syndrome with cooperation.
In "The True Constitution of Government," Andrews vaguely dovetails socialism with opposition to social injustice. When they get down
to cases, such writers as Andrews and George Ripley do not think of
socialism generically, as public control of productive property. To them
it is a proprietary brand name for Fourierism, also known as Association, the secular form of communitarianism funded by joint-stock investment but operated collectively.

Andrews does his best to endow Warren's equitable commerce
with socialist traits. As a foe of exploitation, Warren can be called socialistic; as a defender of private ownership, he is in the tradition of
Locke; and as the advocate of everyone's being his or her own church
and state, on condition of not denying the same right to others, he
is the first American philosophical anarchist. Although "anarchism"
is tempting,[15] there is no precise designation for this blend of three
somewhat conflicting premises. The most appropriate term is "reciprocal libertarianism"; otherwise, why not accept its creator's choice of
"equitable commerce"?

GEORGE RIPLEY'S CRITIQUE OF MODERN TIMES

George Ripley was one who professed "to know enough already." Born
in 1802, four years later than Warren, he won his spurs as a humanist
scholar by way of Harvard, the Unitarian pulpit, the transcendental
effusion, the presidency of Brook Farm throughout its Christian and
Fourierist lives to the post, in 1849, of Margaret Fuller's replacement
as the book critic for the *New York Tribune.*

In July 1852, Ripley reviewed *Equitable Commerce,* the reprint of
Warren's 1846 work, edited and with an introduction by Andrews.[16]
Conceding Andrews's skill in polishing Warren's homespun wisdom,
Ripley agrees that the case for sovereignty of the individual was never
pleaded "more admirably." But, although not conscious plagiarism, Warren's so-called original principle "cannot pretend to novelty." Far from

being a new idea, Warren and Andrews's thesis of sovereignty of the individual is only the latest version of "love thy neighbor," the Golden Rule, or more recent prescriptions for peace and justice. To Ripley, the goal of all reform is to guarantee individual rights. This idea inspired the wisest reformers, especially Charles Fourier, whom Ripley, no less than Andrews, revered as "the most philosophical, the most profound, and the most comprehensive of all teachers of social science in the nineteenth century."[17]

Far from being a premise exclusively Warren's, the emancipation of humanity by means of individual sovereignty is the grand objective of socialism, at least in its form of Association. To Ripley, the "idea of human society" sought by Associative Socialism is not rule by a king, an aristocracy, a privileged class, or even a democracy—which is "the sovereignty of the majority for the time being" only—but governance by "humanity, or the integral Sovereignty of the Individual." This belief in democracy motivates the "great humanitary movement," from Rousseau to the social reformers Saint-Simon and Fourier, who differ from each other and from Josiah Warren "as to the methods of its attainment [but] agree in the supremacy of man over institutions as the true destiny of the race." No doubt, Warren believes that his system is unique, underived from outside sources, but "he exaggerates his own share of its promulgation. He is by no means the exclusive herald of an idea which the age is fermenting."[18]

Ripley misconstrues individual sovereignty, confusing Warren's defiance of organized power with social protest in general, and with Association in particular. He pays tribute to Andrews's previous work, "The True Constitution of Government," but fails to note that Andrews credits Fourier with the aim of enabling each person "to choose and vary his own destiny, untrammeled by social restrictions."

Both Ripley and Andrews endeavor to press Warren's anarchistic principles into a socialist mold that they do not fit. In Andrews's analysis of equitable commerce as the product of Protestantism, democracy, and socialism, the last term of the triad is awkward at best and mistaken at worst. Even in its joint-stock Association form, socialism calls for cooperatively owned and administered property. Andrews stretches its meaning to the limit to cover his own vague definition of socialism as the "emancipation of the Individual from social bondage."[19] His straining to reconcile Fourierism, his first love, with equitable commerce, his current infatuation, resembles John Van Der Zee Sears's recollection of socialism at Brook Farm: "Reduced to a syllogism it might be stated as follows: Major premise: Every human being desires happiness. Minor premise: Socialism provides for the happiness of every human being. Conclusion: Demonstrate this truth and every human being will become a socialist. Q.E.D."[20]

Ripley goes one step further, contending that Warren's cost the limit of price, for all its pretension to exclusive individualism, is actually a form of communism. Communism lumps everyone into an aggregate mass, to which it delivers its aggregate product. Associationism, however, "heaven-wide from Communism," favors the gradual distribution of products, proceeding from present inequality. Warren's system, according to Ripley, which balances equal amounts of labor with no concern for a product's value or utility, is in "irreconcilable antagonism" to individual sovereignty. It deprives producers from freely disposing of the fruits of their labor, thus abrogating their sovereign right of ownership.

It does not follow that a basket of berries and a vase of flowers produced by equal amounts of labor are therefore alike in exchangeable value. Any equalization of labor for labor that fails to depend on "the taste of the parties in the trade" does exactly what Warren declares out-of-bounds — it is an infringement of one person's right by another. "The absolute ownership of the article is thus destroyed by an arbitrary restriction on the process of exchange. Could there be a more flagrant violation of Sovereignty of the Individual?" If the flowers have a market value higher than that of the berries for which they are swapped on the labor-for-labor basis, then Warren's plan is fallacious because it insists on exchange of unequal products on equal terms. "Who," asks Ripley, reaps "the benefit of the difference in value — the individual producer, or the great body of producers? If you say the individual producer, you renounce the principle that cost is the limit of price. If you say the great body of producers, you take the ground of the Communists. But this is to surrender both the principle of individuality and that of the scientific distribution of products."[21]

Ergo, concludes Ripley, sovereignty of the individual is incompatible with cost the limit of price. Warren's commerce is communistic, not equitable, thus vitiating his claim of self-sovereignty by limiting price to cost instead of to market value.

ANDREWS'S DEFENSE

It rankled Warren that Ripley made an issue of who was first to pro-
claim individual sovereignty, an honor that Warren never claimed. He
did not think that Ripley read the book carefully, much less criticized
it fairly. On 4 July 1852, the day after the review appeared, Warren,
at Modern Times, wrote a letter to Andrews, in Manhattan:

> Mr. Gray has just handed me the Tribune of the 3rd. I have noth-
> ing to say to the Editor's three columns. You know that I have
> long ceased to hope anything from Editors or any others who have
> any particular positions or isms to sustain. The true issues will
> come on between the public and their leaders. *The great point is
> to inform the public what we really mean before leaders get a chance
> to misrepresent our views and movements* [emphasis added].[22]

Granted his shabby treatment by editors in the past, why did
Warren not leap at the chance to break into print in a major paper
by answering Ripley's critique? His refusal probably stemmed from sus-
picion of the press, rather than from fear of jousting with the *Tribune*.
Instead of combating Ripley himself, he asked Andrews, the veteran
of many a tilt of words, to ride into battle wearing his colors. The letter informs his partner of "a simple . . . and *unlearned* woman here,"
whose indignant reaction to this "long and labored article" is that "the
fellow is a fool—What a lie! when you [Warren] are always saying that
there is no knowing who originates an idea! and you are always fighting
against vulgar glory! . . . A great big booby! to pretend to criticize a
book and tell other people what they ought to think it is, and he has
never read it himself!"[23]

Maybe Warren believed that this unschooled but commonsensi-
cal sovereign's commitment to Modern Times negated Ripley's disapproval and demolished his critical comments. But Josiah's aversion to
answering Ripley may illustrate more than a show of scorn for what
he perceived as an unfair and shallow detraction. It may also be proof
of a timid retreat from facing up to objections that cry out for the author's response. Warren's typically individualistic advice to Andrews
is "do as you like." Apparently unaware that Ripley wrote the unsigned
review, Warren impeaches Horace Greeley: "It is worthy of note that

the only one who has denied the soundness of Cost as the true limit of price is the Editor of the most prominent reform paper in America—what is prominence for?"[24]

Ripley ends his review with the verdict that Warren's theory of equitable commerce is a failure. In his "Reply to the *Tribune*," Andrews gibes that it is odd to devote three and one-half columns to a failure. Moreover, the *Tribune* does not disagree with sovereignty of the individual—the first of the theory's two pillars—but merely doubts Warren's role as its creator. Immaterial and irrelevant, objects counselor Andrews. Who first enunciated the principle is a question "to which no man would attach less consequence than Mr. Warren himself." The point is whether the premise is true, which Andrews emphatically believes it is.

As he does again the following year in the Introduction to *Love, Marriage, and Divorce, and the Sovereignty of the Individual*, Andrews portrays Warren as a propounder of principles about which there is "nothing flashy nor superficially attractive," but, nonetheless, are "hard, unpretending, but fundamental truths." The rough and simple style of Warren's "Little Manual" will appeal to "common-sense" minded "connoisseurs in social architecture." Scholars and philosophers, Andrews coyly adds, may prefer "my own more elaborate exposition of the same doctrine in 'The True Constitution of Government' and 'Cost the Limit of Price.'"[25]

As a former contributor to both Greeley's *Tribune* and Ripley's *Harbinger*, Andrews was at home with Fourierist rhetoric. Of course individual sovereignty is "implied remotely and prophetically in Fourier's formula of 'Destinies proportioned to Attractions.'" It is also implicit in the Declaration of Independence, which affirms the rights of men to "Liberty and the pursuit of Happiness." The version expressed by Warren stands apart from all others, according to Andrews, because Warren is the first person "clearly to define this idea as a *Principle*, instead of a vague aspiration, to fix it in a *Formula*, to settle its *Legitimate Limitation*, to propound it as one of the *Grand, Practical Solutions* of the *Social Problem*, and to connect it with its *Correlated Principles* in this solution." The concept pervades the writing of modern reformers, but merely to state it is not the same as the "distinct announcement of the 'Sovereignty of each Individual to be exercised at his own Cost,' propounded as a scientific substitute for all Laws and Govern-

ments, and as one of the immediate working instrumentalities of Social Reform."[26]

Social planners prize the usually self-conferred accolade that their
work is "scientific." When calculating the time of the Second Advent
from data stored in Daniel and Revelation, the Rappites were sure they
were scientific as well as inspired. Fourier was convinced that he was
to the social sciences what Newton was to the mechanical, expanding
his predecessor's findings to cover society and the passions. Robert Owen
believed that his plan to resettle the working poor in Villages of Cooperation gave concrete form to the science of society, the same expression that Andrews chose for the title of his book and the purpose of
his life's work. In his preface to Thomas Low Nichols's *Woman, in All
Ages and Nations*, Andrews proclaimed the discoveries of Josiah Warren, "the founder of the American Practical School of Reform, [to be]
superior to the combined orders of Fourier, Owen, and others," and
his own elaboration of them to "furnish, in a simple, truly scientific
and incontestible method, the means of attaining all that has been
aimed at by those eminent reformers, without resorting to those re-
pulsive and erroneous combinations of interest suggested and deemed
essential by them."[27]

Scientific socialism was not yet the registered trademark of Karl
Marx and Friedrich Engels, although they were on their way to corner-
ing the market in Europe. The *Communist Manifesto* did not appear
in English for American consumption until late in 1871, in *Woodhull
and Claflin's Weekly*, translated by none other than the linguist and editor Stephen Pearl Andrews. Charles Shively judges that Andrews respected Marx as the "world famous leader of the 'New Socialism,'" and
the *Communist Manifesto* as the key to his doctrine, but "he considered
it only another socialist pamphlet, important because it confirmed his
own *Science of Society*."[28] This contention is debatable because the *Manifesto* does not confirm the tenets of equitable commerce. The Marxist
progression from feudal through bourgeois to socialist stages resembles
Andrews's projection of equitable commerce as the step-by-step sequence
of Protestantism, democracy, and socialism. But would the property-
owning sovereigns of Modern Times agree they had nothing to lose
but their chains?

History stubbornly fails to validate the future of the United States
predicted "scientifically," either by Marx and Engels or by Warren and

Andrews. Capitalism is not overthrown, bought out, or supplanted; the Marxian forecast of "inevitable" collapse is unrealized, perhaps because the system substantially modified its early image. And Modern Times's example did not lead to a peaceful and gradual change to equitable commerce: cost the limit of price could not prevail over gainful exchange.

Nonetheless, the grip of acquisitive industrialism, although tightening inescapably, had not yet closed on America during the formative years of Modern Times. Communism—"scientific" or Bible-style—socialism, and equitable commerce were substitutes offered by people unwilling to fall in step with the march of the profit system.

Andrews hurls thunderbolts of rhetoric at the supporters of business-as-usual. Cost the limit of price, jargon to some and unknown to most, is now in its infancy, he argues, but "in these words is contained the most Fundamental, the most Potent, and the most Revolutionary Idea of the nineteenth century: a watchword of Reform which comes not humbly, saying 'By your leave,' but with power, saying to the capitalist, 'You must.'"[29]

Attorney Andrews defends his client, the cost principle, against a three-count indictment: first, that he and Warren deny the right of individuals to the product of their own labor; second, that he and Warren oppose either ownership or exchange of property at will; and third, that they want to impose a compulsory law to fix price, thereby contravening their other fundament, sovereignty of the individual. To all counts, answers Andrews, "We simply plead not guilty, and put ourselves upon the country." Yes, everyone deserves title to the product of his or her labor, with the qualification that it be "justly bestowed"—what Marx would call "socially necessary." No, we do not repudiate property and the right to accumulate and exchange it freely, "We only repudiate the right of accumulating other people's property: and as for exchanges, they are the burden of the whole doctrine." No, we make nothing compulsory. Compulsion is unthinkable because it nullifies sovereignty of the individual, and equitable commerce itself.[30]

There is a "however." The fine print in the contract of equity reads that although it prohibited compulsion, "this does not prevent us from . . . acting upon *Principles*. It is precisely this difference between *a compulsory law and a Principle* which our critic has failed to apprehend, and which the world sadly needs to appreciate." No person has the right to do wrong, but all have the right to the freedom to do so. The Modern Times proviso is that any wrong that anyone does be at his or her own cost, "that is, that he do not throw the burdensome consequences of his acts on others."[31]

We do not compel compliance but we want to convince the world of the justice of our principle. The case of cost versus value, that we are now trying, is "One, that of the exchange of equivalent Values, or Benefits; the other, that of the exchange of equivalent Costs or Burdens. One is the *Value Principle*. The one now prevails in the world, the other we contend for—not . . . to enforce it upon any body, but as the true or right thing."[32]

How, inquires Andrews, can the author of the review read *Science of Society* (briefly cited by Ripley) and not be cured of repeating the clichés of "civilized cannibalism," to say nothing of failing to accept the "obvious truth and the high harmonic results of the Cost Principle"? Too hasty a reading betrayed the reviewer into misconceptions, which Andrews politely hopes that mutual accord will resolve.

In conclusion, Andrews restates the lineage of equitable commerce, the infant born of Protestant liberty of conscience and the Democratic ideal of self-government. Without naming it, he alludes to the quiet growth of Modern Times, the equity village settled by searchers for "truer relations among men, and with a real success which will dispense with all criticism at an early age. The time is not distant when the fact that a leading Social reformer and reviewer pronounced the Cost Principle a failure will be quoted among the Curiosities of Literature."[33]

The Saint-Simonian optimism that "the future belongs to us!" is a brave but wishful thought of Andrews's. Equitable commerce never became a popular movement because of the difficulty of convincing people to sever cost from market value and let it stand as the limit of price. Although it agrees with one of mainstream society's fundamental premises—that to own one's house, land, and tools in fee simple is the birthright of *genus Americanus*—it failed to spread because it rejects the correlative premise that what Ripley called "owndom" entitles a person to sell the product of his or her labor at a higher price than its cost. Persuading working people to swap their labor at cost is an assignment as hopeless as making them believe that games are played without winners. Not even at Modern Times, where homestead-

seeking pioneers at first agreed to observe the cost principle, did the
sovereigns long hold out once bidders began to offer them more than
they paid for their acres.

In his reply, Andrews ignores the charge that Warren's program
is more communistic than individualistic because it let the entire community reap the spread between cost and market value. However, in
"Cost the Limit of Price," he states that the system will never "land
in Communism," so long as property remains "owned by individuals,
who will exercise absolute rights over it." The aim is to abolish price
in the coming age of abundance, when every product will be as free
of charge as a glass of water in 1852. Even then, the rights of "owndom"
will persist, as shown in a rather crude example: "You will take a wafer
from my desk without even consulting me. It is not worthwhile to assert my own ownership. But if on doing so repeatedly you render yourself offensive by puffing tobacco smoke in my face, or otherwise, I fall
back upon my right of property, and refuse you the accommodation."[34]

For all of Andrews's parries and ripostes, equitable commerce is
vulnerable to a thrust at its inconsistency. Critics can show the damage to individual sovereignty if the price of the product of personal
labor be limited to its cost. Compulsion is alien to self-sovereignty; the
plan functions only by voluntary rejection of profit. Andrews forecasts
a long campaign for acceptance of an idea designed to end exploitation, on the basis of unforced consent. To exchange labor without a
markup is absent from the agenda of an economy busily forming mass
markets for goods distributed by companies bent on capital gain as
well as on higher net income.

THE PRACTICAL CHRISTIAN REPUBLIC
VS. MODERN TIMES

In attacking *Equitable Commerce* and, by inference, Modern Times,
George Ripley defends his belief in Association against a rival doctrine.
Although finding cost the limit of price fallacious, he hails sovereignty
of the individual as belonging as much to Fourier as to Warren.

Adin Ballou condemns both. To this godly reformer, the founder
of both Practical Christian Socialism and its manifestation at Hopedale,
the concept of individual sovereignty is sinful and Modern Times a

sinkhole. Ballou's hostility boiled over in 1853, when Henry Fish and
"Sister" Seaver, a friend of "Brother" Fish's wife, confessed to adulterous conduct at Hopedale and fled to Modern Times.[35] Had this incident never smudged the purity of his Community, Ballou still would
have linked Modern Times to the Antichrist for its lack of respect for
God's orders.

The tendency of leaders of structured societies to disdain the absence of organization makes it doubly difficult for Adin Ballou to consider Modern Times objectively. Not only is the village depraved, he
contends, it has neither rules nor by-laws. Conversely, Article II alone,
of the Constitution of the Practical Christian Republic, under the heading of "Principles" proclaims eight "Divine Principles of Theological
Truth," eight "Divine Principles of Personal Righteousness," eight "Divine Principles of Social Order," and eleven subprinciples, beginning
with the words "never to." Members are never to kill, hate, or sanction slavery. They are never to fight, envy, oppress, lie, cheat, steal,
commit adultery, fornicate, self-pollute, loaf, curse, brag, or drink spirits
nonmedicinally. They are never to aid, abet, or approve others in any
sinful endeavor. They are never to take part in pernicious amusements,
nor to bet nor gamble, not even to buy a lottery ticket.[36]

Divine principles are the supreme law of the Practical Christian
Republic, which admits applicants only after they swear belief in the
religion of Jesus Christ, as taught and exemplified by the New Testament. Members are free to practice religion as conscience dictated,
hold property, speak openly at meetings, and otherwise pursue any
happiness not forbidden by laws of God and His earthly arbiters.[37]
Nonresister Ballou and his followers, when listing taboos of heavenly
origin, set forth their resolve never to participate "in a sword-sustained
human government, either as voters, office-holders or subordinate as-
sistants, *in any case prescriptively involving the infliction of death or any
absolute injury whatsoever by man on man*; nor to invoke governmental
interposition in any such case even for the accomplishment of good
objects."[38]

The "grand object" of Christian Socialism, Hopedale style, is "to
regenerate the world and save it from its wretchedness and wo [*sic*]."
Its appeal is universal, addressed to rich and poor, employer and worker,
learned and ignorant, talented and unskilled: "Like the Love of the

Great Father, it embodies in its outgushing sympathies, the whole human brotherhood." It preempts the reform movement, embracing the "cause of Anti-Slavery . . . Peace . . . Temperance, and Anti-Capital Punishment, and Anti-Oath-Taking, and Woman's Rights, and Organization of labor," and everything else that promoted goodness. Because it compromises with the forces responsible for poverty and inequality, the "so-called Church" renders itself inefficient, unable to destroy or abolish the evil with which it collaborates. For this Church to reform itself into an agency aimed at ending war, slavery, social injustice, ignorance, and vice, "it must itself be born again— . . . into a higher and nobler life—even into the Christian Socialist life."[39]

Although sharing some of the anarchistic and leveling goals of Modern Times, this mixture of piety and radicalism, of no-government nonresistance and mandatory restraints upon members, is essentially a "peculiar variety of Associationism." Like Andrews and Ripley, Adin Ballou esteems the "great and rare genius" Fourier, with whose works "No other writer on Socialism has produced anything that can be compared." Phalansterianism, the preeminent form of Socialism, "proposes to organize the whole human family, as fast as possible, into associative Phalanxes, provincial confederacies of Phalanxes, and these into one grand Imperial Phalanx of nations."[40]

Charles Fourier predicts a future age of Harmony, when the lands of the earth are completely measured off in Phalanxes, "exactly 2,985,984 of them."[41] Less specifically, the Practical Christian Republic envisions a pyramid tapering upward from Parochial Communities through Communal States to Communal Nations confederated into one Republic under a Supreme Unitary Council of Senators. No need to fear the abuse of authority, for the Constitution assured that "all governmental powers vested in the confederate bodies of this Republic shall be such as are obviously beneficent." The basis of moral and social order at Hopedale, the sole constituency of the Republic, is "Self-government in the individual, the Family and the primary congenial Association."[42]

Unlike Modern Times, where there is no power higher than each individual's, Hopedale's self-government for Practical Christians is "under the immediate sovereignty of Divine Principles,"[43] as interpreted by Adin Ballou and his coadjutors. Infidelity is beyond the pale, the heresy for which Henry Fish and Sister Seaver are driven from the Republic. In the eyes of Ballou's "beneficent" government, they committed the sin of adultery, compounded by taking refuge at Modern Times, the open city of sinners.

In *Free Love in America*, Taylor Stoehr observes that the nonresistants of Hopedale and the sovereigns of Modern Times shared certain values of anarchist libertarianism, but "were of a very different cast of mind. Both groups condemned the coercion of the State, both affirmed the virtues of community. But that was where the resemblance ended."[44]

In contrast to Hopedale, Modern Times had no constitution, no by-laws, no subordination of sovereigns to divine control, no crusade against sin, no sense of holy mission, no belief in itself as a City of God, trapped in the evil city of man. Modern Timers could stand against slavery, hard drink, and central power, but this decision was a choice, not a duty. They could join the army or navy in wartime, or ask the town to hire a substitute. So long as it did not impede another from doing the same, they thought and did whatever they liked, without asking God's approval.

Neither village took part in government—Modern Times for philosophical, Hopedale for moral reasons. Modern Times practised permissive libertarianism; Hopedale engaged in permitted libertarianism. Hemmed in by existing laws and inhibitions, Hopedale's brand of self-government was a counterfeit, Modern Times's the genuine article.

The Long Island haven of free thought inspires the wrath of Ballou in *Practical Christian Socialism*, his three-part work on political science, published in 1854. Part 3 is the author's proof that his system excels every other. Although his plan for the future provides for a confederation of states and nations, Ballou's attitude toward the "sword-wielding" power structure he lived under is uncompromisingly negative.

Why, then, does this foe of coercive authority not recognize in Modern Times, if not his no-government brother, at least a kissing cousin? The concession of "many truths, and . . . valuable suggestions" in Warren's *Equitable Commerce* and *Practical Details*, and Andrews's *Science of Society* cannot compensate for Ballou's objections to the doctrines themselves: "I object to it [equitable commerce], that as a whole its tendency is to promote self-conceit, self-gratification, pertinacity of will, isolation of persons and interests, anarchy and war among human beings."[45]

As for sovereignty of the individual, "It is an irreligious, immoral and licentious doctrine. It ignores God the supreme Sovereign. It knows no God. It knows no essential divine principles. It knows no absolute, universal, all-binding laws to which a common appeal can be religiously made. The Individual is supreme legislator and judge for him or her self on all questions of self-interest. Hear Mr. Warren!" Ballou, proceeding to quote from *Practical Details,* changes the meaning of a crucial line. Warren's "'True religion' is *my* individual religion, and so with every one else's," becomes "True religion [without quotation marks] is *my* individual religion, and so with every one else's." The impression given is that Warren wants his own idea of religion to be adopted as true, whereas Warren plainly means there is no such thing as "true" religion, morality, virtue, or reason, but only what each person chooses to believe: "The idea of any one standard must be given up, and every one allowed to be his own standard before we shall take the first step toward harmonious adjustment."[46]

This flexibility was anathema to the Reverend Adin Ballou, Universalist minister and believer in the rule of God with the Bible as law. Ballou's attack on cost the limit of price is like Ripley's. He wonders who will want to put the "bell" of cost around the neck of the "cat" of the old social system. Why would workers commanding "$2, $3, $5 and $10 per day go into Equitable Villages and accept of $1 per day, or less even, for the sake of actualizing their theory and redeeming society?"[47] Will this idealism not require martyrs, something precluded by Andrews in *Science of Society?*

If less eager to score debating points, Ballou might have reminded readers that man does not live by bread alone. But his criticism was telling, as applicable to Hopedale as it was to Modern Times. The most resourceful self-governors were the bold and independent competers in the marketplace, unwilling to retreat into the shelter of a cooperative but financially unrewarding community. If not martyrs, the ideal villages needed witnesses ready to suffer frugality for the sake of "actualizing their theory and redeeming society."

People are selfish, reflects Ballou. They love a bargain, but not enough to make cost the basis of the economy. "Individual Sovereigntyism" is an unworkable hoax, to be demolished in peroration by a bombardment of adjectives. It is "an irreligious, demoralizing and licentious system, and therefore *ought* never to prevail . . . an incongruous, contradictive, irreconcilable, impracticable system . . . it [is] false in principle, delusive in profession, and necessarily fraught with disappointment to its disciples in its legitimate results." Convinced that he has blown Modern Times out of the water, Ballou surveys the wreckage and modestly muzzles his guns: "The radical and vast superiority of my social system over it I need not more emphatically affirm. I forbear."[48]

Forbearance availed him little—the model community he designed had scarcely two remaining years. Modern Times (1851–1864) outlived Hopedale (1842–1856), though the latter outlasted all other Fourierist villages, including the North American Phalanx (1843–1854). The economic program of Hopedale was joint-stock proprietorship of collectively managed assets, held individually in negotiable shares. Instead of cost as the only limit of price, the Republic held that price should not exceed the fair cost value of anything sold or exchanged, the cost to include prime expenses, overhead, depreciation, waste, risk, labor, and interest or profit at an annual rate not higher than 4 percent. Every member and dependent was guaranteed employment, at least adequate to a comfortable subsistence; relief in want, sickness, or distress; and a suitable sphere of individual enterprise and responsibility.[49]

Its joint-stock format did Hopedale in, when the Draper brothers, its two leading stockholders, took possession of 75 percent of the shares in 1856. Promptly paying all debts, they converted the Republic into their own private business. In his history of ideal villages, John Humphrey Noyes did not condemn Ballou for his overblown "confidence of success, to the verge of presumption," a failing "common to all the socialist inventors: Fourier, without a laboratory or an experiment, was as dogmatic and infallible as though he were an oracle of God; and Owen, after a hundred defeats, never doubted the perfection of his scheme, and never fairly confessed a failure."

At least Adin Ballou rose above these theorizers when, after Hopedale's demise, he manfully owned up that it was total failure. No mere dreamer, he was (like Warren and Ripley) a planner sho "served in the ranks as a common laborer for his cause." There should be a ban, thought Noyes, on American importation of socialist theories that have not been "worked out, as well as written out, by the inventors themselves." Hopedale did not attract the distinction of Brook Farm and other ideal villages that openly called themselves Fourierist, but in comparison was both scientific and sensible, "a Yankee attempt to solve the socialistic problem [deserving] more attention than any of them."[50]

Josiah Warren was one Yankee inventor of social solutions who did not think well of Ballou. In the *Periodical Letter* of March 1855, Josiah replies to an article in the *Tribune* in which Ballou attacked the "Cost principle." Warren resents Ballou's self-righteous habit of stating beliefs as if they are facts, and then placing these "facts" beyond debate because they are emanations of Scripture. "My system," declares Ballou, "ascribes supremacy to the Christian religion over all philosophy . . . religion evolves and patronizes philosophy . . . I make the genuine Christianity of the New Testament in its essential principles absolutely divine, absolutely authoritative." This, snaps Warren, is nothing "more or less than Mr. Adin Ballou's christianity, Mr. Ballou's religion, Mr. Ballou's patronage of philosophy, Mr. Ballou's idea of divinity, and Mr. Adin Ballou's authority which he attempts to raise above every body else, and every fact in nature."[51]

Warren shrugs off Ballou's objections to the cost principle, focused, like Ripley's, on the entitlement of producers to the spread between cost and market value. Ballou defines price as "the reasonable medium between Cost and Value."[52] Who, asks Warren, decides what is "reasonable?" Ballou? The majority? Would not all have different opinions? For Warren, the only yardstick is equity, based on his five-point solution of the social problem:

Individuality.
Sovereignty of the Individual.
Cost the Limit of Price.
Circulating Medium Founded on the Cost of Labor.
Adaptation of the Supply to the Demand.[53]

Because "reasonable" is too vague a term to be useful in determining price, Warren declines to engage in debate with its user any more than he would buy cloth from a "merchant who used a gum elastic yard stick."[54]

Although Ballou wraps himself too much in the Bible, and Hopedale with too many regulations, he and Warren are closer than their dispute suggests. Warren's demon is profit, on which he blames the skewed proportion of poor to rich in a land of enormous abundance. To him, market price is fictitious: a figure, rigged by speculators, that fuels inflation, manipulation, and the cult of acquisition. Yet the only difference between Warren's legitimate factors of price—prime costs, overhead, training, equipment, and his special ingredient of repugnance—and those listed by Adin Ballou is the 4 percent of presumably honest profit allowed at Hopedale.

Neither Modern Times nor Hopedale paid homage to outside government. In *Native American Anarchism*, Eunice M. Schuster notes a similarity in the camps of Warrenite self-sovereignty and of Practical Christian Non-Resistance. While the school of individual anarchism founded by Josiah Warren "would supplant existing law by the laws of nature, the non-resistants would substitute the laws of God as simply set forth by the Golden Rule and by Christ in the Sermon on the Mount—a difference only in name."[55]

As years pass, the difference became more than nominal. B. F. Bowles told the *Sunday Dispatch* that he and his fellow Modern Timers refused to subscribe to nonresistance. A willingness to use force, when needed, received further confirmation from the fifteen soldier-sovereigns who served in the Union forces after the outbreak of civil war.

Throughout the Civil War the Practical Christians kept their vow "never under any pretext whatsoever to kill, assault or injure any human being, even their worst enemy." When the army drafted a former member in the summer of 1863, the "still-adhering" remnant of Hopedale paid his $300 commutation fee "to the government of the United States under military constraint and in respectful submission to the powers that be—but earnestly protesting against the exaction as an infraction of [the member's] natural and indefeasible rights as a conscientious, peaceable subject."[56]

Condemning the "flames of rebellion . . . [lit by] the insane wrath of slave-holding secessionists," Hopedale sympathized with the Union. However, its brand of abolitionism mixed with pacifism did not sanction the use of violence. The warriors of Modern Times received the support of their neighbors; the several Practical Christians who, in spite of their vows, felt the need to enlist had first to resign from the Hopedale congregation, in order not to violate "their former acknowledged obligations."[57]

Josiah Warren was not well-known, much less famous. Except for hostile, patronizing, or muckraking critics, the press ignored him and Modern Times. When reviewing *Equitable Commerce*, George Ripley and Adin Ballou seemed more concerned with justifying their own beliefs than with carefully looking at Warren's. Rather than welcome individual sovereignty, each at his or her own cost, and encourage its testing at Modern Times, they chipped away at its resemblance to statements made by others from Jesus to Fourier. They did not point out that Warren and Andrews not only advocated but implemented the premise of personal freedom. Discussion of polity usually centers on the amount of sovereignty each must yield for government to function. No places are set at the pundits' table for prophets who render *nothing* unto Caesar.

8

Variations on Individual Sovereignty

THE PROGRAM ADVOCATED BY WARREN AND ANDREWS, not widely spread in either country, received more attention in England than in the United States. Henry Edger's reports to the London *Leader* informed socially-conscious British readers of the purpose and progress of Modern Times. An Owenite leader, William Pare, in 1852 wrote a sympathetic account of the village in *Chambers's Edinburgh Journal*, presenting Warren as the preacher and Andrews as the "zealous and eloquent apostle" of equitable commerce. As seekers of "social prosperity not in Socialism or Communism but in the opposite *ism*, 'Individualism,'" they created Modern Times, where "every man charges a fair price for his labour, but no profit." The sovereigns shunned combined interests, each minding his or her own business and letting other people's alone. In this citadel of enlightened selfishness, price was "valued by labour, and labour was . . . valued by time and trouble . . . There is no arrangement for drones; there is no chance for profit, pickings, or plunder." If it can "guarantee the *industry* and *honesty*" of each citizen, Modern Times will "both thrive and live to be Ancient Times; and the same may be said of every community." Pare urged all concerned with reform of society to direct their efforts in this direction, with the objective of "the legitimisation of individuality and selfhood, their economisation as social forces, and their subjection to such regulations as will naturally and necessarily secure 'equitable commerce.'"[1]

In the first number of the *Periodical Letter*, issued from Modern Times in July 1854, Warren dedicated his monthly report "to those who have not lost all hope of justice, order, and peace on earth." He inserted "an item of encouragement" from the 15 October 1853 issue of the London *Leader*, reporting the founding of an organization with the "'somewhat grand'" title of The London Confederation of Rational

Reformers. This group seceded from J. Bronterre O'Brien's National Reformers, who themselves "'seceded from every one.'" Warrenite from the inception, these secessionists from secession defined liberty as the realization of "'Sovereignty of the Individual'—a definition derived from the school of Josiah Warren.'" The *Leader* acclaimed the "'policy and patent good sense of the American Reformers of Modern Times,'" in whose footsteps the London Confederation proceeded by a method the "reverse of the Communistic," seeking reform "by a *segregation*, instead of an *aggregation* [of interests]. Their little tract on the *science of society* deserves a word as a novelty in English democratic literature."[2]

Beneath this announcement Warren printed his letter to Ambrose Caston Cuddon, an English friend, correspondent, recipient of his stereotyping patents for Britain, and secretary of the "new London Confederation." James J. Martin notes that "the English supporters of Warren displayed little timidity in their efforts to spread their beliefs." In addition to drumming up support for equity commerce, visiting Modern Times and Utopia (the Warrenite settlement in Ohio) and reprinting excerpts of Warren and Andrews's works (Martin doubts that any were published in full in spite of plans to do so using Warren's printing devices), Cuddon "brought the matter to the attention of important political personages, including the prime minister, Lord Aberdeen."[3]

Concerning Cuddon's failure to convert another aristocrat, Warren dryly remarked he was not surprised "at the want of sympathy and aid where you looked for it: but I must say that I honor and admire the spirit of that passage in Lord Ashburton's letter to you."[4] Warren never exerted himself to solicit "important political personages," but in a later *Periodical Letter* he quoted from a letter to Cuddon in which he confessed to hoping that "Lord A—*** and Earl S—*** might have been induced to take some interest in our subject." All right, he went on characteristically, these gentlemen may be interested but choose not to say so publicly. "If so, we cannot (with a proper regard to their right of 'Sovereignty') object." At least we have gained the attention of a few of the "rich and powerful . . . If they will examine this, *together with the other* principles of the Equity Movement, they will be surprised to find how little ground there is for antagonism between us."[5]

The statement is no indication that Warren fawned on the wealthy. He was no Charles Fourier, spending his last years vainly "sitting at advertised hours in his small room awaiting the visit of some great capitalist who would offer to finance his schemes to do over the world."[6]

The letter merely conveyed Warren's wishful assumption that all thinking people, rich or poor, would agree with his basic premise if they took the trouble to study it. In the *Peaceful Revolutionist* of May 1848, he expressed his belief in the appeal of equity commerce to working folk: "Throughout the course of the practical developments of the subject, I have been thoroughly satisfied that it would never have aid or cooperation of *capitalists,* until we could prove that we could do without them—until the working classes step out from under them; and then they would *fall* into their proper position." Perhaps his experience at New Harmony with the Welsh-born industrialist Robert Owen and his Scottish associate, William Maclure, induced Warren to think more highly of British than of American capitalists. Most businessmen cannot be expected to strive for profitless enterprise, but, in justice to "the very few Robert Owens and William Mc'Clures [sic] it is necessary to discriminate between them and mere capitalists— they were men as well as capitalists, and we give them a nitch [sic] in our hearts by themselves."[7]

William Pare, the Birmingham Socialist and member of Owen's inner circle, was also a Rational Reformer. He presented the aims of equitable commerce to the Statistical Section of the British Association, meeting at Glasgow in September 1855. Reaffirming Warren's use of "commerce" in its "enlarged *old* English signification of the word 'conversation,' that is . . . the *tout ensemble* of human relations," Pare exalted the plan as a scientific, gradual, and peaceable substitution of new and harmonious relations: "Mr. Andrews, the principal writer or commentator on Mr. Warren's theory . . . avers . . . that when subjected to analysis, and traced to its ten thousand different applications, to ownership, to rent, to wages, &c., that it places all human transactions relating to property upon a new basis of exact justice; that is, it has the perfect, simple, but all-prevailing character of a UNIVERSAL PRINCIPLE."[8]

Its English friends were good press agents, but they never created a British version of Modern Times. Their only practical experiment was made twenty years before the formation of the Confederation of Rational Reformers, when Owen and Pare set up what to them were English models of Warren's time store. Unlike their American prototype, Owen's National Labour Exchanges were repositories for goods that were brought in by members to be exchanged for products of equal cost. Warren was a discount retailer, who bought merchandise in the open market and sold it at cost for cash, plus a small markup for his time that was payable in labor notes. His "equity store" was also a clearinghouse for buyers and sellers of goods and services who were willing to trade their labor at cost, with no need to belong to a co-op or any other group. In contrast, the Owenites ran swap shops, using labor notes as vouchers for purchase of merchandise rather than as contracts to work for a specified time at a given trade. As a result, the bazaars of the National Labour Exchange failed, glutted with unwanted items left in stock after those in demand were taken.[9]

The collapse of Owen's emporia in 1834 did not discourage the opening, ten years later, of a reborn and more effective cooperative movement at Rochdale, in Lancashire. Twenty-eight workingmen, six of them Owenites, became the pioneers of profit-sharing cooperative stores that by 1851, the year of Modern Times's inception, numbered 130 in northern England and Scotland.[10] These co-ops were improved versions of Owen's bazaars, not replicas of Warren's time store. In spite of the short-lived publicity generated by the Rational Reformers, the aspect of equitable commerce pertaining to cost the limit of price did not make headway in Britain.

JOHN STUART MILL'S DEBT TO JOSIAH WARREN

It was sovereignty of the individual, the other half of Warren's doctrine, that found its way into the bloodstream of English liberalism. John Stuart Mill did what Thoreau, Emerson, and other American defenders of individuality did not: in his *Autobiography*, he saluted "a remarkable American, Mr. Warren, [who] had framed a System of Society, on the foundation of 'the Sovereignty of the Individual.'"[11] Mill knew that Warren and a number of followers formed a "Village Community (Whether it now exists I know not), which, though bearing a superficial resemblance to some of the projects of Socialists, is diametrically opposite to them in principle, since it recognizes no authority whatever in Society over the individual, except to enforce equal freedom of development for individualities."[12]

Warren would have added "each at his or her own cost" to the last clause, but Mill's choice of the phrase "equal freedom" showed that he understood what Warren meant. Although Mill was hazy about the specifics, he sharply perceived the distinction between Modern Times and its collectivist, organization-prone counterparts in the ideal village movement.

He committed himself to individualism long before writing the *Autobiography*, in which he explained that his interest began in his youth and culminated in 1859 with the publication of *On Liberty*. As did Warren and Andrews, Mill scoffed at the issue of authorship for a "premise which though in many ages confined to insulated thinkers, mankind have probably at no time since the beginning of civilization been entirely without."[13] He preceded the text of *On Liberty* with a quotation from Wilhelm von Humboldt, the German humanist, hailing as the "grand, leading principle" of government "the absolute and essential importance of human development in its richest diversity."[14] In the *Autobiography* Mill recalled that from the host of past defenders of liberty he chose to cite only Humboldt, "who furnished the motto to the work, *although* in one passage I borrowed from the Warrenites their phrase, the sovereignty of the individual [emphasis added]." Mill qualified his citation of Warren with the disclaimer that "It is hardly necessary here to remark that there are abundant differences in detail between the conception of the doctrine by any of the predecessors I have mentioned and that set forth in the book."[15]

The real difference between Mill and Warren is that between some government and none. The subject of *On Liberty*, posed in its opening sentence, is "the nature and limits of the power which can be legitimately exercised by society over the individual."[16] But Warren, when writing on liberty, argued that society's power over individuals, expressed in law and custom, is so inherently illegitimate that "there is no security, no liberty for mankind, but through the *abandonment of combinations* as the basis of society."[17] Mill's concern is for "Civil, or Social Liberty,"[18] Warren's for total liberty, enabling each to be "so disconnected . . . from others" that he may be SOVEREIGN OF HIMSELF."[19]

On Liberty echoed more than one of Warren's thoughts. In his "Introductory," Mill identified freedom as "pursuing our own good in our own way, so long as we do not attempt to deprive others of theirs, or impede their efforts to obtain it." Individuals should do as they choose without impediment from others as long as what we do "does not harm them, even though they should think our conduct foolish, perverse, or wrong." The "object of this Essay is to assert one very simple principle": that the only warrant for interfering with "the liberty of action of any [person] is self-protection." Prevention of harm to others is the only rightful purpose for restraining a person against his will. The conclusion of Mill's variation on Warren's theme is that "Over himself, over his own body and mind, the individual is sovereign."[20]

This idea is repeated in "Of Individuality," chapter 3 of *On Liberty*, to the effect that men should be free to live "without hindrance from their fellow-men, so long as it is at their own risk and peril." Individual liberty does not permit one to "make himself a nuisance to other people," but otherwise gives the right to "carry his opinions into practice *at his own cost*" [emphasis added].[21] This passage is vintage Warren, bottled by Mill.

Chapter 4, "Of the Limits to the Authority of Society Over the Individual," begins with three crucial questions: "What, then, is the rightful limit to the sovereignty of the individual over himself? Where does the authority of society begin? How much of human life should be assigned to individuality, and how much to society?" Retreating from Warren's stubborn refusal to give up a jot of self-sovereignty, Mill answers equivocally, falling back on the "render unto Caesar" compromise: "Each will receive its proper share, if each has that which more particularly concerns it. To individuality should belong the part of life in which it is chiefly the individual that is interested; to society, the part which chiefly interests society." We must pay for the benefit of protection by society by respecting the rights of others, and by doing our share to defend "the society or its members from injury or molestation." Invoking his brand of the cost principle, Mill sternly declares the entitlement of Society to enforce those obligations "at all costs to those who endeavor to withhold fulfillment."[22]

Mill feared what Alexis de Tocqueville called the "tyranny of the majority,"[23] which may be a patrician's phrase for universal manhood suffrage. Although acknowledging the right to vote and send children to school, some aristocrats of birth or of intellect felt at risk against the rising American tide of egalitarianism. Beneath Mill's complaint that "at present individuals are lost in the crowd . . . [of] collective mediocrity"[24] may lurk the apprehension that common folk who once knew their place might soon demand seats at tables reserved for gentlemen.

In *Considerations on Representative Government*, Mill hitched voting to taxpaying in a would-be disfranchisement of recipients of parish relief: "He who cannot by his labour suffice for his own support, has no claim to the privilege of helping himself to the money of others." He made a modest proposal of five years' probation off the welfare rolls "as a condition for the franchise." Gauging intelligence in proportion to status, he held that employers were smarter than hirelings, foremen than laborers, skilled than unskilled workers, as "a banker, merchant, or manufacturer" is apt to be brighter "than a tradesman, because he has larger and more complicated interests to manage." Not property but intelligence—revealed by one's occupation—should be the measurement for determining whose votes count more than others. Ideally, "two or more votes might be allowed to every person who exercises any of these superior functions." Others deserving a multiple vote are the graduates of universities or even of certain schools where the higher learning was taught "under proper securities that the teaching is real, and not a mere pretence."[25]

Mill was an eloquent champion of freedom of speech, religion, and thought, but his mistrust of plebians detracts from his reputation as the leading spokesman for liberty. What worried Josiah Warren was the tyranny of the minority, whose control of assets empowered it as the majority in decision making. The perceptive Tocqueville had already anticipated this threat to liberty, warning against its menace in *Democracy in America,* in a chapter called "How an Aristocracy May Be Created by Manufactures." The industrial elite "growing up under our eyes is one of the harshest that ever existed in the world" [this prescient observation was made in 1835], but at present could be contained, without danger. "Nevertheless, the friends of democracy should keep their eyes anxiously fixed in this direction; for if ever a permanent inequality of conditions and aristocracy again penetrates into the world, it may be predicted that this is the gate by which they will enter."[26]

Mill's eyes, however, were fixed on the ability of the majority to enforce its standards of thought and behavior. The historian Bernard Semmel believes that the peril to liberty foreseen by Mill was "a conformity imposed by a central power, supposedly to protect citizens, but in fact 'trampling . . . with considerable recklessness, as often as convenient, upon the rights of individuals, in the name of society and the public good.'"[27]

Mill's Platonic remedy made Guardians of the "superior spirits" who know what is best for all: "ultimate control of government must rest with the people, [but] the best government was that 'of the wisest, and these must always be a few.'"[28] Presumably, the majority purged of its tyranny will ratify the power to rule of these few superior spirits. Yet Mill remains, in Semmel's judgment, "the most unchallenged intellectual patron of Anglo-American liberalism."[29] The unposed question is why Mill is a household word and *On Liberty* is required reading, while Warren, from whom Mill derived his key phrase, is stranded in obscurity. To suggest that Warren's essay on "Liberty," in the third section of *Equitable Commerce*, deserves a place on the same shelf as Mill's does not subtract one jot from the latter's dedication to the right of untrammeled dissent.

There are no Guardians in Warren, no Coleridgean clerisy, no weighted voting, no barring of ballots to welfare receivers, no linking of tax-paying to citizenship rights, or rating of intelligence by the position a person holds. Mill borrowed the wording and liked the concept of sovereignty of the individual, but consumers of liberty in its natural state will find Warren's brand undiluted compared with Mill's attenuation. The "Liberty" passage in *Equitable Commerce* was composed at the white-hot pitch of *Common Sense*:

> Each individual being thus at liberty at all times would be SOVEREIGN OF HIMSELF, NO GREATER AMOUNT OF LIBERTY CAN BE CONCEIVED —ANY LESS WOULD NOT BE LIBERTY! Liberty defined and limited by others is slavery! LIBERTY, then, is the SOVEREIGNTY OF THE INDIVIDUAL; and never shall man know liberty until each and every individual is acknowledged to be *the only* legitimate sovereign of his or her person, time, and property, each living and acting at his own cost; and not until we live in society where each can exercise this inalienable right of sovereignty at all times without clashing with, or violating that of others. This is impracticable just in proportion as we or our interests are UNITED *or combined with others*. The only ground upon which man can know liberty is that of DISCONNECTION, DISUNION, INDIVIDUALITY.[30]

As one of many peddlers of liberty, Warren hawked his wares with fewer concessions to orthodoxy than others vending the product, from Mill and Spencer to Thoreau and Emerson. The concept of personal freedom, a scion of the Reformation and the Enlightenment, also reflected the laissez-faire, freewheeling economics of an expanding industrial juggernaut. Yet within the spectrum of liberty a special band belongs to Warren, tying sovereignty of the individual to private but profitless enterprise, and offering Modern Times as an object lesson.

SPENCER'S FIRST LAW OF FREEDOM

Mill was a generous spirit who paid his intellectual debts. Herbert Spencer, however, did not report that he borrowed the thought when, in *Social Statics* (1851), he stated his "law of equal freedom." Whether he was inspired by Warren or not, the premise of sovereignty of the individual could not better be summarized than by Spencer's "First Principle," the law he advanced as the only correct base of equity: *"Every man has the freedom to do all that he wills, provided he infringes not the equal freedom of any other man."*[31] The sticky wicket was Spencer's perception of "equal freedom," as different from Warren's as is competition from cooperation. Spencer is Warren without the cost principle, pushing sovereignty to gluttony. The exploitation precluded by Warren is not only welcome but glorified by Spencer: his phrase "survival of the fittest," giving Darwinist sanction to acquisition, made its coiner the idol of business magnates the likes of James J. Hill, John D. Rockefeller, and Andrew Carnegie.[32]

Spencer's reduction of government's function to keeping the peace attracted the interest of Benjamin Tucker, Warren's successor as spokesman for philosophical anarchism. In his study of American anarchism, David DeLeon comments that Tucker and his associates admired Spencer's emphasis on individuality, "although Tucker could fully endorse only Spencer's 'The Right to Ignore the State' (which he printed separately as 'an anarchist classic') and denounced some of his later writings as reactionary."[33] Perhaps DeLeon was unaware of Richard Hofstadter's comment that the "Spencerian 'right to ignore the state' was dropped from his later writings." According to Hofstadter, Spencer went further than Mill in objecting to giving the vote to the poor: "His categorical repudiation of state interference with the 'natural,' unimpeded growth of society led him to oppose all state aid to the poor. They were unfit . . . and should be eliminated. 'The whole effect of nature is to get rid of such, to clear the world of them, and make room for better.'"[34]

Spencer's homage to individual sovereignty, divorced from War-renite equity, is a shield for the cult of property-seeking, a function of the "instinct of accumulation" in harmony with "the human constitution as divinely ordained."[35] As Warren would put an end to poverty, Spencer would put an end to the poor. Surely Mill makes sounder use of self-sovereignty as the cornerstone of the temple of liberty.

THOREAU AND EMERSON

Individualism came into its own in the middle years of the nineteenth century, as evidenced by the publication of *Equitable Commerce*, *The Science of Society*, *Democracy in America*, *On Liberty*, and *Social Statics*. Expansion of voting rights, the development of a national market, and the opportunity to succeed in business acted as interlocking stimuli, encouraging common folk to shed the notion that fortune and office were closed to them. In a time of transition from farm to factory, country to city, and old world to new, the theme of individualism was both a hymn to opportunity and a pledge to resist the corrupting powers of money and convention. The idea was in the air, a zeitgeist too widespread for claiming by any one thinker. Warren's bar against combination was a unique ramification, as was his claim that liberty depends on melding cost the limit of price with individual sovereignty.

Warren had no copyright on the concept of individuality, nor did he profess it any more cogently than Henry Thoreau or Ralph Waldo Emerson. His lack of recognition does not diminish the testaments of kindred libertarians; they neglected to mention the Peaceful Revolutionist because they either did not know of his work or did not acknowledge knowing it.

Thoreau brilliantly states the no-government posture in "Civil Disobedience," the essay entitled "Resistance to Civil Government" when originally published in 1849. Such gems as "That government is best which governs not at all," "I think that we should be men first, and subjects afterwards," and "Any man more right than his neighbors constitutes a majority of one already" are timeless trophies of anarchism. When asked to pay his share of support for a parson whose sermons he did not attend, he tells the selectmen, "I . . . do not wish to be regarded as a member of any incorporated society which I have not joined." During the years when others hedged on slavery, he declares that no one without disgrace could associate with the American government.[36]

At the end of "Civil Disobedience," Thoreau offers his own incisive brand of sovereignty of the individual:

> There will never be a really free and enlightened State until the State comes to recognize the individual as a higher power, from which all its own power and authority are derived, and treats him accordingly. I please myself with imagining a State at last which . . . would not think it inconsistent with its own repose *if a few were to live aloof from it, not meddling with it, nor embraced by it, who fulfilled all the duties of neighbors and fellow-men* [emphasis added]. A State which bore this kind of fruit, and suffered it to drop off as fast as it ripened, would prepare the way for a still more perfect and glorious State, which also I have imagined, but not yet anywhere seen.[37]

The minority, powerless when it accepts the majority's will, "is irresistible when it clogs by its whole weight."[38] Like Warren, the Peaceful Revolutionist, Thoreau calls for a "peaceable revolution," exemplified by the night he spent in jaul for not paying his poll tax for six years. He knew that most citizens, especially those with families to support, cannot risk the response of government that "will always crucify Christ, and excommunicate Copernicus and Luther, and pronounce Washington and Franklin rebels." They pay their taxes and obey unjust laws, preferring to grumble against slavery or the Mexican War rather than, as he did, "quietly declare war with the State."[39]

In Modern Times fashion, Thoreau urges his compatriots never to put themselves in the position of being an agent of injustice to another: if this be required by the law, "then, I say, break the law."[40] In his *Journal*, in 1854, he advises his native Massachusetts "to dissolve her union with the slaveholder instantly," and each inhabitant "to dissolve his union with the State as long as she hesitates to do her duty."[41] Taking a more ad hoc approach than Warren's, Thoreau recommends withholding loyalty to the government, not simply because it exists but because of the policy it follows. Thoreau's brand of civil disobedience—a means of removing oppression that influenced Tolstoy, Gandhi, and Martin Luther King, Jr.—affected the future more profoundly than Warren's generalized proposition of no state under any condition.

Protesters tend to address specific injustices rather than spend their lives campaigning for the improbable objective of doing away with government. Thoreau perfectly comprehended individual sovereignty and ruled his short life by its precepts, although his writing contains no hint that he is familiar with Modern Times, a congregation of nonjoiners. A passage Thoreau confided to his *Journal* bears an uncanny similarity to the philosophy of the sovereigns:

> I hate the present modes of living and getting a living . . . The life which society proposes to me to live is so artificial and complex . . . I believe in the infinite joy and satisfaction of helping myself and others to the extent of my ability. But what is the use in trying to live simply, raising what you eat, making what you wear, building what you inhabit, burning what you cut or dig, when those to whom you are allied insanely want and will have a thousand other things which neither you nor they can raise and nobody else, perchance, will pay for? . . . Thus men invite the devil in at every angle and then prate about the garden of Eden and the fall of man.[42]

Thoreau was unwilling to place himself in a group situation: "Talking with Bellew this evening about Fourierism and communities," he remarks in an 1855 *Journal* entry, "I said that I suspected any enterprise in which two were engaged together."[43] Apparently, he remained unaware of Modern Times, for which he was an ideal prospect — it was one of the rare places where two or more individuals "engaged together" without compromising their sovereignty.

The circle encompassing Thoreau, Emerson, and Hawthorne did not intersect with the ring of equitable commerce around Warren and Andrews. The *New York Tribune*, the newspaper favored by reformers, carried the long debate between Andrews, Greeley, and James, as well as reviews of Warren's book by Ripley and by Adin Ballou. Both Warren and Andrews spoke frequently in Boston, where Warren lived on and off throughout his sojourn at Modern Times. The "Boston group" at Modern Times was a further link between the two communities. But because of rivalry, indifference, or lack of information, the Warren-Andrews and Thoreau-Emerson-Hawthorne circles seemed oblivious

of each other. Warren's theme of individual sovereignty, hailed in England by John Stuart Mill, remained unheralded by the leading defenders of personal liberty in his native New England.

If Thoreau did not know of Modern Times—where the point of
view approached his own—he was well acquainted with Brook Farm,
a Massachusetts model village organized by friends of his. He took
no interest in the Farm, neither during its early years as a Christian
community nor after it became a Fourierist Phalanx in 1844. Referring
to bank failures during the financial crisis of 1857, he airily observes
in his *Journal* that although "not merely the Brook Farm and Fourier-
ite communities, but now the community generally has failed," the
moon still shone, serene and unchanged: hard times have the value
of showing "where the sure banks are."[44]

Thoreau's senior partner and sponsor, Ralph Waldo Emerson,
was closer to but never a member of Brook Farm, about which he
wrote condescendingly from his perch above the arena. He found it
a gallant test of better living, by projectors who, like Thoreau, felt that
"our ways of living were too conventional and expensive." The founders were high-minded but impulsive young people, intellectual sans-
culottes impatient with business-as-usual. They deserved to be praised
for attempting "what all people try to make, an agreeable place to live,"
free of household routine, a "paradise of shepherds and shepherdesses"
with no head, foreman, or skipper. "On this Farm, no authority," he
noted, in a description that also fits Modern Times, "each was master
or mistress of his or her own actions; hapless, happy anarchists." As
Modern Times must have seemed to its settlers, so Brook Farm was
"the pleasantest of residences," to many of its associates "the most important period of their life," rich in the friendly arts of conversation
and letter writing. "Letters were always flying not only from house to
house, but from room to room," reported Emerson, a moment before
impaling the Farm on the point of his rapier—"It was a perpetual picnic, a French Revolution in small, an Age of Reason in a patty-pan."[45]

Emerson's sarcasm resembles the *Communist Manifesto* passage,
"Critical Utopian Socialism and Communism," in which Karl Marx
and Friedrich Engels deride, with faint praise, the ideal village movement. The new doctrinaires concede that their rival ideologues "attack
. . . every principle of existing society," but write them off as self-delud-
ing indulgers in a fantastic "dream of experimental realization of their

social utopias, of founding isolated *phalansteries*, or setting up a 'Little Icaria'—pocket editions of the New Jerusalem . . . castles on air."[46]

Always the individualist, Emerson saw the world through a filter different from Marx and Engels's, whose thrust at communitarianism aimed to divert the tactics of social change from building model villages to inspiring struggle between the propertied and the working classes. Emerson scolded his friends, the Farmers, and, by implication, all community dwellers, not for declining to wage class war, but for mistakenly assuming that man is a plastic object for molding into a shape designed and willed by leaders. Fourier and his American acolyte, Albert Brisbane, presented a generous and magnificent theory, delivered with enthusiasm. In their ordered and all-too-perfect world, segmented into phalanxes, "Poverty shall be abolished; deformity, stupidity and crime shall be no more. Genius, grace, art, shall abound, and it is not to be doubted but that in the reign of 'Attractive Industry' all men will speak in blank verse . . . It was our feeling," went on Emerson, invoking the editorial 'we,' "that Fourier had skipped no fact but one, namely Life." Builders of ideal villages ignore the human factor, which "spawns and scorns system and system-makers, which eludes all conditions; which makes or supplants a thousand phalanxes and New Harmonies with each pulsation." Of all men, in Emerson's judgment, Thoreau best gave flesh and blood to the purest ethics: "Thoreau was in his own person a practical answer, almost a refutation, to the theories of the socialists. He required no Phalanx, no Government, no society, almost no memory. He lived extempore from hour to hour, like the birds and the angels; brought every day a new proposition, as revolutionary as yesterday, but different: the only man of leisure in his town; and his independence made all others look like slaves."[47]

Emerson's individualism is a mixture of freedom for self-directed thinkers and for self-directed entrepreneurs. The Emerson for whom society is a conspiracy aimed at the manhood of its members, so that "Whoso would be a man must be a nonconformist,"[48] also believes that however "the philosopher and the lover of man" might rail at it, "Trade was the principle of Liberty; that Trade planted America and destroyed Feudalism; that it makes peace and keeps peace, and it will abolish slavery."[49]

He complains that the ideal villages' lofty purpose of sharing work, expenses, and benefits attracts not the bold and capable settlers

needed but rather "those who have tried the experiment of independence and ambition and have failed."[50] Full of talented and humane
young associates, such communities face the problem of "whether those
who have energy will not prefer their chance of superiority and power
in the world, to the humble certainties of the association; whether
such a retreat does not promise to become an asylum to those who
tried and failed, rather than a field to the strong.[51]

BROOK FARM AND MODERN TIMES COMPARED

In his penetrating analysis of the communitarian movement, John Humphrey Noyes expresses resentment toward the negative treatment of
Brook Farm by Emerson and Hawthorne, its two most renowned me-
morialists. He regrest the Farm's bad luck in having its story told by
aliens. Emerson neither belonged to nor sympathized with it; Hawthorne "joined it only to jilt it," and, in *The Blithedale Romance* (1852),
gave the world a "poetico-sneering romance about it."[52] Hoping to set
the record straight, Noyes points out that the Farm was no "picnic"
or "romantic episode" to George Ripley, for one, a man who "went to
work like a hero" to make a fact of brotherhood, "while Emerson stood
by smiling incredulity." Ripley's "whole soul was bent on making a *home*
of it. If a man's first-born, in whom his heart is bound up, dies at six
years old, that does not turn the whole affair into a joke. There were
others of the same spirit, but Ripley was the center of them." Inspired
by the Reverend William Ellery Channing's conception of living up
to Jesus' teaching, the original Brook Farm had no connection with
Fourierism; on the contrary, it was "an original Yankee attempt to embody Christianity as understood by Unitarians and Transcendental-
ists." A joint-stock village that called itself "a Community," it felt its
way toward cooperation, enchanted with "the idea which is the essential charm of all Socialism, that it is possible to combine many families
into one great home."[53]

In 1840 the founders invited Emerson to help to create the Farm
as a laboratory for solving problems resulting from the depression of
the late 1830s. He declined, partly because he disagreed that the Farm
was the answer, and also for a personal reason revealed only in his
Journal: "I do not wish to remove from my present prison to a prison

a little larger. I wish to break all prisons. I have not yet conquered my own house. It irks and repents me. Shall I raise the siege of this hencoop, and march baffled away to a pretended siege of Babylon?"[54]

This confession approaches the border between profundity and neurosis. The paragon of individualism, who summons the self-reliant to "do your work, and I shall know you,"[55] is a loner, unable comfortably to be part of the most congenial ideal village. Rather than lend his persuasive powers to the cause of communitarianism, Emerson sits on the sidelines, keenly exposing problems but unwilling to help to correct them. "We must go alone," he muses. "Isolation must precede true society. I like the silent church before the service begins, better than any preaching."[56] The peerless individualist shrinks from enacting his sentiments; he is an uncommitted soloist who advises but does not consent.

The fire that burned down the new phalanstery in March 1846, on the day before it was set to open, only triggered Brook Farm's demise. The real killer, in Noyes's opinion, was Emerson's adverse influence on the leaders. Noyes objected principally to the individualism and unfocused inspiration, typified by Emerson, that diverted the Farmers from grappling with the root problems of deprivation and inequality. Action played second fiddle to utterance. The tendency "to literature, represented by Emerson and Margaret Fuller," prevailed over the tendency "to religious and social unity, represented by Channing and Ripley."[57]

Lindsay Swift, one of many Farmers to write its history, blames Brook Farm's ruin on "the attempt to transform [it] into a modified Fourierist Phalanx." Swift nominates Brisbane rather than Emerson as the architect of collapse: "It is profitless to speculate as to whether too much system killed the Phalanx, or whether the simple cohesion of the first Association might have averted any serious trouble. There is little doubt, however, that Albert Brisbane, despite his lofty and disinterested character, proved to be the evil genius of Brook Farm."[58]

Whatever or whoever was at fault, Noyes thought that Fourierism was too irreligious for Christian-bred adherents, inclining them toward the semireligion of Swedenborg. The theology of Emanuel Swedenborg (1688–1772) merged his scientific sense of an orderly universe with what to him was intuitive knowledge of angels, spirits, and invisible worlds. He was sure that the Second Coming took place in 1757,

at which time Jesus personally invested him with the power to interpret Scripture. During the 1840s, the Swedenborgian combination of
mysticism with common sense revived in the United States, becoming
popular among seekers of a faith to back up their belief in Fourierism.
Andrew Jackson Davis reports meeting the Swedish seer's ghost several
times in a graveyard near Poughkeepsie. "After 1847," when Davis set
up shop for himself, "Swedenborgianism proper subsided, and 'Modern Spiritualism' took its place," but the doctrines, writes Noyes, are
"identical: Spiritualism is Swedenborgianism Americanized." One of
Emerson's most popular lectures was his ambivalent critique of Swedenborg, "amounting to about this: 'He [Swedenborg] was a very great
thinker and discoverer; but his visions and theological teachings are
humbugs; still they are as good as any other, and rather better.'"[59]

After this display of sarcasm worthy of the sage of Concord,
Noyes proceeds with one of his favorite devices, a faintly mocking
genealogy of a socioreligious movement with which he was not in full
accord. Brook Farm, "which if it had lived would have had Swedenborgianism for its state religion," pursued the following evolution: "Uni-
tarianism produced Transcendentalism; Transcendentalism produced
Brook Farm; Brook Farm married and propagated Fourierism; Fourierism had Swedenborgianism for its religion; and Swedenborgianism led
the way to Modern Spiritualism."[60]

Most ideal communities took their programs so seriously that they
discouraged pleasure for its own sake as sinful or counterproductive.
Not so Modern Times and Brook Farm, its closest analogue. Both delighted in glee clubs, theatricals, pageants, dancing parties, and lively
conversation in which ideology yielded to free expression. Consider-
ing that no more than a few hundred people passed through either
village, the quality of the personnel was conspicuously high.

Because its roster of members and friends includes the cream of
New England's reformers and writers, Brook Farm shines more brightly
in the historical spotlight than shadowy Modern Times. It is fitting to
pay tribute to this brief but brilliant association that numbered among
its retainers and visitors Emerson; Thoreau; Hawthorne; Margaret Fuller;
George Ripley and his wife, Sophia; Theodore Parker; Orestes Brown-
son; Charles A. Dana; Dr. William Ellery Channing and his nephew,
William Henry Channing; Isaac Hecker; Bronson Alcott; Elizabeth

Palmer Peabody; John A. Dwight; and the two major-domos of Fourierism in the United States, Albert Brisbane and Horace Greeley.

It is difficult to comprehend the relative obscurity of Modern Times, through which passed another imposing list of thinkers and doers. The names of Warren, Andrews (whom Noyes regarded as "the American rival of Comte, as A. J. Davis is of Swedenborg") and Edger ("one of the ten apostles de propaganda fide appointed by Comte"[61]) belong on any honor roll of nineteenth-century intellectual activists. So do Thomas and Mary Gove Nichols for their books, periodicals, memoirs, and acts in the fields of medicine, hygiene, reform of sexual-marital standards, and restless progression from cause to cause in search of the mental peace they finally found in Catholicism. Worthy of recognition, too, are Mary Chilton, Theron C. Leland, Ellen Lazarus Allen, Charles A. Codman, Clark Orvis, and Edward Newberry, who contributed to the advancement of rationalist religious thought and egalitarian social relations.

In range of ages, points of origin, marital arrangements, and styles of life Modern Times was more eclectic than Brook Farm, where most of the members were young, single Unitarians from the state of Massachusetts.[62] Once the Farm dissolved it vanished, except on the printed page; Modern Times still exists as Brentwood, its trees, streets, and some of its houses surviving witnesses of the pioneers who made their mark on Long Island's history.

Brook Farm is the setting for Hawthorne's novel, *The Blithedale Romance*, a rather unflattering portrait. Emerson found it wanting. "Hawthorne drew some sketches, not happily," he thought, and "quite unworthy of his genius. No friend who knew Margaret Fuller could recognize her rich and brilliant genius under the dismal mask [of the character Zenobia] which the public fancied was meant for her in that disagreeable story."[63] According to the historian Louis Filler, Hawthorne "found farm work irritating and the optimism of the reformers offensive." Although critical of colonial bigotry and intolerance, he was "upset by Puritan treatment of Quakers in the seventeenth century [but] not disturbed by slavery in his own time."[64] Yet Brook Farm lives on through him.

Modern Times is the subject of a friendlier but less pungent work of fiction, although neither the book nor its author remotely match the popularity of *The Blithedale Romance* or Hawthorne. Few readers know of *Pine and Palm,* an antebellum tale of rivalry between North and South, published in 1887 by Moncure Daniel Conway, the reformer and writer who visited Modern Times and recorded his memorable Sunday. In his novel, also a "romance," Conway portrays a center of equity commerce called "Bonheur," a village where "The social basis was 'individualism'—the freedom of each to think, speak, live, without any limit, save the equal rights of others, to their genius."[65]

Hawthorne modeled Zenobia, the driving spirit at Blithedale, on Margaret Fuller, whom he endowed in the book with the magnetism that was hers and the beauty that was not.[66] Conway patterned his character Maria Shelton on Mary Chilton, his hostess at Modern Times, a woman as comely and bright in life as in her imaginary existence as the spiritual leader of Bonheur. In *Pine and Palm,* remarked Conway in his memoirs, "I have idealized this lovely woman, and indeed the village . . . but her actual history was more thrilling than is there told of Maria Shelton, and the village [Modern Times] appears to me in the retrospect more romantic than my Bonheur."[67]

A whistle-stop on the railroad in a remote corner of New York State, Bonheur is a grove of harmony framed on the theories of "Naboth Warriner, manager of the community." Josiah Warren would flinch at the title of manager but otherwise approve of Conway's village of individual sovereigns, retaining their independence as they cooperate with kindred souls to earn their bread and share their thoughts.

"Whatever [one] might think of their visions," thought Conway, "the visionaries had to be taken seriously." The most charming epitaph of Modern Times is his comparison of the sovereigns with the communitarians Pantagruel visited, much as Conway made his way to the place reached by railway or rainbow. "Though few of them might have heard of Thelema [Thélème], the motto of Rabelais' Utopian abbey had embodied itself in this American forest village: *Fais ce que voudras.*"[68]

9

Changing to Brentwood

A COUNTERCULTURE EVEN SMALLER THAN ITS HOST competed at Modern Times for the hearts and minds of the sovereigns. No sooner did the Nicholses depart than Henry Edger launched his long campaign to change the village from open to closed mentality. Commencing in 1854, this single-minded devotee campaigned to convert his nonconformist neighbors to believe in and be the American base of an orthodoxy designed in France, Auguste Comte's Religion of Humanity.[1]

Conceived by the positivist philosopher as a universal doctrine of reason, the new faith substituted mankind for God as the object of worship. As Andrews ruled the meager roost of the Grand Pantarchy, so Comte proclaimed himself the prophet, pope, and "High Priest of Humanity," the overlord of a projected universal church. Wise men of old replaced the Saints; the new Virgin Mary was Clotilde de Vaux, Comte's platonic lover (deceased); the sacraments yielded to secular ceremonies, the Bible to the works of Comte, the Deity to the *Grand Être* (humanity), and Rome to Paris, toward which must point the axis of every temple and oratory.

Fusing the French Revolution with feudalism, Comte proclaimed industrial chivalry as the religious solution of social problems. He erased present boundaries, with nations supplanted by five hundred industrial republics (shades of Ballou) the size of Belgium or Holland. Temporal power would rest in a "supreme directory of three socially-minded bankers" who, as managers of domestic and foreign policy, exercised "both legislative and executive powers" at every level of government. The superiority given to banking, because of its high theoretical content, coincided with Comte's ranking of the sciences on an ascending scale of complication. On top of mathematics, which he selected as the foundation because it was vital to all the others, he piled astronomy, chemistry, physics, biology, and, at the peak, sociology—a term coined in Comte's prolific mint. His sociology was to the other fields of study what banking was to his lower but necessary pursuits of agriculture, manufacturing, and commerce. Leaders of lesser callings, who dealt with commodities rather than with the bankers' more difficult business of handling abstract wealth, were to receive a modicum of temporal power within the ruling elite. A patriciate of "2,000 bankers, 100,000 merchants, 200,000 manufacturers, and 400,000 agriculturists" would support the top command.[2]

Workers were destined to be disfranchised serfs, assigned to toil not only for their employers but also for the *Grand Être*, for whose weal they would serve without hope of gain. The key word was *submission*, a term antithetical to the concept of individual sovereignty. Comte could shower no higher praise on Edger than to inform his votary that "Your appreciation of true positivism is excellent. You recognize that all positivists must be submissive to the High Priest of Humanity [Comte], the only course of regenerating bonds."[3]

From his seat in Paris the pontiff, self-empowered to ordain, transfer, suspend, or dismiss his priests—would rule the hierarchy. Composed of scholars, artists, and doctors, the clergy complemented the patriciate, directing the hearts and minds of Humanity just as the magnates held dominion over work and government.

Comte excluded women from public life or outside employment, assigning them to be keepers of household tranquility, educated as guardian angels—mothers, wives, and daughters—of the men they would help to achieve a higher degree of cultivation. The role he assigned to women reflected his own experience. According to Richmond Laurin Hawkins, the historian of American positivism, he married "a penniless prostitute whom he had 'picked up' in the wooden galleries of the Palais Royal." After seventeen years of unhappy marriage, Comte and his adulterous wife agreed to separate in 1842, but to honor his maxim, *"L'homme doit nourir la femme,"* he paid her a life annuity and kept the self-imposed pledge of chaste and eternal widowhood that he demanded from every surviving spouse. Three years after his separation, he met Clotilde de Vaux, "a very ordinary and very unhappy woman," thirty-one years of age, whose absentee husband, a light-fingered tax collector, was either fleeing justice or serving time in the galleys, depending upon the source one consults. Comte enjoyed an intense but immaculate (her choice) liaison with *"Sainte"* Clotilde, and upon her untimely death enshrined her as the goddess his flock must adore. As the Mariolatrous symbol of Humanity, Comte ordained, an image of a woman of thirty, with her son in her arms, be placed in every temple. Hawkins predicts that Comte's morbid but notable love for Clotilde will go down in history as the "only one which enabled a lover, during his lifetime, to compel his followers to worship his beloved."[4]

When not astride his hobbyhorse, Henry Edger observed Modern Times objectively. His journal, letters to the London *Leader*, and correspondence with Comte, his "reverend master," served as useful descriptions as well as poignant memoirs of a man whose "attempt to implant the Religion of Humanity in the barren soil of New York State forms one of the most distressing experiences that any mortal has ever gone through."[5]

In April 1851, Edger left his law practice, Christian faith, and mother country of England to come to the United States with his wife and three young children. Applying at once for citizenship in the republican land of freedom which he was sure was his natural home, he perused the list of model communities for a progressive place to live. In response to Robert Owen's letter of recommendation for Edger, Etienne Cabet advised the thirty-one-year-old émigré not to subject his family to the rough surroundings of Nauvoo, the Illinois city founded by Mormons that now was the home of Icarian communists. After hearing of equitable commerce, Edger visited Modern Times in May 1851, two months after its creation, but did not settle permanently until 1854. Meanwhile he tested and found wanting the Fourierist North American Phalanx, near Red Bank, New Jersey, lived for a time in Brooklyn and elsewhere, and finally settled his family in the free-and-easy abode of the sovereigns, his selection as the best place for pursuit of his newly-acquired mission to promulgate the Religion of Humanity.

Three sources inspired Edger: a series on positivism in the London *Leader* by its editor, George Henry Lewes; Harriet Martineau's English translation of Comte's *Cours de philosophie positive*; and his own deep study of the philosopher's works after teaching himself to read French.[6] From 1854 until his death thirty-four years later, Henry Edger, "Comte's most beloved disciple,"[7] devoted himself to the propagation of his reverend master's doctrine. In his description of Modern Times in 1857, Moncure Daniel Conway noted that in addition to reformers, debaters, actors, singers, and dancers, "it is not without an able preacher of Positivism—one who has studied the philosophy of Comte more thoroughly, and can state it more clearly, than any man in America."[8]

The teacher and his adoring student engaged in extensive correspondence. In his first letter, written in February 1854, Edger explained that although "its doctrine is itself anarchical," Modern Times provided his best pulpit. The creedless, deliberately unorganized sovereigns were open to new ideas, so that, in time, "a more favorable reception . . . for rational conceptions" can be expected than in "any ordinary country town either in England or the United States."[9] Later that year he stated that the combination of cost the limit of price, labor notes, and the tolerant ambience furnished by individual sovereignty make "this little village where I live, notwithstanding its preeminent anarchy, a powerful attraction for me." The "silent progress . . . of Equitable Commerce, after swallowing up" Fourierism and most other brands "of socialism long prevalent in this country," is making such inroads into abolitionism, spiritualism, and many other reforms that it threatens "to become a widely ramified movement, and to make of this little village the center of a wide and densely populated district." Carried away by his overstatements, Edger was confident that once "dire realities" proved the fallacy of their idealistic principles, the sovereigns would have the good sense to accept Comte's social program. Therefore, "I cannot help cherishing hopes that I may live in a true positivist Church founded here."[10]

Comte, as anxious to believe Edger's glowing forecast as was Edger to prove his devotion, commends his pupil's analysis of Modern Times, the "bizarre mental milieu . . . [which] constitutes the full development of Occidental anarchy." Agreeing that individualism was preferable to "vague socialism," the pontiff encouraged his only American missionary to found a "positivist Church . . . in the most anarchical community in your anarchical country." Comte and Edger constantly referred to Modern Times as "anarchical," or as a place where "anarchy" prevailed, an accurate designation but one rejected by Warren, Andrews, and the sovereigns because of its pejorative connotation. As for the country he calls anarchical, the Saint Paul of positivism perceived the United States through a glass, very dimly, his lack of understanding revealed by his naïve advice to Edger: "Your age [Edger was then thirty-six] and the social instability of the United States will enable you, in fifteen or twenty years, to convert Modern Times into the spiritual center of a positivist island, which will soon form a separate state in the Union . . . Long Island may thus become the social head of North America, and the religious link between Paris and the New World."[11]

On 1 July 1854, with Comte's *Catechisme positive* as his text, Edger preached his opening sermon at Modern Times to a baker's dozen of sovereigns. His journal listed those present as Clarissa Taylor, Sophia Hayward, William Metcalf, Sarah and Jane Metcalf, [John] Milton Swain, Curran and Henry Swaim, Mr. I. H. Cook, Abigail [Mrs. Peter] Blacker, Eleanor Blacker [Peter and Abigail's daughter], Mrs. Henry Edger, and John Metcalf.[12]

Edger may have confused propensity for going to meetings with zeal for his religion. The sovereigns looked, but few of them bought. The only ones to show interest were the last three persons named. Eleanor Blacker, the brightly promising girl who was the village's first schoolmarm, was fast becoming a convert when she died at the age of eighteen on 16 March 1855. In a letter to Comte, Edger proudly reported her resistance both to her parents' and to Modern Times's "anarchical influences"; he hoped that she might be "elevated into a Local Saint by our final sacrament" of incorporation, the reward of virtuous positivists seven years after their death. In his cautious reply, the First Grand Priest of Humanity regretted "the death of Miss Blacker" and sanctioned "your private adoration of her [but] the question of public adoration will require further study."[13]

Some of those present at the service turned into virulent opponents. After accepting Edger's request to be the godmother of Sophia Clotilde, his fifth child, born in 1855, Mrs. Hayward not only declined but she and the older Metcalfs did their unsuccessful best to dissuade brother John from joining. Do not worry about their hostility, Comte wrote soothingly to Edger, "we should be pleased with the defection of the haughty godmother . . . who does not appreciate the glorious future reserved for women by positivism."[14]

Not counting himself, his wife Milliscent Hobson Edger—a member by marriage more than by faith—and their children, Edger's flock numbered six as of 1859: Caroline Plunkett, of whom nothing further is known except that she was on the list of converts in Edger's journal; Ellen Lazarus Allen (the sister of Marx Edgeworth Lazarus), a former

Brook Farmer and the widow of John Allen, one of the Farm's leading traveling spokesmen; Mr. and Mrs. Richard Parker, an English couple who lived in Brooklyn; John Metcalf, William's younger brother, who was Edger's most ardent disciple; and John's wife, the former Clara Christiana Osborne.[15]

John Metcalf resented the hostility his brother and Mrs. Hayward showed toward Edger's views, compounded by their disapproval of John's loaning money to his mentor to help him start a fruit tree nursery. In 1855, as he reported in his first letter to Comte, his "Most reverend Father," John Metcalf left Modern Times for Manhattan where he worked, "making castings for a machine shop," and spent his free time trying to convert Catholic "proletaries" to the Religion of Humanity. Comte answered that he approved of Metcalf's mission among the Catholics, and speaks of "the holy league . . . to rally the Catholics to the positivists against the Protestants."[16]

In New York, Metcalf fell in love with Clara Christiana Osborne, a Catholic, whom he married according to Comtean ritual on 28 Gutenberg 71 (9 September 1859). With Henry Edger officiating, the bride and groom swore vows of "eternal widowhood," a condition of positivist upon that called for lifelong abstention from sex by whichever spouse survived. After declaring them man and wife "In the name of Humanity, and by the authority delegated to me by Auguste Comte," Edger ended the ceremony by removing from his arm the green ribbon symbolizing the Faith, and fastening it to the bride's wrist.[17]

After the wedding, John and Clara moved into their own home at Modern Times. Later on, according to Robert E. Schneider, Henry Edger, for all "his respect for the sanctity of the positive bonds of matrimony which he had tied . . . had intimate relations with Clara, the wife of his devoted disciple."[18] John Metcalf—whether Clara went with him is unclear—moved to Berlin Heights, Ohio, forty-five miles west of Cleveland, an experimental community founded in 1856. In his study of the free-love movement, John C. Spurlock describes this model settlement as committed to ideas familiar from Modern Times: "individual sovereignty, equitable commerce, women's rights, and free love," with free love apparently serving "as informal divorce." By the end of the 1850s, comments Spurlock, with such substantial communities as Modern Times and Berlin Heights, "free love constituted a small, but vigorous, counterculture within American Society."[19] The answer to this allegation is that although Modern Times was a refuge for victims of unhappy marriage and a shelter where lovers could live together and not be considered immoral, the crusade for free love peaked and faded with the Nicholses' defeat in 1854: thereafter, free love at Modern Times remained more a perception in the public mind than a reflection of what went at the village. It is not known whether John made up with Clara, but he kept his faith in positivism and eventually reconciled with Edger.

The Religion of Humanity was an elitist and hierarchical creed that repelled most sovereigns of Modern Times. Andrews found it offensive, although he admired the French philosopher as a blazer of historical and sociological trails, and thought of himself as America's Comte. In his *Basic Outline of Universology*, Andrews contrasted Comte's authoritarianism with Warren's sovereignty of the individual, a premise enhanced by himself, Mill, and Spencer: "Comte . . . leans . . . wholly to the opposite extreme. He explicitly denies Rights to the *Individual* in Society altogether. He affirms that Society alone has Rights, and that the Individual has Duties to perform only."[20]

Codman depicted the sovereigns' reaction to Edger's campaign to enroll Modern Timers in Comte's religion. "Mr. E.", a man of culture, inspired "a desire for music and literature in the Village," directed the Glee Club, led the orchestra, and wrote several hymns and songs. However, his acceptance of Comte's "Religion of Humanity . . . which he . . . made the basis of his life work until he died in Paris, France in 1889" [Edger died in 1888], did not rub off on the villagers: "He made but few converts, for the pioneers were thoroughly individualistic." All the same, "though they could not accept any plan of Salvation but their own, they recognized the right of all others to believe and advocate what seemed a solution to each one's mind."

Warren resented Edger's efforts, convinced that he "was a Jesuit sent here to work against the Equity movement." This judgment was unfair, thought Codman: had Warren better understood the "Positive doctrine," he would have realized that it aimed at *"Human Unity"* just as he did. Warren's was an "external method," Comte's one "of scientific morality."[21]

Codman failed to acknowledge that Edger's rigid orthodoxy was indeed a secular form of Jesuitism, in diametrical opposition to freedom of individual choice. In an 1855 letter to Edger on the importance of soliciting Catholics, Comte referred to his new work, *Appel aux Conservateurs*, "which indicates especially the holy league of Catholicism and positivism." He hoped his American disciple would "enter into relations with the Jesuits, who are, I suppose, the principal directors of Catholicism in America. Their successes prepare the triumph of our cause, since the conversion of Protestants to Catholicism is the best preliminary to their conversion to positivism."[22]

In 1857, Edger informed Comte of his interest in the Irish Catholic laborers coming into the vicinity as employees of wealthy neighbors, and of his hope of entering "ere long into relations with the Catholic priest of this district." After applauding his disciple for this effort to win over Catholics, Comte reported dispatching "my convert, the former revolutionary Alfred Sabatier," to Rome to negotiate "in my name with the general of the Jesuits [to] organize a league to save the Occident from the immense disorder by which is threatened." Of course, added Comte, "positivism alone can preside over this league." The Jesuit general Rex, who had never heard of Comte, shunted Sabatier off to a subordinate: "Needless to say that the negotiations between Comte and Rex ended then and there."[23]

Codman's amiable effort to bridge the gap between the disparate views of Warren and Edger resulted from his conversion by Edger. In his memoir, Codman acknowledged that he "accepted and to this day maintains Comte's doctrines as an all-sufficient solution."[24] When his second wife, Emily Studley Codman, died in 1886, she received a positivist funeral addressed by Codman and two other veterans of Modern Times, Dr. Edward Newberry and Henry P. Brown. "Our sister," remarked Newberry, one of the longest-lived of the pioneers, ". . . was an appreciative student of Swedenborg, Owen, Fourier, Warren, Andrews, Comte, and of all who are worthy of remembrance in the history of human progress." Brown recalled how Emily left New England to join the Modern Times effort to apply "the principles taught by Josiah Warren," aimed at escaping "the great and growing inharmony in human society and the unequal distribution of wealth, from which so many evils spring." Brown's eulogy concluded in the rhetoric of Comte's religion: "Thus passed Emily Codman from objective life into the collective Humanity."[25]

The pontiff selected Edger as one of the first three apostles of an eventual board of seven composing the British-American high command, set up "to assist the High Priest of Humanity in the general direction of the Occidental transition." In March 1856, Comte praised the "founder of our American church" for his plan to establish "an agricultural domain exploited by true positivists," and financed by a rich patron, "which would make Modern Times into a metropolis of American positivism, civic as well as religious." "We must become the directors of western opinion," the pontiff added eight months later: "In the long run we shall triumph; we shall rule the entire world."[26]

But within a year—and before the Religion of Humanity ruled the world, the United States, or even the village of Modern Times—stomach cancer caused Comte's "transformation" from objective to subjective life. In other words, he died, succeeded as pontiff by his chosen and far lesser prophet, Pierre Laffitte.

The heartsick Edger continued to ply his faith at Modern Times and in New York City. In 1860, he reported lecturing to forty people at Pearson's Hall, Modern Times, on 26 Moses 74 (26 January 1862).[27] His holding of meetings on Sunday aroused the wrath of ministers, one of whom denounced "Mr. Edger, who borrows the Christian Sabbath to popularize French Atheism."[28] Yet the "Family Oratory," constructed above the log cabin in which he dwelt, was the only church erected during the lifetime of Modern Times, as well as "the First Altar, probably, ever raised in America to the adoration of the true and definitive Great Being." In the tower of the oratory, itself surmounted by belfry and spire, Edger secreted a bottle containing a memorandum headed:

> Au culte de l'Humanité: This building is erected by Henry Edger, born at Chelwood, Fletching, Sussex, England, 22 Jan. 1820, now residing at Modern Times, Long Island, upon this very spot; cultivator of the soil, Member-elect of the British Contingent of the Positive Committee . . . it is solemnly consecrated to the Domestic Worship of Humanity . . . Witnesses [all were Modern Timers who worked on constructing the oratory but did not convert to positivism]: I. S. Loveland, G. S. McWatters, Clark Orvis, J. M. Swain, W. [Walter] Smith (6 August 1856).[29]

By 1864, the year in which Modern Times became Brentwood, Edger's sermons and pamphlets may have caused some of the pioneers to doubt the purpose for which they came to live in the pine barrens. Perhaps there was a nugget of truth in Edger's brave boast to Comte that a change was coming over "the spirit of the people, especially observable in the growing loss of faith in the chimeras of Equitable Commerce."[30]

Schneider states that, in the immediate aftermath of his affair with Clara, Henry Edger "beat a hasty retreat, going to England alone in the spring of 1870," where he remained for the next six months. Soon after he left, his wife Milliscent died, "violently insane, in a lunatic asylum at Hartford, Connecticut." The sad news was imparted to Edger in a letter from his friend, the kindly Charles Codman, who "assumed the responsibility for the funeral" and burial in Brentwood Cemetery. Mrs. Edger's illness was undiagnosed except for Schneider's suggestion that "poor Milliscent's brain, already overtaxed by constant conflict between the beliefs bred by a staunch Protestant upbringing" and all the new ideas to which she was exposed, may have succumbed to the blow of her husband's departure.[31] However, she was no newcomer to such institutions when she went to Hartford, having been confined as far back as 1867 at Utica's Lunatic Asylum, the nineteenth century's ugly term for mental hospital.

Comte recommended sex in marriage for procreation only, and preferably not at all once the family was achieved, but Henry Edger, the favored disciple, could not control his appetite. As early as 1857 he felt compelled abruptly to announce, at the end of a letter to "his Reverence," that he was duty-bound to confess that "the regimen of complete chastity has been beyond my force of resolution." Comte received the news calmly. After letting his acolyte know that "I praise your *The Positivist Calendar* in my eighth annual circular," the high priest, perhaps mindful of his own experience, advised: "Do not be discouraged because your resolution of chastity has failed. Persevere and you will become wholly chaste." But Edger, then straining every ounce of strength in his work of becoming a priest, again reported his weakness a few months later. Admitting his utter failure even to approximate chastity, he reported doing "battle with lust" every night; he feared the "gradual approach of that horrible form of insanity which has been termed nymphomania."[32]

His remorse at indulging in pleasures that most sovereigns took for granted was one more indication that Edger marched to a different drummer than mainstream Modern Timers. After Milliscent's death, he scrapped his never well-kept pledge of eternal widowhood, remarried, and sired four more children, his lapse of chastity failing to shake one jot of ardor for Comte's religion. After twenty-six years at Modern Times–Brentwood, he gave up his busy but unrewarding work in America and moved to Paris to spend his final years near the shrine of his idol. In April 1888 he died at Versailles and was buried at Montreuil cemetery.[33]

His American franchise to represent Comte was of little value. The Religion of Humanity was too godless for the godly, too Catholic for Protestants, too blasphemous for Catholics, too liturgical for freethinkers, too rigid for libertarians, too hostile to personal initiative for most of the sovereigns of Modern Times.

But Edger truly was a "cultivator of the soil," his nursery of fruit trees one of the village's earliest going concerns. When rechristening Modern Times, the settlers chose the name of Brentwood, the London suburb where Henry Edger and Milliscent Hobson had married.[34] The sovereigns did not honor the Edgers for their promotion of an authoritarian doctrine, but for their ten years of civic service to the village of Modern Times.

THE LONGEVITY FACTOR

Secular model villages were short-lived and often abruptly ended. New Harmony collapsed in its third year, torn with dissent and burdened with opportunists whose motive for coming had been to share the fortune but not the vision of Robert Owen. Brook Farm did not long survive the fire that ravaged the new phalanstery in 1846, on the day before it was due to open. The North American Phalanx suffered a similar shock in 1854 when mills, workshops, and stores burned down, a terminal disaster for the largest American project of Fourierism. Hopedale suddenly succumbed in 1856, when its two major shareholders staged what today would be called a corporate raid. Adin Ballou was convinced it was "their decision to withdraw their portion of the common funds from the treasury that precipitated our overthrow," after which the Practical Christian Republic became a hard-headed lucrative company owned by the "Brothers Draper."[35]

Such crises afflicted neither Modern Times nor Utopia. Warren's equity villages "did not fail," thought William Bailie, "in the sense that New Harmony, Brook Farm, and numerous other socialistic experiments failed."[36] Utopia, the Ohio River community founded in 1847, created in two years what settler E. G. Cubberly neatly termed "a reciprocating society." One dozen families found themselves with homes, "who never owned them before." Using "labor capital," Cubberly was able to build a brick cottage "one and a half stories high, and all the money I paid out was $9,81 cts.—all the rest was effected by exchanging labor for labor, Mr. Warren is right: and the right way to get back as much labor as we give, is by the labor cost prices—Money prices, with no principle to guide, have always deceived us."[37]

Of such was the kingdom of equitable commerce. Twenty-five years later, reflected Warren, people asked him how big was Utopia now, and why a hundred villages like it were not in full operation. He could think of no short or comprehensive answer to these legitimate questions. For one thing, the lands surrounding Utopia's eighty quarter-acre plots "were controled [sic] by speculators" demanding prices so high that they stymied future expansion. After about four years, "the largest portion of the first settlers moved together to Minnesota, where land was abundant and cheap." Had these equitists kept the faith in Minnesota? As far as Warren knew, they had. His only report was of a potato speculator's offering one of them thirty-five cents a bushel, five cents over the going rate, to which the unconditional answer was "No, I will not sell them for speculation at any price—twenty-five cents a bushel will pay me for my labor and I shall supply my neighbors with them at that price."[38]

A second obstacle to Utopia's growth was that the three-year contract with the site's owner to hold the price of lots unchanged expired before all were taken up. "It is labor and trouble thrown away" to invest them when the *"prices of lots can be raised,* just as they become desirable." The third handicap, endemic to sponsors of equitable commerce, was that the "common, mercenary news papers could not or would not do it any justice, so that the public learned very little about it." Ignorance led to lack of interest: even if books on the subject were published, people seldom took an interest in that about which they knew nothing.[39]

Modern Times secured a five-year contract of price stability, two years more than Utopia's, but this period was not long enough, either. "At the expiration of this term, speculation grasps at the unsold lots," after which it was "no longer worth while to do any thing for further growth." With the aims of the movement so little known, concluded Warren, "I would suggest ten years, in which to fill up a settlement of, say, a thousand acres."[40]

Warren imprudently surmised the existence of land owners willing to grant ten-year terms. And, in the unlikely event that there were, where would settlers be found to fill "a thousand acres"? In 1855, Warren reported that each Equity Village held no more than eighteen or twenty families. "Twenty families cannot sustain an Equitable Store; but five hundred could." The same applied to eating-houses, factories, laundries, schools, and cultural facilities. A few dozen families could not furnish a broad enough base for the circulation of labor notes, "but a thousand families, embracing the right proportions of the different professions, could render the common barbarian money almost useless among themselves and place each in a state of ease and pecuniary independence by the employment of two or three hours a day." Before giving up comfort and risking the hardships of starting life again in the wilderness, families should wait until a substantial number agreed to support the new movement. Once two or three hundred families did, then "the pivot or centre man [Warren was not on speaking terms with the word 'leader'] can suggest a time and place for concentration." Whether and when to join was the free choice of individuals, but chances were that at least two hundred of the three hundred sympathetic families "might be ready to move at or near the time contemplated."[41]

It was wishful thinking to assume that even two hundred families were ready to leave their present homes to build a no-gain society in the wilderness. Too few producers were willing to swap their labor at cost; too few potato growers were prone to reject a bid for their crop at five cents over the market rate. Smaller still was the number of businessmen who handed back valuable paper at cost, and long before its expiration, the way Warren surrendered his valuable lease in the heart of downtown Cincinnati.

Even if trading purists turned up with the integrity to renounce unearned increment, what landowner was apt to sign a ten-year agreement binding him and his heirs to hold acreage for sale at a fixed price? Moreover, size was itself a dilemma. A village of seventy or one hundred people was too small a trading unit to flourish, but a prosperous town of one thousand might be an unfriendly host to self-sovereignty, which depended on small-scale polity for success, its effectiveness inverse to number. If the response to the Nicholses' edict to forsake reputation for free love's sake threatened the individuality of a scant six dozen sovereigns, how would schisms be reconciled in a village ten or more times that size?

In her study of ideal communities, Rosabeth Moss Kanter defines "success" in terms of longevity. Her measurement of success is "the length of time in existence": a community has to last at least twenty-five years, "the definition of a sociological generation . . . to be considered successful." This time stipulation restricts her list of successes to eleven of ninety examples, with one (Icaria) considered "unclassifiable."[42]

But longevity for its own sake was not a criterion highly esteemed at Modern Times. For thirteen years the sovereigns strove to demonstrate a way of life in place of emerging industrialism, but, according to William Bailie, the Warrenites did not "expect their villages, even if these became numerous, to solve the social problem." Accepting the world as it was, their intent was to show what could be done by the practice of Equity, "by labor, free from the curse of monopoly and the blight of authority." The main cause of Modern Times's "nonsuccess [was the] scarcity of employment other than that of agriculture"; the sovereigns were too short of capital to start factories in which to make goods for sale in the outside world. If a rumored boxworks existed, it ended swiftly or maybe died a-borning in the 1857 depression. The only industry mentioned by Codman was the proposed cigar-making enterprise that the sovereigns, in spite of their need for income, rejected because they abhorred the "vile weed." Labor-for-labor notes were handy as internal currency but no help in dealings with people who "neither understood the principle nor accepted the practice of Equitable Commerce."[45]

Why emulate Shakers and Rappites, prolonging a fossilized existence for generations after the Millennium, for which they were shaped, failed to fulfill its prediction? The sovereigns made their point to a heedless and often disdainful world, after which they quietly dropped out of the model community movement into the easygoing life-style of their adopted Long Island habitat.

THE WAR OF THE REBELLION

Bailie was right that the village lacked industry, but he exaggerated the damage inflicted by the 1857 crash. A slow but steady influx of settlers continued: although lacking a factory, Modern Times–Brentwood became a small but solvent garden and fruit-growing center. Bailie was more accurate when he blamed the curtailment of growth on the impact of the Civil War. A village devoted to personal freedom could not easily cope with legalized murder. To condone placing sovereign individuals in a kill-or-be-killed situation, and to pay taxes to a government of whose authority they are skeptical, placed defenders of equitable commerce in an anomalous position.

Warren's view of war as the ultimate violation of individual sovereignty clashed with the pro-Union sentiments of many Modern Timers and was a factor in his final decision to leave the village in 1862. To Josiah, secession was guaranteed by the same Declaration of Independence that vested the people with the right to alter or abolish their government. However, this power was no blank check to be filled in by the slave owners. As slaveholding states had the right to secede, so slaves had the right to secede from their masters. To take up arms to defend a mythical "Union" was to kill or be killed for centralization. Such action protected the most primitive *"clanship . . .* for nationality is no more or less than clanship, and clanship is the worst feature of barbarism."[44]

Neither side was intentionally wicked. On the contrary, stated Warren, the whole ordeal was "a lamentable mistake, the unavoidable result of a blind reverence for *precedents,* for legal technicalities and formal institutions" instead of the "deep underlying *principles* which *gave rise to* the institutions."[45] Not clanship but self-sovereignty was the central idea around which to rally:

> One party denies the right of secession or self-sovereignty, to the whites of the South and to their white subordinates at home, and in the same breath assert that right in favor of the blacks of the South. The other party leaders claim that right for themselves, but to deny it to their white subordinates, and to the black people of the South! That is the difference between the parties! That is, no difference at all. Both . . . become entangled in a web of

confusion, from which nothing but the simple admission of that great inalienable right of sovereignty in *every person* (within his or her own sphere . . .) can possibly extricate them.[46]

The solution of Warren and Andrews was to break "Unions" into components, and these into smaller components, and these into individual fragments of which each was a nation and each a sect. From then on, "political slavery of all colors is logically at an end." The question more crucial even than chattel slavery was "the enslavement of *Labor*," a subject concerning whites and blacks alike, "but which can find no solution until the Equitable compensation for labor is understood. If I get an hour's labor of you more than I am justly entitled to, I have enslaved you pecuniarily to that extent; but how can we tell what I am entitled to for an hour of my services?" The answer, ignored by the politicians, was to give up the search for national legislative solutions to tariffs, navigation of seas and rivers, foreign trade, and protection of manufactures. Only by "disintegrating," or "individualizing" our subjects, and applying to each its appropriate regulator, could we approach true civilization.[47]

This statement, tinted with Fourierist prevision of "true civilization," resembled William Lloyd Garrison's call to disintegrate present government. There was an element of similarity between Warren, the "Peaceful Revolutionist," and Garrison, the perpetrator of "revolution without taking up arms."[48] Yet Warren was neither Fourierist nor Garrisonian, but essentially self-propelled. His antistatism paralleled but did not coincide with the movement of Garrison and Ballou to separate from the Federal Union.

In his *Address to the Friends of Freedom and Emancipation in the United States,* Garrison forswore allegiance to a Constitution subjecting slaves to hopeless bondage. His theme was "NO UNION WITH SLAVE-HOLDERS . . . Secede, then from the government . . . send no Senators or Representatives . . . for what you cannot conscientiously perform yourself, you cannot ask another person to perform as your agent. Circulate a declaration of DISUNION FROM SLAVE-HOLDERS, throughout the country. Hold mass meetings—assemble in Conventions—nail your banners to the mast!"[49]

Garrison recognized Jesus as the only master worth serving. He had been stimulated to take this position by a letter from John Humphrey Noyes in 1837, advising Christians to boycott or secede from the government. The United States, wrote Noyes, "was a bloated, swaggering libertine, trampling on the Bible — its own constitution — . . . the petitions of its citizens: with one hand whipping a negro tied to a liberty-pole, and with the other dashing an emaciated Indian to the ground."[50]

At the first annual meeting of the Non-Resistance Society, held in Boston in 1839, Adin Ballou raised God's jurisdiction above that of paltry humans, whose government, "as contradistinguished from the divine [was] a mere cypher." When "it opposes God's government it is nothing; when it agrees with his government it is *nothing*; and when it *discovers* a new item of duty — a new application of the law of God — it is nothing." Dross can neither be purified nor reformed, nor is it the duty of Christian nonresistants to subvert or overthrow their governments. "By no means. We utterly disclaim any such object. We are not Jacobins, Revolutionists, Anarchists, though often *slanderously so denominated.*" Then what is the object? "The resolution of this convention calls not for the overthrow or subversion of governments, but only to *supersede* them . . . with the kingdom of Christ. *How?* By the spiritual regeneration of their subjects . . . by giving them *heavenly* instead of *earthly motives.*"[51]

Warren was not an abolitionist Christian like Garrison, a perfectionist Christian like Noyes, or a fundamentalist Christian like Ballou. Nonetheless, as a pragmatic secularist, he arrived at some of the antistatist conclusions reached by moralists of the disunion faction. In the chapter in *Equitable Commerce* on "The Greatest Practicable Amount of Liberty to Each Individual," he proclaimed that "We can dispense with government only in proportion as we can reduce the amount of public business to be managed. This, then, is the movement for the restoration of the liberty of mankind; it is to *disconnect*, to *individualize*, rather than to combine or "UNITE" our interests!" To delegate power through representation is not a solution. Government completely controls a community that owns all its property. Should that community own only half of its property, its government's power is cut in two. The way to eliminate government is to individualize all interests, thus ensuring enjoyment of liberty in a society finally harmonized.[52]

Friends of freedom should "come out" of the Union, but not because it mistreated blacks and Indians, or failed to imitate Christ. By its very existence, government denied personal sovereignty. An un-wavering nominalist, Warren believed that people are real, combined interests fictitious. In a republic as large as the United States, he grudg-ingly conceded, "perhaps the vote of the majority is the best expedient, but it is only an expedient." The culprit was neither the Whig nor the Democratic party: "the fault . . . is inherent in *the Republic itself* . . . The RIGHT is to have no Combined *National interests*, but only INDIVIDUAL INTERESTS." In an era of sectional conflict, when the issue was the rela-tive sovereignty of the states and the federal government, Warren stuck to his individualist guns in hopes that the future would be his: "It may be perfectly *right* for me to go in a straight line directly north to get to my friend's house; but if the streets are crooked I *must* go a little wrong." Because of its "unspeakable" beauty, those people who under-stand will take the shortest practicable road "in the right direction, and embrace as *little* wrong as possible."[53]

At the end of his article on Modern Times, Moncure Conway stated his reason for its decline. It was not cranks like the man "who worked and walked about in a state of nudity,"—he was a provocateur, sent in by "some ill-disposed persons [of which he was one], wishing to break up the village." The crucial issue was the war, which along with taxation was foreign to the purpose for which Modern Times ex-isted. Labor notes would not be "regarded by Mr. Chase [the Secretary of the Treasury] as equivalent to greenbacks"; beyond that lay the con-scription of sovereigns "for a kind of service at variance with their prin-ciples." In a dramatic, if inaccurate, coda, Conway adorned his rational statements about the war with one of his novelist's flights of fancy: "One day a small ship spread its white wings and bore southward from Montauk Point, *on which were nearly all of those whom I saw at Modern Times* [emphasis added]: it did not pause along all that coast of fire . . . two thousand miles and more it sailed, and anchored at last near a pleasant, peaceful shore in South America, where those voyag-ers have fixed their tents for the present. And there may Peace attend them!"[54]

Conway's red-string-around-the-finger story was probably only a yarn, but his reported exodus of the sovereigns was a dyed-in-the-wool fabrication. The only known embarkees were Dr. Newberry's three sons, who, according to Dyson, struck it rich in Argentina.[55] Because they were boys of twelve, ten, and four years of age on the 1860 census schedule, their departure furnishes flimsy proof of a mass migration in protest against the Civil War. Subsequent censuses, real estate deeds, and the markers in Brentwood Cemetery conclusively show that most of the sovereigns stayed put, and that those who left went to other states of the Union, not to South America. Yet Conway's legend passed for gospel to many observers of Modern Times. Madeleine B. Stern, for example, swallowed his bait—hook, line, and sinker—but without giving Conway the credit. After Modern Times changed to Brentwood, she wrote, as if Conway's fancy required no proof, "A ship sailing from Montauk Point would carry the survivors of the equity village to South America."[56]

When the quarrel between the sections erupted into warfare, the formerly no-government pioneers became as patriotic or more than their town-of-Islip neighbors. The first brass band in Suffolk County, formed about 1860, consisted of a dozen sovereigns led by Joseph Owram. Performing beyond the village borders, wrote Codman, the band was "much in evidence . . . during the early years of the War of the Rebellion," playing at "'patriots' parades, Flag raisings and Public Meetings." Josiah Warren, a skilled musician, "composed a 'South Bay Quickstep' which was quite popular."[57]

Of the 168 sons of Islip serving in the Union forces, fifteen hailed from the village conceived in anarchy, its proportion of soldiers to population higher than that of the town as a whole.[58] Two gave their lives—George Baxter in battle and Charles Miller of disease contracted while serving with the 8th New Jersey Regiment. A third presumed fatality was Henry Fish, the Hopedale exile, who marched with the 84th New York and is listed as missing in the record of Suffolk County soldiers.[59] Three others "returned sick . . . recovered from the 'Army Fever' and are yet alive," noted Codman,[60] who modestly refrained from noting his hitch with the 102nd Infantry, a New York regiment favored by men from western Suffolk County. Henry Alexander Edger, against the will of his father, also joined the 102nd.

Their experience in the marching band prepared Charles H. Bishop, Frank E. Blacker, Thomas C. George, Isaac Haines, and William Jenkins to enlist as army musicians. They "were assigned to the 5th N.J. Regiment and were with General Mc Lellan [sic] at the battle of   [probably Antietam tho' not named by Mr. Codman] and through all the campaign of 'the Peninsula.'" All returned, but a leg wound suffered at Gettysburg lamed George for the rest of his life.[61] Other wounded men who came back were Edward C. Pierce, 14th New York, and Henry Dahlems, 39th New York. The fourteenth and fifteenth Modern Times soldiers, Robert White and Edward Dow, both served in the 9th New Jersey Infantry.[62]

Codman related the ordeal of Isaac Gibson, a potential sixteenth soldier from Modern Times, who after being drafted "appeared before the Examining Board of the Army Surgeon [and] told them he was a Quaker, was opposed to fighting, that he would not handle a musket or fire a gun; but that he would be willing to join the Hospital Corps and act as a Nurse." When the army found him "physically unfit for soldiering," perhaps because of his tubercular history, he "returned to his farm—to the arts of Peace." Gibson, told in 1854 that he would die within a year unless he came to the Long Island pine woods, "was a good man, always ready to lend a helping hand. He lived alone most of his sojourn here and died without a struggle, being found dead in his bed on the morning of Mar. 15, 1898."[63]

At first, the sovereigns accepted a sparse scale of living as the price of renouncing market ethics, but the prosperity marking the final years of the Civil War sapped their devotion to labor exchange without capital gain. The New York State census of 1865 required each marshal to answer a series of questions about the impact of the conflict. As the census taker for the Third Election District of Islip, in which Modern Times was contained, Charles W. Fordham reported that since 1860 the average pay of farm laborers had risen from twenty to thirty dollars a month. This increase of 50 percent affected debt between individuals "favorably—cash is the rule." What was the war's effect on credit? "Never was better than now." Yes, the war promoted prompt payments. In Fordham's judgment, possibly influenced by his being a minister's son, "our men came home better citizens, many have become Christians, all seem more steady, thoughtful, manly." Honored by friends and neighbors, the veterans gained in self-esteem: *"They are too proud to be mean* [emphasis added]."[64] Fordham's simple but eloquent statement deserved a better fate than burial in the census archives.

What "other changes in social conditions of the people" did Fordham notice "since 1860? First, a great growth in patriotism in the sentiment of nationality, confidence in the power and integrity of the nation, and a truthful perception of the pernicious effects of slavery."

Without amplification, Fordham reported "intense hatred toward England" as another of "inward social changes."[65] It is unclear whether he referred to British sympathy for the Confederacy, diminished but not erased by Emancipation, or to local support for Irish freedom; no hard evidence supports this purported Anglophobia.

As for "outward" results of the war in Islip, it *"quickened trade, money was never more plentiful. Farmers never raised so much and never had more money in their pockets* [emphasis added]." Unlike his cryptic reference to anti-English sentiment, Fordham attached a terse postscript to his finding that farmers rolled in money: "It's a mystery but a *fact* in my district."[66] The "mystery" was the abundance of cash in a year when drought had reduced the yield of potatoes and other crops to half or less the usual amount.

The other two Islip census districts confirmed a drought, but not of money: farm wages were up and debt was down, with cash payments greatly increased. In the First Election District, census marshal John W. Yarrington noted "a tendency to extravagance in the way of dress and manner of living."[67] In the Second Election District, Seth R. Clock worried that morality did not stand "so high today as it did in 1860, especially . . . the *Temperance Cause* [is] at a low ebb." Clock ticked off the same sequence of lessened debt, for shorter terms, with prompter payments.[68]

These changes must have been apparent to the pioneers living on "scant rations" at Modern Times. Once the five-year span of fixed pricing expired in 1856, upward pressure on real estate values eroded the practice of equitable commerce. The nudists, cranks, and ultras were gone. The aura of free love persisted, but its militant patrons were elsewhere—the Nicholses, now in Ohio, were soon to take refuge in English exile and Roman religion, while Andrews diminished his interest in Modern Times in favor of groups of his own in Manhattan.

Warren failed to come to terms with the waging of full-scale war by rival combinations. Pushing individual sovereignty to its limit, he held that just as the South had the right to secede from a Union it did not support, the same "right of self-sovereignty in every human being which gives you [the South] the supreme right to leave us without asking our leave, gives to your slaves the same right to leave you . . . I hardly know which of the two classes is most enslaved, or most to be pitied, slaves or masters."[69]

After secession and Fort Sumter, few Northerners wasted their pity on masters; individual sovereignty could not hold out against the demands of the state for men and money. To Warren, the issue transcended black slavery because the "enslavement of *Labor* is another subject which concerns whites and blacks alike." No solution would be found short of "Equitable compensation for labor." Majority rule was, at best, an expedient: "only by *'disintegrating,'* or *'individualizing'* our subjects . . . can we approach true civilization."[70] Viewing war as the ultimate violation of individual sovereignty, he packed up and left Modern Times for the last time, his name gone from the record after the school district meeting of October 1862.

MODERN TIMES BECOMES BRENTWOOD

No future crisis matched the drama of Mary Gove and Thomas Nichols's call on the sovereigns to pledge, in support of free love, their names, lives, and sacred honor. Once Stearns's defection, the *Tribune* debate, and the rout of the Nicholses were past if not forgotten events, the village settled down for a spell of calmer growth. The "Boston group" and other settlers who came after 1854 were friendly to equitable commerce without being militant in its defense. The self-reliant life-style of Islip did not differ much from their own, but did not require its people to storm the ramparts of Mammon and Grundy.

The modest pull of the ideal village movement, to which location was incidental to program, yielded to the force exerted on Modern Times by its Suffolk County habitat. In the late 1850s and early 1860s, some wealthier pioneers arrived. Unconcerned with remaking society, these newcomers were attracted by the healthy climate and natural charm of the pine woods, where land was cheap but the setting ideal for a rich man to build an estate.

The new factor of opulence impressed Modern Timers accustomed to functional poverty. When land prices rose on Long Island, the sovereigns did not go to Minnesota but stayed put, bent their ideals, and took what the traffic would bear. Quietly but irrevocably, the cost principle broke against the power of the dollar.

At the same time that rising property values lowered the sovereigns' commitment always to trade at par, the pressure of patriotism superseded their antistatist bias. As if to prove the changed mood of the village, fifteen of its men enlisted in the army fighting to save the Union. On 7 September 1864, the residents of Modern Times decided to give their village the name of Brentwood. "As time passed, and free lovers left, made happy marriages, or died," observes John C. Spur-lock, "the town . . . became more moderate and discreet, changing . . . from a bastion of radicalism into a sleepy village with a shady past."[71]

10

Looking Backward

JOHN HUMPHREY NOYES STRETCHED THE TRUTH in his pedigree of Modern Times: "Owen begat New Harmony; New Harmony (by reaction) begat Individual Sovereignty; Individual Sovereignty begat Modern Times; Modern Times was the mother of Free Love, the Grand Pantarchy, and the American branch of French Positivism."[1] This line of descent was only partially accurate. The egalitarian Warren rejected Owen's top-down style of leadership in particular, and the need for organization is general; he conceived of equitable commerce as the antidote to combination and, a quarter-century after the discord at New Harmony, tested the concept at Modern Times. But the Long Island village had no maternal relationship with the three other movements cited. Far from being the child of Modern Times, free love was an interloper, rejected by the settlers after its partisans called for commitment. The Grand Pantarchy was Andrews's New York City nucleus for a projected world union of which he was the intellectual overlord; his dream of becoming the Sovereign of individual sovereigns was as foreign to Modern Times's purpose as would be a pope of free-thinkers. Finally, "the American branch of French Positivism" applied not to Comte's philosophy but to its distortion by its author into the dogmatic Religion of Humanity, promoted at Modern Times by his lonely apostle, Henry Edger.

BRENTWOOD JOINS THE OUTSIDE WORLD

Book B of the Suffolk County *Certificates of Incorporation* recorded a series of changes in the months before and after the transition from Modern Times to Brentwood. On 18 August 1864 (three weeks before the change), a meeting in the schoolhouse formed "an incorporated

184

Society of the 1st. Congregational Church of Thompson Station." Trustees elected were F. M. A. Wicks, who now owned property in the village; Stephen Sharp, a landowner in the vicinity; and Horace Pike, a non–Modern Timer of whom nothing more is known. Also involved was Elisha F. Richardson, an owner of farms and orchards adjacent to the village of which he was a friend but not a resident.[2]

On 8 November 1864, a meeting of "the inhabitants of the village of Brentwood (late Modern Times) and vicinity," provided for a public cemetery. For this purpose, fourteen former sovereigns united with five of the prosperous farmers and businessmen now in contention for leadership of the "late Modern Times." As if by prearrangement, the group chose three pioneers as trustees along with Wicks, Richardson, and Robert W. Pearsall,[3] a magnate of the status quo who forcefully took the leading role once unobtrusively played by the Peaceful Revolutionist.

On 21 January 1865, an assembly at the schoolhouse elected Pearsall president of the Farmer's Club of the Suffolk County Agricultural Society, the purpose of which was "the increase of knowledge on, and interest in all horticultural and agricultural subjects." This gathering of nine from the village and seven outsiders voted for F. M. A. Wicks as vice-president, and for two former Modern Timers, C. B. Brown and Isaac Gibson, as secretary and treasurer.[4]

On 3 October 1865, pursuant to an Act of the Legislature passed 13 April 1854 and entitled "an Act for the incorporation of Societies to establish free churches," the Christ Church Association of Brentwood commenced to organize an Episcopal church that began as a branch of St. Mark's of Islip. Of seven trustees, William Metcalf and Peter I. Blacker (both born in England) represented the once godless village, along with five non–Modern Timers, including the busy Robert W. Pearsall.[5]

Early in 1865, as a newly elected Trustee of Common School District 12, Pearsall presented a petition signed by the fifteen voters required, requesting a meeting to debate "whether an Union free school be formed." Union Free Districts, created by law in 1853, are enlargements of common districts from grade to high-school size. On 28 January, with Pearsall in the chair, the unanimous vote of the twenty men present created Union Free School District 12; on 22 February, the voters elected Pearsall president and William Metcalf clerk and librarian.[6]

The expansion of District 12 so quickly after the name change, together with the formation of churches, a branch of the Farmer's Club, and the Cemetery Association, testified that Modern Times's nonconformist policy failed to answer the pioneers' need for formal organization. It also signaled the advent of a new class of wealthier settlers, attracted by the sovereigns' proof that the once despised pine barrens offered a cheap but rewarding site for development.

Still, the former Modern Timers did not abandon their nonchalance for cant and respectability. At the school district meeting of 1868, Aaron Stone made a dual motion: first, that a portion of the Bible be read "in the usual manner without note or comment at opening of school . . . each morning," with provision to excuse any children whose parents or guardians object; and second, "that music be introduced as a portion of regular exercise of the school." A sizeable part of the old guard never surrendered. The meeting rejected the first resolution "by a decisive vote: none in the affirmative"; the second "carried unanimously."[7]

Dyson describes Robert W. Pearsall as "an aristocrat . . . and a capitalist."[8] Pearsall and his wife, Elizabeth, went on buying sprees during the early 1860s, acquiring every lot they could get within or near the village. Mrs. Pearsall's mother, Elizabeth B. Phelps, also bid up property values. After acquiring the hundred-acre plot that Andrews bought and resold to the Nicholses for the doomed project of Desarrollo, Mrs. Phelps donated it to her daughter for "the consideration of love and affection and the sum of one dollar."[9] The Pearsalls matched this purchase of land on the western side of the village by buying a large tract to the east and south, on which they built a mansion "modeled after a famous chateau in France . . . [with] furnishings . . . imported from Europe—luxurious draperies, costly period furniture, Persian rugs, oil paintings, and marble statues." In 1870, Pearsall hired Frederick Law Olmstead, the landscape artist renowned for designing both Central and Prospect Parks, "to come to Brentwood and beautify his estate . . . [the] grounds became radiant with flower beds, flowering shrubs, velvety lawns, hedges, walks, and lily ponds, an artificial lake, and a 'Lover's Lane,' silent and shady between the rows of tall pines planted by the colonists of Modern Times."[10] William Hayward, another prosperous resident with no attachment to equity commerce, erected an elegant house on his charter purchase, "the most imposing residence in the village next to Pearsall's chateau."[11]

THE LEGACY OF MODERN TIMES

Although no longer willing to live in the village he founded, Warren maintained his interest and affection for Modern Times long after the residents changed its name. In *Practical Applications*, his final work, he listed the contributions of Modern Times to Brentwood. In the midst of the pine barrens now stood a "very pretty village . . . improving faster than any other in the neighborhood." With nothing except their "hands and their good sense . . . a few industrious individuals . . . have made themselves homes and business." Where there was not even a cowpath at first was now an avenue nearly a mile long and a hundred feet wide, with a grid of other streets and avenues crossing each other at right angles. There was a railroad station, a post office, and a connecting road "running out into the country in one direction and extending to the Great South Bay in the other, and running right through the town." Having been defamed by past detractors, "The name of the place is changed, and the annoyance from that source is at an end." There were "No demands for jails—No grog shops, No houses of prostitution." Theft, trespass, murder, or crimes of any sort were absent: "Few, if any doors are locked at night, and the fear of robbers and *fire* probably disturbs no one's sleep."[12]

More than thirty years later, William Bailie asserted that even if the original aims of the pioneers were lost by the wayside, the village never "wholly departed from its original spirit and character." The former sovereigns did not quarrel over property or the form of government. Cooperation among residents as well as a pleasing setting remained, although when Bailie wrote, in 1906, only "three of the early pioneers survive."[13]

At the end of his memoir, Codman pondered the pros and cons. "As an Equity Village, 'twas a success as far as it went." Concerned with value rather than cost, the political economists missed the point of "Equity in Trade." The grubby ethic that things were worth what they fetched in the market had led to "'Corners,' 'Monopolies,' and

the monstrous inequalities of present conditions." Religion and char-
ity could not solve the problem of social equity without "a true com-
prehension of what Justice is." Modern Times was nevertheless a failure,
at least as the word was understood. After all, reckoned Codman, only
5 percent of all business succeeded, especially in the field of morals.
Our "fundamental mistake" was thinking that "more than a handful
of those who clamor for justice are honest and in earnest: those who
prate and shout for it . . . are far from ready to practice."[14]

The village lacked a "Leader with the gift for addressing the public and presenting our plan." There was no capital to establish an industry, no fertile soil in the early years, no waterpower for organizing
"some kind of manufacturing and by it [earn] a living." Because of his
past unsatisfactory experience with the press, Warren refused to seek
publicity. It is wonderful "that the hope and faith of the Pioneers" sustained them for thirteen years." Codman captured the essence of Modern Times as a model of counterculture: "None of us had the desire
for riches. Equity was the ruling motive, that was what we were here
to establish. We are lacking in the art of buying Low and selling high.
Our aim was to show by example that better conditions for living were
possible – that Equity could be made actual . . . We may have been speculators in Morality – but not in Land products." The sovereigns endured
privations, left opportunity behind – by the "standard of worldly ambition we failed." Yet at least their experiment had "assisted in keeping alive the aspiration for Social progress." The millennium that he
thought was in sight seemed more distant than ever to Codman, the
gentle generalizer. Perhaps it did not exist, or was "only a Chimera.
I dunno . . . the ideal of Poets philosophers and Saviors seems a long
way ahead."[15]

In *Practical Applications*, Warren measured the "gains of the residents . . . as not only what they have *got*, but what they have *not got*."[16]
They had a garden village rescued from the wilderness, with trains and
mail and highways, and a name now free of scandal. They did not
have murder, theft, greed, or vice: no fences ringed the strawberry gardens, no policemen guarded the streets. Missing from Josiah's list of
what the former sovereigns lacked was the benefit of organizations that
did for individuals what they could not do alone.

Contending that public control over capital goods prevents degradation of labor, socialists want to put an end to planless and private production. Defenders of profit disagree, insisting that prospect of gain is the true incentive that gets work done efficiently and guards the people's liberty. The purpose of equitable commerce was to blend these rival doctrines by maintaining private ownership but precluding exploitation. Yet to bar profit but cherish enterprise was as arbitrary and wishful a dream as the Nicholses' demand that Modern Timers face martyrdom for free love, or Comte and Edger's fantasy of the Positivist State of Long Island. To expect Americans in the age of growth to forego gain in favor of equity was a noble aspiration, but unwelcome to the folk it proposed to save.

By proving the viability of the pine barrens and the railroad, Modern Times played a meaningful role in the development of Long Island. But a raft of cooperation could not stay afloat in a sea of competition. The village was handicapped economically, unendowed with business acumen. Its program helped pioneers short of cash to acquire homesteads, but otherwise was a form of subsistence richer in ideas than output. Labor-for-labor exchange suited handmade production or self-performed service, but not the rising regime of mass production for a swelling national market.

Modern Times was too small, too underfinanced, and too restricted to private but profitless enterprise for its sovereigns long to accept their self-imposed frugal standard of living. Although it empowered settlers to own their own homes in fee simple, it denied them the equally prized American drive to sell the fruit of one's labor for more than it cost to produce. Most of the skilled mechanics and food producers the village needed for its base were disinclined to trade at par with no provision for financial gain. To seekers of advancement bold enough to take a risk, the United States may have seemed the real utopia, poised on the threshold of growth, and abounding in opportunity. If, in Arthur E. Bestor's eloquent phrase, the ideal villages were "patent office models of the good society," the patent at Modern Times remained pending.[17]

Sovereignty of the individual clashed with cost the limit of price: personal freedom meant little to sellers barred from setting the value of the goods they produced or the service they rendered. Anarchism was not a system of government but rather a vision of pure freedom,

hard put to operate even a hamlet because, at the first sign of controversy, majority vote or the will of a leader subverted the splendid premise that each be his or her sect and nation.

Josiah Warren and Stephen Pearl Andrews made a gallant but
quixotic effort to maximize every individual freedom except the right
to make a profit. Offered as the ultimate in personal laissez-faire, their
experiment precluded craftsmen from selling a product for more than
it cost to make. In an era of rising political tension, it ignored the need
for concerted action. The problems of slavery, sectional rivalry, urban
and industrial growth, immigration, and supervision of the Territories
could not be solved by turning back the nation's clock to simpler times
of barter and local autonomy.

Yet Modern Times was remarkable for the creativeness of its polity, the zeal of its reformers, and the quality of its pioneers. During
its thirteen years of existence, it made a significant effort to plant the
seeds of individual sovereignty and cost the limit of price. Its settlers
built homes for the homeless, respected each other's independence,
and demonstrated that man was not made for the company, state, or
Sabbath. There was no incidence of crime in spite of the absence of
police and court. And by defying restrictions on cohabitation and raising the issue of woman's rights, the village pointed the way toward
parity between the sexes.

An asylum for fugitives from unhappy marriage, Modern Times
refused to become the bastion of all-out war on the institution. Yet
the sovereigns practiced the mating customs for which they refused to
be hucksters. Prematurely removing the stigma from cohabitation, each
pair selected its form of bonding, a process now taken for granted. The
hot light of marital reform seared Modern Times's reputation but pointed
the way to the future.

The sovereigns perceived the Millennium as a metaphor, not as
a real event. Although their mission of sweeping change encouraged
such an allusion, they did not think of themselves as heralds of a
thousand-year reign of peace and freedom. To them Modern Times was
no union of saints prepared to walk in the New Jerusalem, but a work-
able combination of reason with social justice. They were testers of
equitable commerce, immersed in the current order, their role that of
scientists bent on proving that profit was not a function of owning,
or law a need of association. As a substitute for religion they empha-

sized freedom of thought, which to them was the purpose of Protestantism. The sovereigns of Modern Times revived the ideals of the earlier
pathfinders hailed by the Reverend Nathaniel S. Prime, the pioneers
who took up "their residence in the trackless wilderness, for the rights
of conscience and the enjoyment of liberty."[18]

Notes
Selected Bibliography
Index

NOTES

1. SCALE MODEL OF LIBERTY

1. Rosabeth Moss Kanter, *Commitment and Community: Communes and Utopias in Sociological Perspective* (Cambridge, Mass.: Harvard Univ. Press, 1972), 244–45. Kanter condenses the number to 91 to avoid repetition of Shaker, Harmonist, Oneida, and other communities with two or more branches among the 124 settlements listed by Arthur E. Bestor, "Checklist of Communitarian Experiments," appendix to *Backwoods Utopias: The Sectarian Origins and the Owenite Phase of Communitarian Socialism in America: 1663–1829* (Philadelphia: Univ. of Pennsylvania Press, 1953; reprint, Philadelphia: Univ. of Pennsylvania Press, 1981), 277–84.

2. Albert Brisbane, *Association: or, A Concrete Exposition of the Doctrine of Association, or Plan for the Reorganization of Society* (New York: Greeley & McElrath, 1843), quoted in Bestor, "Checklist," 231.

3. For a comprehensive nineteenth-century study of model communities including Modern Times, see John Humphrey Noyes, *History of American Socialisms* (1870; reprint, New York: Hillary House, 1961). I cite other works on the subject below; see chapter 9 for rebuttal of Rosabeth M. Kanter's "longevity factor" as the measure of success or failure.

4. Josiah Warren, *Practical Details in Equitable Commerce, Showing the Workings, in Actual Experiment, During a Series of Years, of the Social Principles Expounded in the Works Called "Equitable Commerce," by the Author of This, and "The Science of Society," by Stephen Pearl Andrews* (New York: Fowlers & Wells 1852), 13.

5. Josiah Warren, *The Peaceful Revolutionist, Devoted to the Practical Details of Equitable Commerce* 2 (May 1848): 132. Although the passage alludes to Utopia (Smith's Landing, Ohio), a village of equity formed by Warren in 1847, it applies to Modern Times as aptly as the sobriquet "Peaceful Revolutionist" fits Warren.

6. Warren, *Practical Details*, ix.

7. Josiah Warren, *The Periodical Letter on the Principles and Progress of the "Equity Movement," to Those Who Have Not Lost All Hope of Justice, Order, and Peace on Earth* 1 (Feb. 1855), 106. This monthly newsletter written, printed, and published by Warren from 1854 to 1858 is (except for a few numbers issued from Boston) datelined Thompson P.O., Long Island, N.Y. For more on Thompson, short for Thompson's Station, the post office address for Modern Times, see chap. 2 below.

8. Stephen Pearl Andrews, *The Science of Society* (New York: Fowlers & Wells,

1852; reprint, Weston, Mass.: M & S Press, 1970), 127. This edition comprises two works by Andrews interpreting Warren's philosophy: *The Science of Society. No. 1. The True Constitution of Government in the Sovereignty of the Individual as the Final Development of Protestantism, Democracy and Socialism*, and *The Science of Society, No. 2. Cost The Limit of Price; A Scientific Measure of Honesty in Trade as one of the Fundamental Principles in the Solution of the Social Problem*. See chap. 5 below for analysis of *Science of Society*.

     9. Charles A. Codman, "A Brief History of 'The City of Modern Times' Long Island, N.Y.– and A Glorification of Some of Its Saints," (Brentwood, N.Y., ca. 1905), 1; a pencilscript in the Modern Times Collection of the Suffolk County Historical Society, Riverhead, N.Y. Pages cited are from the 27-page typewritten copy held by the Society, copies of which are in the public libraries of Brentwood, Smithtown, and Huntington, Long Island, N.Y.

     10. Ibid., 15. See chap. 9 below for a discussion of the failed but strenuous effort of Henry Edger to make Modern Times the American seat of Auguste Comte's Religion of Humanity.

     11. Ibid., 26–27.

2. THE SITE AND THE FOUNDERS

     1. Edgar Fenn Peck, M.D., to R. M. Bayles, Brooklyn, L.I., 8 Oct. 1873, appendix to Richard M. Bayles, *Historical and Descriptive Sketches of Suffolk County with a Historical Outline of Long Island* (1873; reprint, Port Washington, N.Y.: Ira J. Friedman, 1962), i–iii.

     2. Lawrence G. Paul, *The Pine Barrens of Ronkonkoma: A Guide for the Hiker to the Long Island Pine Barrens* (New York: New York–New Jersey Trail Conference, 1986), 6.

     3. Timothy Dwight, *Travels; In New-England and New-York* (New Haven: the author, 1822), 3:302. The dour Calvinism of Dwight (1752–1817), a grandson of Jonathan Edwards, did not cloud the accuracy of his posthumous travelogue.

     4. Winslow C. Watson, "The Plains of Long Island," *New York State Agricultural Society, Proceedings for 1859* (Albany: Charles Van Benthuysen, 1860), 495.

     5. Paul, *Pine Barrens*, 6.

     6. Edger F. Peck, *Description of the Lands on Long Island* (Brooklyn: the author, 1858), 4. This four-page pamphlet was a reprint issued "more than ten years since the first publication . . . of the brief description of the wild lands of Long Island" (ibid., 1).

     7. *Sixth Annual Report of the American Institute, of the City of New York, Made to the Legislature, March 25, 1848* (Albany, 1848), 669, 692–93; see also Daniel Denton, *A Brief Description of New York Formerly Called New Netherlands* [sic] (London, 1670), in *Historic Chronicles of New Amsterdam, Colonial New York, and Early Long Island*, ed. Cornell Jaray (Port Washington, N.Y.: Ira Friedman, 1968).

     8. William H. Ross, M.D., "A Study of the Climate of Long Island," *Brooklyn Medical Journal* 18 (Mar. 1904): 83.

9. Peck, "Letter," i.

10. Codman, "Modern Times," 8–9.

11. Paul, *Pine Barrens*, 1, 6.

12. Peck, "Letter," ii.

13. Ibid.

14. Ibid., ii–iii. The eight listed investors were R. E. Johnson; H. I. Wheeler; Uel West (not Mel West as reported by Brentwood's historian, Verne Dyson, *A Century of Brentwood* (Brentwood, N.Y.: Brentwood Village Press, 1950), 5); Nathan Stephens; Christopher Wray; J. [Joseph] Agate; R. J. Richards; and S. P. Townsend. Wray and his wife Sophia Jane, and Agate and his wife Maria, were the most frequent grantors of acreage bought by Modern Timers. Two of "the other" grantors not listed by Peck were Alanson Briggs and his wife Sarah, and William J. Bauer and his wife Mary.

15. Ibid., iii. Peck omitted the names of wives but the deed *Libers* show that Catherine Fleet, Samuel's wife, was the grantor in all Modern Times transactions involving the name of Fleet (see chap. 3 below).

16. Josiah Warren, *Practical Applications of the Elementary Principles of "True Civilization" to the Minute Details of Every Day Life. Being Part III, the Last of the "True Civilization" Series, and the Facts and Conclusions of Forty Seven Years Study and Experiments in Reform Movements through Communism To and In Elementary Principles, Found in a Direction Exactly Opposite to and Away from Communism, But Leading Directly to All the Harmonic Results Aimed at by Communism* (Princeton, Mass.: the author, 1873), 25. For the meaning of communism and socialism in the 1840s and 1850s, and Warren and Andrews's position, see chap. 7 below.

17. "A Card–To the Public," *New York Daily Tribune*, 4 Apr. 1853, 5.

18. Codman, "Modern Times," 4.

19. "Map of the City of Modern Times," *Liber of Maps* 34:19, Office of the Suffolk County Clerk, Riverhead, N.Y. This map, made 20 Mar. 1851 by Ebenezer Hawkins, surveyor, and recorded 18 Jan. 1859, is the reference map for all deeds executed at the village.

20. Codman, "Modern Times," 6.

21. Stephen Pearl Andrews, Preface to *Practical Details in Equitable Commerce* by Josiah Warren, vi.

22. Warren, *Periodical Letter* 1 (Sept. 1854): 34.

23. Warren, *Periodical Letter* 1 (May 1854): 47. The stump removers, a trio of Midwestern brothers named Swaim–Curran, Henry, and one whose name cannot be found–should not be confused with Swain, another Modern Times family.

24. There may be other advertisements for the village, but "A Card–To the Public" is the only one located.

25. A remark about Dr. Peck preceding the summary of his speech in *Sixth Annual Report*, American Institute, 687.

26. Peck, "Letter," iii.

27. Moncure Daniel Conway, "Modern Times, New York," *Fortnightly Review* 1 (July 1865): 421, published eight years after his weekend visit; this account of sexual and intellectual attitudes at Modern Times is examined in chap. 4 and 5 respectively.

28. The Long Island Railroad Company: Diamond Jubilee (1834–1909) (Jamaica, N.Y.: N.p. 1910), iii.

29. Mildred H. Smith, *Early History of the Long Island Railroad: 1834–1900* (Uniondale, N.Y.: Salisbury Printers, 1958), 2.

30. Manorville (also known as Manor) derives its name from St. George's Manor, the 1697 patent granted by William and Mary to Col. William "Tangier" Smith; this immense tract stretched across Long Island from Riverhead to Fire Island (Paul, *Pine Barrens*, 9).

31. *The Long Island Railroad: 100th Anniversary (1834–1934)* (Jamaica, N.Y.: Osborne Co., 1934), 6, citing the 1834 report of Major D. B. Douglass, the line's top engineer; another source claims that "The new route to Boston . . . reduced the 16-hour water trip by half" (David Robinson George, "A Brief History of the Long Island Railroad," in *Long Island—A History of Two Great Counties, Nassau and Suffolk,* ed. Paul Bailey [New York: Lewis Historical Publishing Co., 1949], 2:397).

32. J. H. French, *Gazetteer of the State of New York 1860* (Syracuse: R. Pearsall Smith, 1860), 71). Rail and ferry combinations also were set up for New Haven traffic bound for Hartford, Worcester, and Boston. See also Henry Varnum Poor, *History of the Railroads and Canals of the United States of America* (New York: John H. Schultz & Co., 1860; reprint, New York: Augustus M. Kelley, 1970), 1:69, 264–65 for the Long Island Railroad; 210–11 for the New York and New Haven; 287 for the New York and Harlem; and 187–88 for the New York, Providence and Boston.

33. George, "A Brief History," 400. For the line's collapse see Edwin L. Dunbaugh, "New York to Boston Via the Long Island Railroad," in *Evoking A Sense of Place,* ed. Joann P. Krieg (Interlaken, N.Y.: Heart of the Lakes Publishing, 1988), 75–84.

34. Ralph Henry Gabriel, *The Evolution of Long Island: A Story of Land and Sea* (1921; reprint, Port Washington, N.Y.: Ira J. Friedman, 1968), 134.

35. Nathaniel S. Prime, *A History of Long Island, from Its First Settlement by Europeans, to the Year 1845, with Special Reference to Its Ecclesiastical Concerns* (New York: Robert Carter, 1845), 1:59–60.

36. The patent of Sagtikos Manor, issued in 1697, included the 150-acre estate on which the manor house (now a museum) stands, the Apple Tree Neck (or Wicke), a sliver of land extending five miles north from the bay. The widow of Stephanus Van Cortlandt, the first patentee, and her sons Oloff, Phillip, and Stephen, sold the property to Timothy Carll of Huntington. Carll's grandson Selah sold it some fifty years later, in 1758, when a Setauket man, "Jonathan Thompson purchased for his son, Isaac, the estate . . . known as Sagtikos Patent or Manor . . . For this beautiful property he paid 1,200 pounds New York money, which sum he brought over from the North side in his saddle bags on a handsome gray horse" (Sarah D. Gardiner, "The Sagtikos Manor 1697, An Address Read before the Annual Meeting of the Order of Colonial Lords of Manors in America on April 26, 1934" [New York: Publications of the Order of Colonial Lords of Manors in America, 1935], 9–10).

37. George Lewis Weeks, *Some of the Town of Islip's Early History,* (Bay Shore, N.Y.: Consolidated Press, 1955), 42. Thompson's Station stood on the northwest corner of today's Fifth and Suffolk Avenues (Fifth was known as Telegraph Avenue be-

cause of the line from Thompson's to Bay Shore). Suffolk Station (later North Islip, then moved and renamed Central Islip) sometimes is cited incorrectly as the railroad station for Modern Times – the claim belongs to Thompson's. Two and one-half miles east of Thompson's at the present "Five Corners" intersection of Suffolk and Islip Avenues, Suffolk Station was the main connection for rail and carriage transit "over south" to Islip village. F. M. A. Wicks also operated stages north and south from Thompson's Station. Neither Thompson's nor Suffolk Station now exists.

38. Peck, *Lands on Long Island,* 3.

39. James J. Martin, *Men Against the State: The Expositors of Individualist Anarchism in America, 1827–1908* (1953; reprint, Colorado Springs: Ralph Myles Publisher, 1970), 66. Masquerier shared Warren's passion for individualism, maintaining that "the principle of individuality of rights and property makes each man and woman an equal and independent owner of an individual homestead, with the sublime liberty of self-direction, self-employment, and self-government" (Lewis Masquerier, *Sociology, or, the Reconstruction of Society, Government, and Property* [1877; reprint, Westport, Conn.: Greenwood Press, 1970], 52). However, Warren disagreed with Masquerier's belief in majority rule once "all are located on their own soil," a practice antithetical to individual sovereignty (Warren, *Practical Details,* 102).

40. Andrews, Preface to Warren, *Practical Details,* vi.

41. "A Card–To the Public," *Tribune,* Apr. 1853.

42. Conway, "Modern Times," 422–23.

43. For Warren's printing inventions, see pp. 20, 199n.61 below; for his two systems of musical notation (1844 and 1860), see Ann Caldwell Butler, "Josiah Warren: Peaceful Revolutionist" (Ph.D. diss., Ball State Univ., 1979), addendum E, 189–91. Butler's thoughtful biography does not deal in depth with Modern Times.

44. "The Genealogy of Josiah Warren," in Martin, *Men Against the State,* appendix 2, 292–93. Dr. Warren then (1970) lived in St. Petersburg, Fla. (ibid., 292).

45. Warren, *Periodical Letter* 1 (May 1854): 14, and (Sept. 1854): 33–34.

46. George W. Warren, "Josiah Warren" [Evansville, Ind., 1893], unpaginated typescript, Warren MSS, Workingmen's Institute Library, New Harmony, Ind.).

47. The Rappites were Pietist dissenters from German Lutheran orthodoxy. Led by George Rapp and his adopted son and business manager, Frederick, they came from Württemberg to Pennsylvania during the first decade of the nineteenth century, there to await the Millennium. They moved to Indiana, prospered by making wine to drink and whiskey (and other products) to sell, and returned to Pennsylvania, where they grew old and rich, survived the turn of the century, and dissolved with a distribution of assets among the few remaining members. The best studies of the Harmonists, or Rappites, are by Karl J. R. Arndt: *A Documentary History of the Indiana Decade of the Harmony Society, 1814–1824,* 2 vols. (Indianapolis: Indiana Historical Society, 1975): *George Rapp's Harmony Society, 1785–1847,* rev. ed., Rutherford, N.J.: Fairleigh Dickinson Univ. Press, 1972; and *George Rapp's Successors and Material Heirs, 1847–1916* (Rutherford, N.J.: Fairleigh Dickinson Univ. Press, 1972). For Robert Owen and New Harmony, see John F. C. Harrison, *Quest for the New Moral World: Robert Owen and the Owenites in Britain and America* (New York: Charles Scribner's Sons,

1969); Bestor, *Backwoods Utopias;* "Proceedings of the Preliminary Society and Minutes of the Convention for Forming a Constitution for the Society at New Harmony, 1825–1826," New Harmony MSS, Workingmen's Institute Library; and *The New-Harmony Gazette,* New Harmony, Ind., 1825–1828. A recent study of Harmony and New Harmony is Anne Taylor, *Visions of Harmony: A Study in Nineteenth-Century Millenarianism* (Oxford, U.K.: Clarendon Press, 1987).

48. Robert Owen's address to the pioneers of New Harmony, delivered 12 Apr. and published 1 Oct. 1825 in the first issue of the community's organ, the *New-Harmony Gazette.*

49. Ibid.

50. Warren, *Periodical Letter* 2 (July 1856): 55.

51. Owen's associate William Maclure assembled the "boatland of brains" in 1826. Maclure, a Scottish businessman who made enough money to retire from work in his middle age, became an American citizen concerned with geological research and the promotion of Pestalozzian (progressive) educational methods in his adopted country. To make New Harmony a nucleus for experimentation in every field, he recruited the zoologist Thomas Say, the naturalist Charles LeSueur, the ichthyologist Constantine Rafinesque, and the Pestalozzians Joseph Neef, Phiquepal d'Arusmont, and Madame Marie Fretageot. Most of these intellectuals remained in New Harmony after the collapse of the first community, as did Robert Owen's sons William, Richard, David Dale, and Robert Dale Owen, to whom their father deeded his holdings after returning to Britain for thirty more years of campaigning for political and economic reform. Another New Harmonyite, if only briefly, was the free-spirited Frances "Fanny" Wright, the Scottish-born fighter for the rights of women, labor, and victims of slavery. For Robert Owen and socialism, see the discussion in chap. 7.

52. Labor notes, suggested for Owen in 1820, were first used in 1826 by New Harmony's "three independent communities . . . a School or Educational Society, an Agricultural and Pastoral Society, and a Mechanic and Manufacturing Society . . . [which] traded with one another by labor notes" (Bestor, *Backwoods Utopias,* 184–85; see also Harrison, *Quest for the New Moral World,* 202. For Warren's Mechanical College, see chap. 3 below.

53. Warren, *Periodical Letter* 2 (July 1856): 56.

54. Noyes, *History of American Socialisms,* 94.

55. George W. Warren, "Josiah Warren," 4. The land in the heart of downtown Cincinnati stretched from Elm to John Streets, between Fifth and Ninth.

56. William Bailie, *Josiah Warren, the First American Anarchist: A Sociological Study* (Boston: Small, Maynard & Company, 1906), 23–24.

57. Alexander Bryan Johnson, *A Treatise on Language* (New York: G & C Carvill, 1828).

58. *Peaceful Revolutionist* 1 (5 Apr. 1833): 13.

59. Warren, *Practical Details,* 92–93.

60. George B. Lockwood, *The New Harmony Communities* (Marion, Ind.: The Chronicle Co., 1902), 298. The press "was capable of striking off from forty to sixty copies per minute, an achievement in printing never heard of or imagined" (George W. Warren, "Josiah Warren," 5).

61. George L. Kubler, *History of Stereotyping* (Brooklyn: Brooklyn Eagle Commercial Printing Division, 1927), 301. Patent #4479, signed by Secretary of State James Buchanan, is in the Warren MSS, Workingmen's Institute Library. Specimens of Warren's stereotyping and printing are in the Institute's collection; printing equipment made by Warren is on display at the Old Print Shop in the Historic New Harmony complex.

62. The firm consisted of the Fowler brothers – Lorenzo and Orson – and Samuel Wells (one of the two defaulting charter buyers at Modern Times). Their prime interests were phrenology and spiritualism, but they also "undertook the dissemination of a series of modest volumes which brought the core of native American anarchist thought before a sizeable cross-section of the nation's reading public" (Martin, *Men Against the State*, 71). Orson Fowler's avocation was architecture, especially the design and construction of octagon houses (see Walter Creese, "Fowler and the Domestic Octagon," *Art Bulletin* 28 [June 1846]: 89–102). Two octagons, both standing, were built at Modern Times: the schoolhouse, now on the high-school grounds, and the home of William and Jenny Dame, on present-day Brentwood Avenue, now a residence of the Sisters of St. Joseph.

63. *Circular*, City of Modern Times, Long Island, N.Y., Sept. 1852, in Andrews, Preface to Warren, *Practical Details*, viii.

64. Martin, *Men Against the State*, 48.

65. Warren, *Peaceful Revolutionist* II (May 1848): 1. For Owenite and Fourierist concepts and examples of community organization, see Noyes, *History of American Socialisms*, 181–232, and passim. For Fourier's philosophy, see *Harmonian Man: Selected Writings of Charles Fourier*, ed. Mark Poster (Garden City, N.Y.: Doubleday, 1971), and *The Utopian Vision of Charles Fourier*, eds. Jonathan Beecher and Richard Bienvenu (Boston: Beacon Press, 1971); and Ralph Waldo Emerson, "Fourierism and the Socialists," *Dial* 3 (July 1842): 86–89.

66. Warren, *Practical Details*, 115.

67. Ibid.

68. Codman, "Modern Times," 17; free love is the subject of chap. 4 below.

69. Caroline Cutter Warren to Josiah Warren, 21 Oct. 1855, Josiah Warren Papers, Labadie Collection. Univ. of Michigan Library, Ann Arbor.

70. Caroline Cutter Warren to Josiah Warren. These lines, written 21 August, were on p. 8 of a multiply-dated letter begun 20 July and finished 24 August 1856. Labadie Collection, Michigan.

71. Warren to Andrews, 5 Jan. 1852, Warren MSS, Workingmen's Institute Library.

72. Warren to Andrews, 9 Jan. 1852, John Ishill Collection, Houghton Library, Harvard Univ., Cambridge, Mass.

73. Warren to Andrews, 31 Mar. 1852, Ishill Collection, Harvard.

74. Warren to Andrews, 28 Apr. 1852, Ishill Collection, Harvard.

75. Warren to Andrews, 4 July 1852, Ewing Cannon Baskette Collection on Freedom of Expression, Univ. of Illinois Library, Urbana-Champaign, Ill.

76. Bailie, *Josiah Warren*, 97–98. The Metcalf sisters were Jane and Sarah: the "Kate" who nursed Warren is either a third sister, not counted in the 1860 census,

or the nickname for one of the others. For Warren's reasons for leaving Modern Times, see chap. 9 below.

77. The best study of Andrews is Madeleine B. Stern, *The Pantarch: A Biography of Stephen Pearl Andrews* (Austin: Univ. of Texas Press, 1968); see also Harvey Wish, "Stephen Pearl Andrews, American Pioneer Sociologist," *Social Forces* 19 (May 1941): 447–82. For Universology, see Stephen Pearl Andrews, *The Basic Outline of Universology. An Introduction to the Newly Discovered Science of the Universe; Its Elementary Principles, and the First Stages of That Development in the Special Sciences* (New York: Dion Thomas, 1872). For Alwato, the precursor of Esperanto, see Stern; a letter by Andrews in Alwato appears on p. 145.

78. Stern, *The Pantarch*, 87.

79. Ibid., 87–90.

80. Ibid., 93–95.

81. John Townsend Trowbridge, "A Reminiscence of the Pantarch," *The Independent* 58 (26 Feb. 1903): 499. Trowbridge thought Andrews was sane and—give or take human foibles—sincere, "but a colossal egotist and sterile pedant" (501). To George E. Macdonald, a rationalist editor, Andrews was a man of vast learning, "very strong on social freedom" (George E. Macdonald, *Fifty Years of Free Thought: Being the Story of the Truth Seeker, with the Natural History of Its Third Edition* [New York: The Truth Seeker Co., 1929], 406).

82. Trowbridge, "A Reminiscence of the Pantarch," 500.

83. For Andrews and *Woodhull and Claflin's Weekly*, see Emanie Sachs, [pseud.], *"The Terrible Siren": Victoria Woodhull (1838–1927)*, New York: Harper & Brothers, 1928), passim; for Andrews, the Claflin sisters, and the First International, see Charles Shively, introduction to Stephen Pearl Andrews, *Love, Marriage, and Divorce, and The Sovereignty of the Individual: A Discussion between Henry James, Horace Greeley and Stephen Pearl Andrews, and a Hitherto Unpublished Manuscript, Love, Marriage, and the Condition of Woman by Stephen Pearl Andrews* (1853; reprint, Weston, Mass.: M & S Press, 1975), 9; for Victoria Woodhull's public endorsement of free love, see n.55, in chap. 4 below.

84. G. Macdonald, *Fifty Years of Free Thought*, 1:181–82; the freethinkers' recommendation was modified to exempt "a limited amount of church property" (182).

85. Codman, "Modern Times," 7.

3. HOMES FOR THE HOMELESS

1. *Liber of Deeds, Town of Islip* 59:288, Office of the Suffolk County Clerk, Riverhead, N.Y.

2. Remarks attributed to William Metcalf by "B. D. J.," *New York Sunday Dispatch*, 9 Oct. 1853, in A. J. Macdonald, "Materials for a History of Ideal Communities" (New Haven: The Yale Collection of American Literature, Beinecke Rare Book and Manuscript Library, Yale Univ.), 138. After Macdonald died, in 1854, John Humphrey Noyes acquired the manuscript, made it the foundation for his *History of American Socialisms*, and then gave it to Yale, his alma mater, in 1870.

3. For Mary A. Andrews's purchase of lot 139, see *Liber of Deeds* 83: 303; on 3 Apr. 1855 she sold it to Emily Baxter, a Modern Timer from Boston (*Liber* 83:322).

4. The record date of Kellogg's purchase from Catherine Fleet (*Liber of Deeds* 77: 336, 4 Apr. 1851), is 13 June 1854, the record date of Andrews's and Warren's deeds. It is tempting to infer that this was Edward Kellogg, the currency reformer who became the posthumous father of Greenbackism, but as far as I can ascertain he had no middle initial.

5. Dyson, *A Century of Brentwood*, 47, 157; for Hayward's sale of his third lot to Thomas Low Nichols and his wife Mary Gove Nichols, see chap. 4 below.

6. Ibid.

7. *Liber of Deeds* 302:16.

8. Greeley's seven lots are in *Liber of Deeds* 77:342; for the debate on love, marriage, and divorce, between Andrews, Greeley, and Henry James, Sr., see chap. 4 below.

9. Greeley was treasurer of the Sylvania Association (Phalanx) in the present town of Greeley, Pike County, Pa.; Sylvania, organized in New York City in 1842, broke up two years later. The North American Phalanx, near Red Bank, N.J. also originated in New York City, with Greeley as vice-president and a stockholder; this largest of Fourierist communities lasted from 1843 until it petered out after a fire almost destroyed it in 1854. Greeley had friendly relations with Brook Farm (discussed in chap. 8 below), which, after evolving from Transcendental to Fourierist ideology in 1844, suffered a ruinous fire two years later, resulting in its demise. Noyes shrewdly attributes the collapse of Associationism to Fourier's "devotion to theory [and] Brisbane's . . . devotion to propagandism," both at the expense of execution. One well-realized example of Fourierism would do "infinitely more for the cause than all his [Brisbane's] translations and publications" (Noyes, *History of American Socialisms*, 249–50). However, no Phalanx came close to enjoying the requisites prescribed by Fourier – three-square-mile acreage, 1,680 settlers, and $100,000 invested capital.

10. Horace Greeley, "Land Reform," in *Hints Toward Reform, in Lectures, Addresses, and Other Writings* (New York: Fowlers & Wells, 1853), 317. For Greeley's campaign for land reform and the Homestead Act (finally enacted in 1862) see Roy M. Robbins, "Horace Greeley: Land Reform and Unemployment, 1837–1862," *Agricultural History* 7 (1933): 18–41; see also *Our Landed Heritage: The Public Domain, 1776–1970* (Lincoln: Univ. of Nebraska Press, 1976), 112–14, and passim.

11. Horace Greeley, *New York Daily Tribune*, 28 Dec. 1849 and 6 May 1852, cited in Robins, *Our Landed Heritage*, 108.

12. *Liber of Deeds* 77:342, 5 Apr. 1851. In his autobiography Greeley kept mum about buying land at Modern Times. His 1851 reference closest to this date concerns his leaving New York for Europe on board "the staunch American steamship *Baltic* . . . on the 11th of April" (Horace Greeley, *Recollections of A Busy Life* [1868; reprint, Port Washington, N.Y.: Kennikat Press, 1971], 1:270.

13. Warren, *Practical Applications*, 17.

14. Codman, "Modern Times," 4; Warren, *Practical Applications*, 17.

15. Codman, "Modern Times," 4–5.

16. Henry Edger, London *Leader* 3 (27 Mar. 1852): 299.

17. Codman, "Modern Times," 25.

18. "A Card—To the Public," *New York Tribune*, 4 Apr. 1853. Gray was a close associate of Warren's; Leland was Andrews's colleague in phonography, the term for the Isaac Pitman method of shorthand that Andrews brought from England and promoted in the United States.

19. *Liber of Deeds* 75:38.

20. *Liber of Deeds* 87:118.

21. Codman, "Modern Times," 18.

22. Edger, *Leader*, 299.

23. Warren, *Periodical Letter* 4 (Nov. 1854): 59–60.

24. B. D. J., *Sunday Dispatch*, 138.

25. *Circular*, City of Modern Times, Long Island, N.Y., Sept. 1852, in Andrews, Preface to Warren, *Practical Details*, viii. The sovereigns did not shrink from admitting that some couples were not married. For the relationship between Jane Cran and Josiah Warren, see chap. 2 above.

26. Ibid., vii–viii.

27. Edger, *Leader* 4 (8 Jan. 1853): 32.

28. Warren, *Periodical Letter* 1 (Dec. 1854): 69.

29. The retrospective observations on "cranks, faddists, and other bizarre 'professed friends'" are from Warren, *Practical Applications*, 17–20.

30. Codman, "Modern Times," 21; William J. Gaynor, *Brooklyn Eagle*, 5 June 1904. For Dame's purchase of three acres (he bought a fourth on 24 Dec. 1855), see *Liber of Deeds* 88:331.

31. For the Blackers, see Dyson, *Century of Brentwood*, passim; for Eleanor Blacker's interest in the Religion of Humanity, see the section on Henry Edger in chap. 9 below.

32. Codman, "Modern Times," 23, 3. See *Liber of Deeds* 82:362, for Codman's purchase of lot 156 on Sixth Street between Second and Third Avenues. For Charles and Ada Codman's divorce, and Charles's subsequent marriage to Emily Studley, see chap. 4 below. Charles A.'s cousin from Dorchester, Charles H. Codman, came to Modern Times in 1859 and bought lot 130 (*Liber of Deeds* 103:445). No record remains of "cousin Charlie's" involvement; he probably returned to Dorchester after selling his Modern Times property eight years later (*Liber of Deeds* 147:287).

33. Dyson, *Century of Brentwood*, 52. Gibson died in 1898, forty-eight years after contracting tuberculosis and forty-four years after coming to Modern Times. He and a score of the sovereigns are buried at Brentwood Cemetery, Madison Avenue, Brentwood, N.Y.

34. Charles A. Codman was not the last survivor of Modern Times. He passed away on 28 July 1911, at the age of eighty-four, but Jenny Dame lived a few weeks longer, dying when she was seventy-four, on 15 Sept. Codman, his second wife Emily, his father, and William and Jenny Dame and their two daughters are buried in Brentwood Cemetery.

35. Codman, "Modern Times," 13.

36. *Census of the State of New York for 1855*, Albany, 1855. (Millwood, N.Y.: KTO Microform, 1948), fiche A267, card 1.

37. Manuscript Census of Population, Town of Islip, Suffolk County, New York, *Eighth Census of the United States, 1860* (Washington, NARS Microfilm, 1967), reel 865:68–70. For details, see chap. 6 below.

38. Warren, *Practical Letter* 1 (Feb. 1855): 99.

39. "Remarks of Edward F. Linton at the Village Cemetery at Brentwood, Long Island, 'Decoration Day,' May 30th, 1905," in *1855 – Fifty Years After at Brentwood, Long Island, May 30th 1905* (Brooklyn: Eagle Press, 1905), unpaginated.

40. Census of Population, Town of Islip, 1860.

41. Dyson, *A Century of Brentwood*, 47.

42. Codman, "Modern Times," 24.

43. Warren, *Periodical Letter* 1 (Sept. 1854): 43.

44. Ibid., 44–45.

45. Codman, "Modern Times," 11–12. Newberry's cane, which doubled as a medicine case, and his striking paintings of heads are among the memorabilia in the Modern Times Collection, Brentwood Public Library.

46. Ibid. John Humphrey Noyes coined the pre-eugenics word *stirpiculture* for his method of "scientific propagation" by members of the Oneida Community (covered in chap. 4 below). "The time will come," wrote Noyes, "when random and involuntary procreation will cease, and when scientific combination will be applied to human generation as freely and successfully as it is to animals" (cited in Maren Lockwood Carden, *Oneida: Utopian Community to Modern Corporation* [1969; reprint, New York: Harper & Row, 1971], 61). Because of the limited number of subjects, stirpiculture at Oneida was less systematic than Newberry's union of opposites; a committee decided which Oneida Community members should mate to breed superior children (Carden, ibid., 61–65; see also Lawrence Foster, *Religion and Sexuality: Three American Communal Experiments of the Nineteenth Century* [New York: Oxford Univ. Press, 1981], 118–19).

47. Codman, "Modern Times," 11–12.

48. The Nicholses were long departed from Modern Times at the time of the 1860 census – for their brief but implosive stay see chap. 4 below. For the water-cure see Thomas Low Nichols, *Esoteric Anthology (The Mysteries of Man): A Comprehensive and Confidential Treatise On the Structure, Functions, Passional Attractions, and Perversions, True and False Physical and Social Conditions, and the Most Intimate Relations of Men and Women* (1853; reprint, New York: Arno Press, 1972), 206–24.

49. Sarah Josepha Hale, *Woman's Record, or, Sketches of All Distinguished Women, from the Creation to A.D. 1848* (New York: Harper & Brothers, 1855), 756–61. For Thomas Low Nichols and more on Mary Gove, see chap. 4 below.

50. B. D. J., *Sunday Dispatch*, 138.

51. Codman to Edger, 28 Dec. 1858, in Edward Schneider, *Positivism in the United States: The Apostleship of Henry Edger* (Rosario, Argentina: the author, 1946), 251–53.

52. See George S. McWatters, ed., *Detectives of Europe and America, or Life in the Secret Service, A Collection of Celebrated Cases in Great Britain, France, Germany, Italy, Spain, Russia, Poland, Egypt, and America* (Hartford, Conn.: J. B. Burr, 1881), 25, 29. George S. McWatters and his wife, Charlotte M. McWatters, are buried in Brentwood cemetery.

53. Bailie, *Josiah Warren*, 78.

54. Codman, "Modern Times," 15.

55. Warren, *Periodical Letter* 1 (Sept. 1854): 35.

56. Ibid., 5.

57. Ibid.

58. Dyson, *A Century of Brentwood*, 52.

59. Codman, "Modern Times," 25.

60. *Liber of Deeds* 102:321.

61. Josiah Warren, handbill, 10 Dec. 1842, Warren MSS, Workingmen's Institute Library.

62. Codman, "Modern Times," 20.

63. Facsimile labor-for-labor note, Modern Times Collection, Brentwood Public Library, Brentwood, N.Y. Original notes are in the Modern Times Collection of the Suffolk County Historical Society, Riverhead, N.Y.

64. Mark Holloway, *Heavens On Earth: Utopian Communities in America 1680–1880* (New York: Dover Publications, 1966), 137.

65. Warren, *Peaceful Revolutionist* 2 (May 1848): 6, in A. J. Macdonald, "Ideal Communities," 137.

66. Harrison, *Robert Owen*, 207.

67. Warren, *Peaceful Revolutionist* 2 (May 1848): 6, in A. J. Macdonald, "Ideal Communities," 133.

68. Warren, *Practical Details*, 89.

69. Josiah Warren, *Modern Education* (Thompson P.O., Long Island: the author, Dec. 1861), 1.

70. Ibid., 1–2.

71. Codman, "Modern Times," 18.

72. Ibid., 8.

73. "Minute Book of School District 12," Office of Superintendent of Schools, Brentwood, N.Y. Because the book is unpaginated, I hereinafter cite meetings in the text by their dates.

74. *Liber of Deeds* 89:259, 261.

75. Codman, "Modern Times," 17.

76. Ibid., 18, a note inserted in Codman's memoir by Dr. William H. Ross.

77. Andrews, never a resident, did not attend school meetings. Ironically, his longest stay was in 1885, the year before he died, when he spent several weeks at Codman's home attempting to recover from bladder trouble. In a letter to Edger, Codman reported reading to Andrews "your Manuscript of proposed League of All Religions and he says it meets his cordial approval" (Schneider, *Henry Edger*, 208; see also Stern, *The Pantarch*, 149). Andrews died 21 May 1886, at the age of seventy-four.

78. Census of Islip, 1860, 68–70.

4. MARRIAGE AND FREE LOVE

1. Louis J. Kern, *An Ordered Love: Sex Roles and Sexuality in Victorian Utopias— the Shakers, the Mormons, and the Oneida Community* (Chapel Hill: Univ. of North

Carolina Press, 1981), 5. See also Lawrence Foster, *Religion and Sexuality*, 15–20 and passim.

2. "Mr. Warren has a great repugnance to being *represented* by or held responsible for others. He is an individual and scarcely ever uses the personal pronoun plural" (Thomas Low Nichols, "Individuality–Protest of Mr. Warren–Relations of the Sexes," *Nichols' Journal of Health, Water-Cure, and Human Progress* 1 (Oct. 1853): 52. Even while battling with Warren over marital practice at Modern Times, the Nicholses respected his unyielding individualism, much as Warren always spoke highly of Robert Owen, with whose top-down style of leadership he completely disagreed.

3. Noyes, *American Socialisms*, 638, 624.

4. Carden, *Oneida*, 16.

5. John Humphrey Noyes, "History of the Battle Axe Letter," *Oneida Circular* 11 (24 Aug. 1874), 276–77, cited in Taylor Stoehr, *Free Love in America: A Documentary History* (New York: AMS Press, 1979), 497–99. The correct name of the paper published in Philadelphia by Theophilus Gates was *The Battle-Axe and Weapons of War*.

6. Foster, *Religion and Sexuality*, 82.

7. Noyes, *American Socialisms*, 626.

8. Matt. 5:48, 19:21.

9. Carden, *Oneida*, 15.

10. Ibid., 4.

11. Noyes, *American Socialisms*, 628, 625.

12. Carden, *Oneida*, 63.

13. Kern, *An Ordered Love*, 237; Carden, *Oneida*, 51; see also G. J. Barker-Benfield, "The Spermatic Economy and Proto-Sublimation," in *The Horrors of the Half-Known Life: Male Attitudes Toward Women and Sexuality in Nineteenth-Century America* (New York: Harper & Row, 1976), 175–88.

14. Kern, *An Ordered Love*, 217.

15. Noyes, *American Socialisms*, 638–40.

16. Carden, *Oneida*, 106.

17. Kern, *Ordered Love*, 239.

18. Foster, *Religion and Sexuality*, 85.

19. Carden, *Oneida*, 61–62.

20. George Stearns, in William S. Heywood, "Modern Times," *Practical Christian*, 9 Oct. 1852, 3. *Art of Living* is not preserved; the George Stearns who went to Modern Times should not be mistaken for the abolitionist George L. Stearns.

21. Adin Ballou, *History of the Hopedale Community, From Its Inception to Its Virtual Submergence in the Hopedale Parish* (1897; reprint, Philadelphia: Porcupine Press, 1972), 241, 247.

22. Ibid., 248–49.

23. Ibid., 249.

24. "Christian Chastity," *Practical Christian* 14 (16 July 1853), 3.

25. Stephen Pearl Andrews, *Love, Marriage, and Divorce, and the Sovereignty of the Individual: A Discussion between Henry James, Horace Greeley, and Stephen Pearl Andrews, and a Hitherto Unpublished Manuscript–Love, Marriage, and the Condition of*

Woman by Stephen Pearl Andrews (1853; reprint, with an Introduction by Charles Shively, Weston, Mass.: M & S Press, 1975).

26. Victor Hennequin, *Love in the Phalanstery*, trans. and preface by Henry James, Sr. (New York: Dewitt and Davenport, 1849); for a summary, followed by a selection, see Stoehr, *Free Love*, 393–403. Phalanstery, or Phalanx, was Fourier's term for an ideal village of 1,800 people, organized in groups and series to carry on the community's work. James's translation at first was anonymous, but his style was too familiar to escape recognition.

27. Marx Edgeworth Lazarus, *Love vs. Marriage* (New York: Fowlers & Wells, 1852).

28. Lazarus, *Love vs. Marriage*, 159, quoted by Charles Shively, in his Preface to *Love, Marriage, and Divorce* by Stephen Pearl Andrews, 3. Authors for the *Phalanx* (its earlier name) and the *Harbinger*—the weekly newspaper edited by George Ripley that was the organ of Brook Farm until its demise in 1847—included Lazarus (52 articles), James (32), Ripley (315), Greeley (2), and Andrews (1) [a list compiled by Noyes, *American Socialisms*, 212].

29. For the connection between Victorian sexual mentality and the accumulative phase of capitalism in England and the United States, see Steven Marcus, *The Other Victorians—A Study of Sexuality and Pornography in Mid-Nineteenth-Century England* (1966; reprint, London: Transworld, 1969); see also G. J. Barker-Benfield's discussion of the "spermatic economy" (*The Horrors of the Half-Known Life*, 175–88).

30. Shively, Introduction to Andrews, *Love, Marriage, and Divorce*, 2 (the excerpts quoted by Shively are from Albert Brisbane, *Social Destiny of Man*, [Philadelphia: C. W. Stollmeyer, 1840]), 175, 145, 333).

31. Ibid., 3, citing Lazarus, *Love vs. Marriage*, 236.

32. Lazarus, *Love vs. Marriage*, in Stoehr, *Free Love in America*, 85.

33. Lazarus, quoted by Stoehr, *Free Love in America*, 78. Lazarus believed in Fourierist collectives more than in the do-it-yourself reliance of communities of equity commerce. He argued that woman will never know freedom "save in the large home, the varied and attractive industry of the Phalanx." There she can mingle with friends as she moves among thirty occupations each month, and enjoy the "real charm of maternity" with the assistance of "unitary nurseries," in which children are cared for tenderly "either in the presence or the absence of the mother" (ibid., 85).

34. People would rather indulge in love or other pleasures than in work: "On the one hand love comes into opposition to the interests of civilization; on the other, civilization threatens love with substantial restrictions" (Sigmund Freud, *Civilization and Its Discontents* [New York: W. W. Norton, 1962], 50).

35. Shively, Introduction to Andrews, *Love, Marriage, and Divorce*, 3.

36. Andrews, *Love, Marriage and Divorce*, 36, 35.

37. Ibid., 54.

38. Codman, "Modern Times," 16.

39. For the critiques of George Ripley and Adin Ballou, see chap. 7 below.

40. Andrews, *Love, Marriage, and Divorce*, 24, 25.

41. Ibid., 39.

42. Ibid., 31–33.

43. Ibid., 44, 45.

44. Ibid., 46.

45. Ibid., 48.

46. Ibid., 40.

47. Ibid., 28.

48. Shively, Introduction to Andrews, *Love, Marriage, and Divorce,* 7.

49. Greeley, cited in Stoehr, *Free Love,* 91.

50. Andrews, *Love, Marriage, and Divorce,* 72. The practice of abortion was at a high level, not only to prevent illegitimacy but as a means for women to control the number and frequency of their children. In her history of birth control in the United States, Linda Gordon cites Thomas Low Nichols as a source for data on the frequency of infanticide in mid-nineteenth-century urban America. Nichols, writing in the 1860s, "speculated that the huge amounts of laudanum being sold were used not just to quiet crying children but also to kill infants painlessly" (Thomas Low Nichols, *Human Physiology: The Basis of Sanitary and Social Science* [London: Trübner, 1872], 21–27, as summarized in Linda Gordon, *Woman's Body, Woman's Rights: A Social History of Birth Control in America* (New York: Grossman Publishers, 1976), 51.

51. Andrews, *Love, Marriage, and Divorce,* 71.

52. Edgar Allan Poe, "The Literati of New York City," *Godey's Magazine and Lady's Book* (July 1856), 16. Mary Gove wrote a perceptive account of her visits to Poe at his Fordham cottage, including impressions of his wife, mother-in-law, and friends (*Reminiscences of Edgar Allan Poe* [New York: Six Penny Magazine, Feb. 1863; reprint, New York: Union Square Bookshop, 1931].

53. Mary Sargeant Gove Nichols, *Mary Lyndon, or, Revelations of a Life: An Autobiography* (New York: Stringer & Townsend, 1855), 343–44, 384, 388.

54. Janet Hubly Noever, "Passionate Rebel: The Life of Mary Gove Nichols, 1810–1884" (Ph.D. diss., Univ. of Oklahoma, 1983), 8.

55. Stoehr, *Free Love,* 9. Fanny Wright, the dynamic Scots-born reformer, briefly associated with Warren at New Harmony, and again in 1830, when, with Robert Dale Owen, they planned to transfer the New Harmony newspaper to New York City, only to cease operations when Owen withdrew to handle a family problem. Wright opposed "'the tyranny usurped by the matrimonial law' [but never] came out as a free lover in public" (ibid., 4). Victoria Woodhull was the most flaming free lover of all, exemplified by her 1871 declaration: "Yes! I am a free lover! I have an inalienable, constitutional, and natural right to love whom I may, to love as long or as short a period as I can, to change that love every day if I please" (Sachs, *"The Terrible Siren,"* 135). The author of this famous speech was probably Stephen Pearl Andrews, but, as Emanie Sachs observes, "if some of the light was . . . Andrews', all of the heat was hers [Victoria Woodhull's]" (ibid., 139). After tempestuous careers as free lovers and radicals, Victoria and her sister, Tennessee Claflin, each married a wealthy Englishman and spent the second half of her life in England as a dignified matron.

56. Ellen Lazarus Allen was a Brook Farmer, as was her father. She became the second wife of the Rev. John Allen, the Universalist minister who was one of the

Farm's leaders and traveling spokesmen. Years after his death, she moved to Modern Times with her four young children, where she was one of Henry Edger's few converts to the Religion of Humanity. After Modern Times became Brentwood, she remarried and, after experiencing Judaism, Universalism, and the Positivist faith, she completed her religious metamorphosis by becoming a staunch Episcopalian (see chap. 9 below).

57. The *Tribune* editorial paragraph, the letter from "A Villager," and Thomas Low Nichols's rebuttal are from "Calumny," an article in *Nichols' Journal* 1 (Sept. 1853): 44.

58. The one hundred acres of "arable and fertile land" noted in *Nichols' Journal* 1 (July 1853): 31, were not the "free gift" of Andrews. The Nicholses paid him the $2,400 cost (*Liber of Deeds* 70:304), with the help of a $2,000 mortgage (*Liber of Mortgages* 44:175, Office of the Suffolk County Clerk, Riverhead, N.Y.), on which they defaulted after they left Modern Times. A lawsuit against them was settled by the payment of the debt by Valentine Nicholson, of Cincinnati, the publisher of the Nicholses' marriage manual (1854) and of Thomas L. Nichols' utopian novel of free love, *Esperanza* (1860). After paying Mary Gove Nichols (only her name was on the deed) the token sum of $1 on 3 Feb. 1855 (*Liber of Deeds* 84:542), Nicholson sold the land to Elizabeth Phelps on 5 May 1856 for only $700 (*Liber of Deeds* 99:450; the $1,300 difference may be a loss taken by Nicholson as a consideration for royalties owed to T. L. Nichols). The Nicholses also defaulted on the Modern Times cottage they bought from William Hayward, on lot 77, at Fifth Street and Third Avenue (*Liber of Deeds* 46:51). When they failed to pay a $100 installment, with interest, on the $400 mortgage held by Hayward, the latter obtained a judgment and sold the property at public auction on 19 Jan. 1856 (*Liber of Deeds* 49:149). The 24 Oct. 1855 date of the judgment is proof that the Nicholses lived at Modern Times for a little more than two years.

59. Thomas L. Nichols, "The Water Cure Establishment at Port Chester," *Nichols' Journal* 1 (Sept. 1853): 44.

60. "To the World's Reformers," *Nichols' Journal* 1 (July 1853): 31.

61. "American Hydropathic Institute," *Nichols' Journal* 1 (Aug. 1853): 38.

62. "Institute of Desarrollo—A School for Life," *Nichols' Journal* 1 (Oct. 1853): 49; Codman, "Modern Times," 19.

63. Noyes, *American Socialisms*, 93.

64. Codman, "Modern Times," 16.

65. Robert Owen, "A Declaration of Mental Independence," *New-Harmony Gazette* 1, 12 July 1826, 330.

66. "City of Modern Times," *Nichols' Journal* 1 (Aug. 1853): 39.

67. Mary Gove Nichols, "The City of Modern Times," *Nichols' Journal* 1 (Aug. 1853): 15.

68. Josiah Warren, *Positions Defined* (Modern Times: the author, Aug. 1853).

69. Ibid.

70. Thomas Low Nichols and Mary S. Gove Nichols, "Marriage: Defining Positions," *Nichols Monthly* 1 (Jan. 1855): 31–32, in Stoehr, *Free Love*, 272. This statement in the first person within an article bylined by both of the Nicholses typified their constant mixing of "I" with "we." The article attacked the entrance into matrimony of one of its foremost enemies, Marx Edgeworth Lazarus. Lazarus, as the Nicholses,

lived up to the adage "Do as I say, not as I do." When he drafted Victoria Woodhull's ultra–free-love manifesto in 1872, Andrews may have remembered Mary Gove's endorsement of amorous variety.

71. Warren, *Periodical Letter* 1 (July 1854): 9, 13, two references to Thomas Low Nichols and Mary Gove Nichols, *Marriage: Its History, Character and Results: Its Sanctities and Its Profanities, Its Science and Its Facts Demonstrating Its Influence as a Civilized Institution, and the Happiness of the Individual and the Progress of the Race* (Cincinnati: Valentine Nicholson & Co., 1854).

72. Codman, "Modern Times," 7, 17.

73. Warren, *Practical Applications*, 24–25.

74. Bailie, *Josiah Warren*, 134.

75. "Individuality – Protest of Mr. Warren – Relations of the Sexes," *Nichols' Journal* 1 (Oct. 1853): 52.

76. See Bertha-Monica Stearns, "Memnonia: The Launching of a Utopia," *New England Quarterly* 15 (June 1942), 280–95.

77. Ibid., 294. This statement by "the former head of Memnonia" was a communication to *The New England Spiritualist*, 25 Apr. 1857, a periodical in which Nichols earlier had expressed his views on free thought, free speech, and free love.

78. Stoehr, *Free Love*, 51. Noyes commented that, in the same year of 1853 (the Nicholses' peak as sexual radicals), Dr. Nichols "published his 'Esoteric Anthropology' . . . and issued his printed catalogue of names for the reciprocal use of affinity-hunters all over the country" (Noyes, *American Socialisms*, 93, referring to Thomas Low Nichols, *Esoteric Anthropology (The Mysteries of Man): A Comprehensive and Confidential Treatise On the Structure, Functions, Passional Attractions, and Perversions, True and False Physical and Social Conditions, and the Most Intimate Relations of Men and Women* (1853; reprint, New York: Arno Press, 1972).

79. Neither of the Nicholses returned to the United States. After Mary died in 1884, Thomas continued to write, edit, and work for food reform and other causes. Toward the end of his life he moved to France, where he died in 1901 at the age of eighty-five. For the Nicholses in England, see Bernard Aspinwall, "Social Catholicism and Health: Dr. and Mrs. Thomas Low Nichols in Britain," in *The Church in Healing: Papers Read at the Twentieth Summer Meeting and the Twenty-First Winter Meeting of the Ecclesiastical History Society*, W. J. Sheils, ed. (Oxford: Basil Blackwell, 1982), 249–70.

80. Thomas Low Nichols, *Forty Years of American Life, 1821–1861* (1864; reprint, New York: Stackpole Sons, 1937), 241.

81. Warren, *Practical Applications*, 20.

82. Conway, "Modern Times," 425.

83. Ibid., 17.

84. B. D. J., *Sunday Dispatch*, in A. J. Macdonald, "Ideal Communities," 139.

85. Conway, "Modern Times," 427.

86. See *Liber of Deeds* 302:16, recording an 1887 transaction in which William and Sophia take part as Mr. and Mrs. Metcalf.

87. Richard M. Bayles, "History of Suffolk County," in *History of Suffolk County*,

New York, with Illustrations, Portraits, and Sketches of Prominent Families and Individuals (New York: W. W. Munsell, 1882), 72. An unanswered question is whether the Hyman Seaver who, in 1861, defeated Theron C. Leland for the office of clerk of School District 12 was related to "Sister" Seaver.

88. Codman, "Modern Times," 17.

89. Codman to Edger, 28 Dec. 1858, in Schneider, Appendix 3, 251 (see chap. 9 below for a thorough discussion of Edger).

90. Ibid.

91. *Liber of Deeds* 279:235–37. The $500 was put together as follows: the deed of a four-acre lot in Modern Times; E. D. Linton's mortgage of a sailboat; notes and due bills of Frank Blaisdell [Ada's brother] and E. D. Linton; the balance in cash and two promissory notes, payable Aug. 1859 and Aug. 1860.

92. *Liber of Deeds* 102:321, and *Liber* 114, 358. Myndert and Rebecca Fish were from Onondaga, N.Y.

93. *Liber of Deeds* 83:186.

94. Stoehr, *Free Love*, 333.

95. A selection from James Arrington Clay, *A Voice from the Prison, or, Truths for the Multitude, and Pearls for the Truthful, by James A. Clay, Written During His Confinement in Augusta (Me.) Jail* (Boston: Bela Marsh, 1856), in Stoehr, *Free Love*, 279.

96. Ibid., 278.

97. *Liber of Deeds* 88:94; for the sale deed see *Liber* 108:174.

98. Clay, *A Voice from the Prison*, 388.

99. *Liber of Deeds* 108:174.

100. Stoehr, *Free Love*, 332–33.

101. T. D. Seymour Bassett, "The Secular Utopian Socialists," in *Socialism and American Life*, eds. Donald Drew Egbert and Stow Persons (Princeton: Princeton Univ. Press, 1952), 1:200.

102. Andrews, *Love, Marriage, and Divorce*, 49.

103. Thomas Low Nichols and Mary Gove Nichols, "Marriage: Defining Positions," *Nichols Monthly* 1 (Jan. 1855), in Stoehr, *Free Love*, 272.

104. D. P. W., "Modern Times," *New York Weekly Leader*, 29 July 1854, cited in Schneider, *Henry Edger*, 49. Schneider found this article (from an otherwise unpreserved newspaper) clipped and inserted on p. 21 of Henry Edger's journal (see chap. 9 below).

105. Codman, "Modern Times," 22. In June 1853, Mary Gove Nichols reported that "for nearly two years I have worn the Bloomer dress [except] for rest, and for ornamental occasions, I like drapery—it is beautiful to me." Thousands of women converted to the new costume for "its usefulness and convenience": she would not resign her "comfortable walking dress (a house Bloomer) for any price." If women were to do anything "*worthful* they must have liberty to dress for the work." They have been "parasites so long that freedom is a stern, strange idea." She urged women with the strength and courage to "step out of their (so-called) sphere," and damn the conservatives—full speed ahead (Mary Gove Nichols, "Dress," *Nichols' Journal* 1 (May 1853): 13.

106. D. P. W., *New York Weekly Leader*, in Schneider, *Henry Edger*, 49–50. The

I. H. Cook mentioned by D. P. W. is probably James H. Cook – phrenologist, Fowlers & Wells employee, and sexual radical – who lived at Modern Times for six months in 1852 and four years later joined the free-love community of Berlin Heights, Ohio (see John C. Spurlock, *Free Love: Marriage and Middle-Class Radicalism in America, 1825–1860* (New York: New York Univ. Press, 1988), 124–25, 157.

    107. Schneider, Appendix 4, *Henry Edger,* 255–56. Devout freethinkers celebrated Tom Paine's birthday (29 Jan. 1737).

    108. Codman, "Modern Times," 21–22.

    109. See Barker-Benfield, "The Spermatic Economy," 175–88.

    110. Codman, "Modern Times," 15.

5. EQUITABLE COMMERCE

    1. Warren, *Practical Details,* 82.

    2. Andrews, Preface to Warren, *Practical Details,* vi.; Webster's 1861 *Dictionary* capitalized "Christian," but many contemporary writers did not, with no disrespect intended.

    3. Codman, "Modern Times," 14. There is no other hint of Shakers (most of whom lived in Shaker villages) at far-from-celibate Modern Times. The only known Quaker is Isaac Gibson.

    4. "Come-Outers" took their designation from Revelation 18:4: "And I heard another voice from heaven, saying, Come out of her, my people, that ye be not partakers of her sins, and that ye receive not of her plagues." "Her" was any church perceived by Come-Outers as acquiescent to slavery. James A. Clay was an anarchistic abolitionist of the Come-Outer brand. Andrews, Thomas and Mary Nichols, Edger, Leland, and other sovereigns were former Fourierists; Ellen Lazarus Allen, born in the Jewish religion, rotated from Fourierism at Brook Farm to Edger's Positivist church at Modern Times to active membership in the (post–Modern Times) Brentwood Episcopal Church, of which William Metcalf and Peter Blacker were founders (see chap. 9 below).

    5. "A Card – To the Public," *Tribune.* In his extensive interview in the *Sunday Dispatch,* Bowles never refers to his clerical background, which is unmentioned by any unobserver of Modern Times; perhaps he was an unordained lay preacher.

    6. G. Macdonald, *Fifty Years of Freethought* 1:231, 232, 303, 383–85. Macdonald married Grace Leland, the daughter of Mary Chilton and Theron C. Leland. Like William Metcalf and Sophia Hayward, and Charles Codman and Emily Studley, the Lelands cohabited at Modern Times before they married for life.

    7. *Suffolk County Certificates of Incorporation, Book B,* 100–101, Office of Suffolk County Clerk, Riverhead, N.Y. Only Metcalf and Blacker were Modern Timers; the five other incorporators lived in nearby communities.

    8. Codman, "Modern Times," 14.

    9. The innovative, influential *Fortnightly Review,* "a frank and self-confessed rebel in the world of periodicals," was the first English magazine to carry articles signed

by authors, an experiment launched by the founding editor, George Henry Lewes. Its policy was "to be impartial and absolutely honest, thoroughly eclectic, opening its columns to all opinions, without any pretensions in editorial consistency or harmony" (Walter Graham, *English Literary Periodicals* [1930; reprint, New York: Octagon Books, 1966], 258–60).

10. Conway, "Modern Times," 425–26.

11. Ibid., 426. The reference is to "Thespian Hall," a building probably named from Warren's recollection of New Harmony's "Thespian Club."

12. Ibid., 426.

13. Ibid., 426–27. Conway admired Emerson, whom he met while studying at Harvard Divinity School; Emerson influenced him to change his denomination from Methodist to Unitarian (before he switched again to become a Congregationalist minister).

14. Ibid., 427.

15. Ibid., 428.

16. Ibid.

17. Ibid., 429–30.

18. Ibid., 429.

19. B. D. J., *Sunday Dispatch,* in A. J. Macdonald, "Ideal Communities," 138.

20. Poster, *Charles Fourier,* 10.

21. Warren, *Peaceful Revolutionist* 2 (May 1848): 3.

22. B. D. J., *Sunday Dispatch,* 138.

23. Lewis Perry, *Radical Abolitionism: Anarchy and the Government of God in Antislavery Thought* (Ithaca: Cornell Univ. Press, 1973), 59.

24. For the impact of the war on Modern Times, and the names of its soldier sovereigns, see chap. 9 below.

25. B. D. J., *Sunday Dispatch,* in A. J. Macdonald, "Ideal Communities," 138.

26. John Locke, *Second Treatise of Government,* ed. C. B. Macpherson (Indianapolis: Hackett Publishing Co., 1980), 8.

27. B. D. J., *Sunday Dispatch,* in A. J. Macdonald, "Ideal Communities," 138.

28. Benjamin R. Tucker's "Explanatory" to his edition of Andrews's *The Science of Society* (Boston: Sarah E. Holmes, 1888) is included in the modern reprint of Andrews's 1852 work (Weston, Mass., M & S Press, 1970.

29. Andrews, *Science of Society,* 12.

30. Ibid., 10.

31. Ibid., 7.

32. Ibid., 10, 35.

33. Ibid., 11.

34. Ibid., 10.

35. Andrews, *Love, Marriage, and Divorce,* 9.

36. Andrews, *Science of Society,* 11.

37. Ibid., 22.

38. Poster, *Charles Fourier,* 40.

39. Warren, *Equitable Commerce,* 101–102, 103.

40. Andrews, *Science of Society*, 23.

41. Ibid.

42. Ibid., 38–39.

43. Ibid., 34.

44. Ibid., 27.

45. Ibid., 33.

46. Josiah Warren, *True Civilization An Immediate Necessity and the Last Ground of Hope for Mankind: Being the Results and Conclusions of Thirty-Nine Years' Laborious Study and Experiments in Civilization As It Is, and in Different Enterprises for Reconstruction* (Boston, 1863; reprint, New York: Burt Franklin, 1967), 169–70.

47. Andrews, *Science of Society*, 34.

48. Andrews, ibid., 24. See also Charles Codman's explanation for the choice of the name "Modern Times," cited above on the frontispiece.

49. Andrews, *Science of Society*, 24.

50. Ibid., 25.

51. His biographer comments that during the late 1870s Andrews taught Alwato at the Normal University of his Pantarchy (the ideal community in which he played the role of philosopher-king to a few devotees), but "to later generations inhabiting the modern Tower of Babel, Alwato was unfortunately consigned to the domain of the dead languages" (Stern, *The Pantarch*, 134).

52. Ibid., 28–29.

53. Micah 4:3–4.

54. Percy Bysshe Shelley, *Hellas. A Lyrical Drama* [1821], in *The Complete Poetical Works of Percy Bysshe Shelley* (Boston: Houghton Mifflin, 1974), 11. 1060–65.

55. Poster, *Charles Fourier*, 56, 39, 40, 55.

56. Ibid., 10.

57. Thomas Paine, *The Age of Reason* [1794–1795] in *The Selected Work of Tom Paine and Citizen Tom Paine*, ed. Howard Fast (New York: Modern Library, 1943), 290–91.

58. Ibid., 291.

59. Warren, *Periodical Letter* 1 (Aug. 1854): 29.

60. Warren, *True Civilization*, 144–45.

61. Thomas Paine, *Rights of Man* [1791–1792], in Fast, *Tom Paine*, 206.

62. Ibid., 155–56.

63. Thomas Paine, *The Age of Reason*, 330.

64. Thomas Paine, *Common Sense and The Crisis* (Garden City, N.Y.: Doubleday, 1960), 13, 59, 42.

65. Andrews, *Science of Society*, 39–40.

6. THE LONG ISLAND MILIEU

1. Nathaniel R. Howell, "History of Islip," in Bailey, *Long Island*, 1:324. The other eight towns, in order of formation, were Southold and Southampton (1640),

214 NOTES TO PAGES 110–12

East Hampton (1648), Shelter Island (1651), Huntington (1654), Brookhaven (1655), Smithtown (1663), and Riverhead (1791, originally part of Southold). The town of Babylon (which, like Islip, has no coast facing New England) split off from Huntington in 1872. The colonial government authorized a government for "the precincts of Islip" in 1710; a 1666 grant to the "European settlers of Setauket . . . for such lands as they might thereafter purchase" included what is now eastern Islip, but, although a few squatters may have come in, "no such purchase was ever made, and the land was afterward confirmed by patent to William Nicoll," who sent "one man or more to possess it . . . and became a permanent resident in 1701" ("The Town of Islip," in *History of Suffolk County, New York, with Illustrations, Portraits, and Sketches of Prominent Families and Individuals* [New York: W. W. Munsell & Co., 1882], 5).

2. Carl A. Starace, ed., *Book One of the Minutes of Town Meetings and Register of Animal Ear Marks of the Town of Islip 1720–1851* (Islip, N.Y.: Town of Islip, 1982), v. Dr. Abraham Gardiner Thompson, the squire of Sagtikos Manor during the lifetime of Modern Times, was a prominent physician, civic leader, assemblyman [1857], and landowner. His middle name indicates the Thompsons' linkage by marriage to the family whose American founder, Lion Gardiner, was the first English settler of Long Island (see Roger Wunderlich, "An Island of Mine Owne: The Life and Times of Lion Gardiner, 1599–1663," *Long Island Historical Journal* 2 (Fall 1989): 3–14). The historian and jurist Benjamin Franklin Thompson belonged to the same family.

3. Howell, "History of Islip Town," 324.

4. Bayles, *Suffolk County*, 196.

5. "The Town of Islip," in *History of Suffolk*, 6.

6. See Prime, *Long Island*, 1:78.

7. Ibid., 77.

8. Benjamin Franklin Thompson, *History of Long Island from Its Discovery and Settlement to the Present Time*, 3rd ed., rev. and enlarged with additions and a biography of the author of Charles J. Werner (New York: Robert H. Dodd, 1918 [completed by Thompson in 1849, the year of his death]), II:365.

9. Howell, "History of Islip Town," 317. Matthias, William Nicoll's father, spelled his surname Nicolls, according to surviving documents, several of which are in Brookhaven Town Hall (ibid., 319). Islip was granted in 1666 to the people of Setauket, but, except possibly for a few squatters, they took no action to claim it.

10. George L. Weeks, *"Isle of Shells" (Long Island)* (Islip: Buys Bros., Inc., 1965), 265. Beside Nicoll and Van Cortland, the patentees were Andrew Gibb, clerk of the Queens County Court, and a friend of William Nicoll's, for the land that now is the village of Islip; John Mowbray, a tailor (or teacher) of Southampton, for what is Bay Shore today; and the brothers Thomas and Richard Willet, a pair of Rhode Island Quakers, for the West Islip lands between Sagtikos Manor and Babylon.

11. Thompson, *History of Long Island*, 2:347.

12. "The Town of Islip," in *History of Suffolk*, 5.

13. Starace, *Town Meeting Minutes*, 18, 21, 22, 27. The spelling in this and other excerpts is as it appears in the original "Minutes of Town Meetings, 1720–1875" in Islip Town Hall, Islip, N.Y.). Not until 1821 were hogs in Islip prohibited from running

"on the common lands or public highways . . . under the penalty of fifty cents for every offence," to be applied "for the use of the poor of S^d town" (ibid., 83).

14. Ibid., 27.

15. Ibid., 10, 16, 47.

16. Ibid., 41, 43.

17. Sarah D. Gardiner, "The Sagtikos Manor 1697," 10.

18. Rosalie Fellows Bailey, "The Nicoll Family and Islip Grange: An Address Delivered before the Order of Colonial Lords of Manors in America, April 21, 1938, with Additions" (New York: Publications of the Order of Colonial Lords of Manors in America, 1940), 28, 29.

19. For Washington's diary of his trip, see Bayles, *Suffolk County*, 64–65.

20. Census of Population, Islip, *Eighth Census of U.S., 1860*, 68–70.

21. *Census of the State of New York for 1855*, Albany, 1857 (Millwood, N.Y.: KTO Microform, 1948), A267, xl.

22. Manuscript Schedule of Products of Industry, Town of Islip, Suffolk County, New York, *Eighth Census of U.S., 1860*, (Washington, NARS Microfilm, 1967), reel 686.

23. Ibid., 1–2. Scudder required only two pages for his census of industry.

24. Thompson, *History of Long Island* 2:359–60.

25. Judith Treistman, "What is a Bayman?" *Suffolk Maritime Folklife* (Hauppauge, N.Y.: Suffolk, County Maritime Folk Festival, 1981), unpaginated pamphlet.

26. Lawrence J. Taylor, *Dutchmen on the Bay: The Ethnohistory of a Contractual Community* (Philadelphia: Univ. of Pennsylvania Press, 1983), 69. The community of baymen (mainly oystermen) was itself a model village, in which residents shared ideals and objectives and lived in harmony as an extended family. The best place to learn about the bay folk from descendants of the Hollanders who came to Tuckertown, is the Suffolk Marine Museum, Suffolk County Park, West Sayville, N.Y.

27. Manuscript Schedule of Productions of Agriculture, Town of Islip, Suffolk County, New York, *Eighth Census of U.S., 1860*, reel 681.

28. The only servant at Modern Times in 1860 was Mary Giles, fifty-three years old, an English-born, illiterate employee of Ann Gliddon, a fifty-two-year-old widow from England who lived with her twin sister, Mary. This household of fiftyish Englishwomen played no apparent part in the affairs of Modern Times. Perhaps they purchased the property for reasons apart from ideology—such as climate, price, or friends.

29. Howell, "The Town of Islip," 324.

30. Prime, *Long Island*, 1:247–48.

31. French, *Gazetteer 1860*, 637.

32. Census of Islip, *Eighth Census of U.S., 1860*, reel 865. The four ministers were Henry Davis, Episcopal; Joseph Nimmo, Presbyterian; and Moses Bedell and Ralph Smith, Congregationalist.

33. Alson J. Smith, "Methodism on Long Island," in Bailey, *Long Island*, 2:110.

34. "The Town of Islip," in *History of Suffolk*, 7.

7. CRITICISM AND DEFENSE

1. John Van Der Zee Sears, *My Friends at Brook Farm* (New York: Desmond Fitzgerald, 1912), 148.

2. Raymond Williams, *Keywords: A Vocabulary of Culture and Society* (New York: Oxford Univ. Press, 1976), 239.

3. Harrison, *Quest for the New Moral World*, 46–47. Harrison's "science of society" is not an allusion to Andrews's book.

4. Acts 2:44–45, 4:32.

5. Richard T. Ely, *Recent American Socialism* (Baltimore: Johns Hopkins Univ., 1885), 11–12.

6. *Practical Christian* 11 (25 May 1850): 6. Cabet wrongly assumed that Hopedale was communist—the Practical Christians were joint-stock socialists. Cabet's authoritarian leadership caused a schism within his movement, which died out in spite of heroic efforts to cope with the hardships of frontier life. See "Icarian Community," in William A. Hinds, *American Communities* (1878; reprint, Secaucus, N.J.: Citadel Press, 1973), 62–80; see also "Icaria," in Mark Holloway, *Heavens on Earth: Utopian Communities in America 1680–1880* (New York: Dover, 1966), 198–211.

7. Carol Weisbrod, *The Boundaries of Utopia* (New York: Pantheon, 1980), 126–27.

8. Ibid., 209. The case is *Schriber v. Rapp,* 5 Watts (Pa.) 351 (1836).

9. Weisbrod, *Boundaries of Utopia,* 136.

10. Ibid., 137.

11. Ibid., xvii. In 1874, James W. Towner moved from the Berlin Heights, Ohio, free-love community to Oneida, where he led the faction that challenged such features of Noyes's dictatorial rule as his reluctance to share the role of "first husband" to virgins; the "Townerite" vs. "Noyesite" wrangling anticipated Oneida's breakup in 1879 (see Carden, *Oneida,* 100–101). Towner then moved to Southern California, where he became a superior court judge (Weisbrod, *Boundaries of Utopia,* 251–52; for Towner's article, "Decadence of Marriage," which Stoehr calls "a thumbnail history of free love in America," see Stoehr, *Free Love in America,* 510–13; for Towner's exchange of letters on the same subject with the Nicholses, see ibid., 469–77. For Towner's career, writes Weisbrod, "see Robert S. Fogarty, 'Nineteenth Century Utopian,' *Pacific Historian* 16 (Fall 1972): 70–76" (Weisbrod, 231).

12. Charles Nordhoff, *The Communistic Societies of the United States, from Personal Visit and Observation* (1875; reprint, New York: Dover Publications, 1966), and Noyes, *History of American Socialisms.*

13. Noyes, *History of American Socialisms,* 616.

14. Ibid., 3, 13.

15. The 1861 edition of Webster's *American Dictionary* defines *anarchism* in two words: "confusion, anarchy." An anarchist is "one who excites revolt, or promotes disorder in a state," and anarchy means "want of government; a state of society where there is no law or supreme power, or the laws are not efficient, and individuals do what they please with impunity; political confusion."

To "do what they please with impunity," though probably not a barb aimed specifically at Modern Times, nonetheless fit the caricature of the village sketched by critics of equitable commerce. George Ripley, Adin Ballou, and other opponents conveniently ignored the condition for individual sovereignty, which linked a person's right to act freely on his or her's acceptance of the right of another to do the same (Ripley's and Ballou's critiques are dealt with later in this chapter).

A generation passed before anarchism would be discussed as a doctrine proposing the replacement of state power with voluntary cooperation. As he burrowed backward in time to uncover "The Evolution of the Socialist Vocabulary," Arthur E. Bestor found that Pierre Joseph Proudhon was the first to "convert a word signifying lawlessness and social disorder to a word denoting a definite political and social order." Proudhon, who was to French philosophical anarchism what Warren was to American, styled himself as an *anarchiste* and his doctrine as *anarchisme* in *Qu'est-ce que la Propriété?*, a pamphlet published in 1840. *Anarchy* and *anarchist* are ancient words, but Bestor reported a new word – *anarchisme* – created in time to be in the 1865 Larousse *Grand Dictionnaire universel*. More than forty years elapsed from Proudhon's use of *anarchism* until it entered the English language, Bestor found: "the first printed use of the old word in the new sense seems to have been in the title of a Boston periodical, the *AnArchist, Socialistic-Revolutionary Review*, in 1881. In 1891, John Rae (in his book on *Contemporary Socialism*) stated that 'seven or eight years ago the word was scarcely known'" (Bestor, "The Evolution of the Socialist Vocabulary," *Journal of the History of Ideas* 9 (June 1948): 285–86).

No sooner did anarchism gain admission to dictionaries than its perception as a philosophy suffered from the violent image projected by "propagandists by the deed." This is one more reason to reach into the bin of ideas to retrieve those of Warren and Andrews, buried under the fame of that wing of the anarchist movement that resorted to guns, bombs, and dynamite, rather than words or model villages.

16. In the style of the period, the title did not skimp on words: Josiah Warren, *Equitable Commerce, a New Developement [sic] of Principles, as Substitutes for Laws and Governments for the Harmonious Adjustment and Regulation of the Pecuniary, Intellectual, and Moral Intercourse of Mankind, Proposed as Elements of New Society* (New Harmony, Ind.: the author, 1846; rev. ed., New York: Fowlers & Wells, 1852; reprint, New York: Burt Franklin, 1967. For Ripley's review and Andrews's rebuttal, see Appendix to Andrews, *Science of Society*, 153–65.

17. George Ripley, "A Review. Equitable Commerce. A New Development of Principles, Proposed as Elements of New Society, by Josiah Warren," *New York Tribune*, 3 July 1852, reprinted in Andrews, Appendix 1 to *Science of Society* 154, where Andrews noted that the unsigned review "was supposed to have been written by George Ripley, a prominent disciple of Fourier and at one time president of Brook Farm."

18. Ibid., 156.

19. Ibid., 10.

20. Sears, *Brook Farm*, 148.

21. Ripley, "Review," 158–59.

22. Warren to Andrews, 4 July 1852, Ewing Cannon Baskette Collection, Illinois.

23. Ibid.

24. Ibid.

25. Andrews, Preface to *Equitable Commerce* by Josiah Warren, vii.

26. Andrews, *Science of Society*, 161–62.

27. Stephen Pearl Andrews, Preface to *Woman, in All Ages and Nations; A Complete and Authentic History of the Manners and Customs, Character and Condition of the Female Sex, in Civilized and Savage Countries, From the Earliest Ages to the Present Time*, by Thomas L. Nichols, M.D. (New York: Fowlers & Wells, 1854), vi.

28. Charles Shively, Introduction to Andrews, *Science of Society*, 13.

29. Andrews, *Science of Society*, 165.

30. Ibid., 162.

31. Ibid., 164–65.

32. Ibid., 165.

33. Ibid.

34. Ibid., 151.

35. For the defection of Fish and Seaver, see the organ of Hopedale, *Practical Christian* 14 (2 July 1853): 3, and Adin Ballou, "A Free Love Episode," in *History of the Hopedale Community from Its Inception to Its Virtual Submergence in the Hopedale Parish* (1897; reprint, Philadelphia: Porcupine Press, 1972), 246–49. See also chap. 4 above.

36. Ballou, *Hopedale Community*, 397–99.

37. The Constitution, By-Laws, Rules, and Regulations of the Hopedale Community spelled out these rules to the last letter; see Ballou, *Hopedale Community*, 368–400.

38. Ibid., 399.

39. Ballou's associate and son-in-law, William S. Heywood, "The Importance of Christian Socialism," *Practical Christian* 14 (8 Oct. 1853): 47.

40. Adin Ballou, "The Different Kinds of Socialism," *Practical Christian* 13 (12 Mar. 1853): 90–91.

41. Holloway, *Heavens on Earth*, 138.

42. Ballou, *Hopedale Community*, 403–5.

43. Ibid., 403.

44. Stoehr, *Free Love in America*, 416.

45. Adin Ballou, *Practical Christian Socialism: A Conversational Exposition of the True System of Human Society; In Three Parts, Viz: I. Fundamental Principles. II. Constitutional Polity. III. Superiority to Other Systems* (Hopedale, Mass.: the author, and New York: Fowlers & Wells, 1854), 3:638.

46. Ibid., 623–24.

47. Ibid., 636.

48. Ibid., 638–39.

49. Noyes, *History of American Socialisms*, 125, citing an "exposition in tract form by Mr. Ballou in 1851."

50. Ibid., 140–41.

51. Warren, *Periodical Letter* 1 (Mar. 1855): 113–14.

52. Ibid., 117.

53. Warren, "Means of the Solution," *Equitable Commerce*, xi.

54. Warren, *Periodical Letter* 1 (Mar. 1855): 117.

55. Eunice M. Schuster, *Native American Anarchism: A Study of Left-Wing American Individualism* (New York: Da Capo Press, 1970), 71.

56. Ballou, *Hopedale Community*, 313, 320. Many residents of Hopedale maintained their nonresistant, abolitionist fervor long after the demise of the Practical Christian Republic.

57. Ibid., 312.

8. VARIATIONS ON INDIVIDUAL SOVEREIGNTY

1. William Pare, "Triallville [*sic*] and Modern Times," *Chambers' Edinburgh Review* 18 (18 Dec. 1852): 395–97. The name "Trialville" applies to the Ohio River settlement of Utopia and, less frequently, to Modern Times to camouflage them from sensation seekers. Pare, an activist in the British cooperative movement and Birmingham city politics, wrote a book on *Equitable Commerce as Practised in the Equity Villages of the United States* (London, 1856).

2. Warren, *Periodical Letter* 1 (July 1854): 14.

3. Martin, *Men Against the State*, 90.

4. Warren, *Periodical Letter* 1 (July 1854): 14.

5. Warren, *Periodical Letter* 1 (Jan. 1855): 94.

6. Robert L. Heilbronner, *The Worldly Philosophers: The Lives, Times, and Ideas of the Great Economic Thinkers* (New York: Simon & Schuster, 1961), 101.

7. Warren, *Peaceful Revolutionist* 2 (May 1848), in A. J. Macdonald, "Ideal Communities," 132.

8. William Pare, Esq., "Equitable Villages in America" [read before the Statistical Section of the British Association at Glasgow, Sept. 1855], *Journal of the Statistical Society of London*, Series A, 19 (June 1856), 127; ibid., 127, 131.

9. Harrison, *Robert Owen*, 207.

10. David Thomson, *England in the Nineteenth Century (1815–1914)* (1950; reprint, New York: Penguin, 1981), 150.

11. John Stuart Mill, *The Autobiography of John Stuart Mill*, ed. John Jacob Coss (1873; reprint, New York: Columbia Univ. Press, 1924), 179.

12. Ibid., 179. It is not clear whether Mill refers to Modern Times or Utopia; he finished the *Autobiography* in 1867, three years after Modern Times became Brentwood, but, in compliance with his instructions, it was not published until he died, in 1873.

13. Ibid., 178.

14. John Stuart Mill, *On Liberty*, in *Utilitarianism, on Liberty, and Considerations on Representative Government*, ed. A. D. Lindsay (New York: Dutton, 1922), 62.

15. Mill, *Autobiography*, 179–80.

16. Mill, *On Liberty*, 65.

17. Warren, *Equitable Commerce*, 60.

18. Mill, *On Liberty*, 65.

19. Warren, *Equitable Commerce*, 61.

20. Mill, *On Liberty*, 72, 73, 75.

21. Ibid., 114.

22. Ibid., 131–32.

23. Alexis de Tocqueville, *Democracy in America* (1835; reprint, New York: Random House, 1945), 1:269 ff.

24. Mill, *On Liberty*, 121–22.

25. Mill, *Representative Government* (1861), 282, 285.

26. Tocqueville, *Democracy in America*, 2:171.

27. Bernard Semmel, *John Stuart Mill and the Pursuit of Virtue* (New Haven: Yale Univ. Press, 1984), 99. The quotation from Mill is in "De Tocqueville on Democracy in America" (1840), *Collected Works*, ed. J. M. Robson (Toronto: Univ. of Toronto Press), 189–90; Mill admired *Democracy in America*, perhaps because it reflects his own reservations about the assumption of power by the plebs.

28. Ibid. Semmel's source is J. S. Mill's other essay on "De Tocqueville on Democracy in America" [1835], *Collected Works* 18:74.

29. Semmel, *Mill*, 3.

30. Warren, *Equitable Commerce*, 57.

31. Herbert Spencer, *Social Statics or the Conditions Essential to Human Happiness Specified, and the First of Them Developed* (London: John Chapman, 1851), 103.

32. Richard Hofstadter, *Social Darwinism in American Thought* (1944; rev. ed., Boston: Beacon Press, 1967), 45.

33. David DeLeon, *The American as Anarchist: Reflections on Indigenous Radicalism* (Baltimore: Johns Hopkins Univ. Press, 1978), 75.

34. Hofstadter, *Social Darwinism*, 40–41.

35. Spencer, *Social Statics*, 133.

36. Henry David Thoreau, *The Major Essays*, ed. Jeffrey L. Duncan (New York: Dutton, 1972), 106, 108, 116, 120.

37. Ibid., 129.

38. Ibid., 117.

39. Ibid., 114–15, 124. Thoreau's crucifixion remark resembles a Modern Timer's comment at the Sunday discussion reported by Conway (see p. 94 above).

40. Ibid., 115.

41. Henry David Thoreau, *Thoreau: People, Principles, and Politics*, ed. Milton Meltzer (New York: Hill and Wang, 1963), 91.

42. Ibid., 125–26.

43. Ibid., 124.

44. Ibid., 144.

45. Ralph Waldo Emerson, "Brook Farm," from "Historic Notes of Life and Letters in New England," in *The Works of Ralph Waldo Emerson*, ed. James Elliot Cabot (Cambridge, Mass.: Houghton Mifflin, 1883), 10:339–46.

46. Karl Marx and Friedrich Engels, *The Communist Manifesto with Selections*

from the Eighteenth Brumaire of Louis Bonaparte and Capital, ed. Samuel H. Beer (New York: Appleton-Century-Crofts, 1955), 43–44.

47. Emerson, "Brook Farm," 327, 331, 335–36.

48. Ralph Waldo Emerson, *Self-Reliance* [1841], in *Works* 3:51.

49. Ralph Waldo Emerson, "The Young American. A Lecture Read before the Mercantile Library Association, in Boston, at the Odeon, Wednesday, 7 February, 1844," *Dial* 4 (Apr. 1844): 496.

50. Emerson, "Brook Farm," 346.

51. Ralph Waldo Emerson, "New England Reformers. A Lecture Read Before the Society in Amory Hall, On Sunday, March 3, 1844," in *Works*, 3:251.

52. Noyes, *History of American Socialisms*, 107.

53. Ibid., 108, 117.

54. Ralph Waldo Emerson, *Journal*, cited by Zoltan Haraszti, "Brook Farm Letters," *Bulletin of the Boston Public Library* 12 (Feb. 1937): 57.

55. Emerson, *Self-Reliance*, 55.

56. Ibid., 71.

57. Noyes, *History of American Socialisms*, 562.

58. Lindsay Swift, *Brook Farm: Its Members, Scholars, and Visitors* (1899; reprint, New York: Corinth Books, 1961), 14, 281.

59. Noyes, *History of American Socialisms*, 544.

60. Ibid., 550.

61. Ibid., 94.

62. "It consisted in the main of young people—few of middle age, and none old" (Emerson, "Brook Farm," 339): "Of about seventy persons now assembled there, about thirty are children sent thither for education: . . . there are only four married couples (C. L. [Charles Lane], "Brook Farm," *Dial* 4 (Apr. 1844): 355); "Nearly all the first members were Unitarians and many of the later comers were of the same faith" (Sears, *My Friends at Brook Farm*, 98).

63. Emerson, "Brook Farm," 342.

64. Louis Filler, *The Crusade Against Slavery 1830–1860* (1960; reprint, New York: Harper & Row, 1963), 111.

65. Moncure Daniel Conway, *Pine and Palm: A Novel* (New York: Henry Holt & Co., 1887), 236.

66. Taylor Stoehr, *Hawthorne's Mad Scientists: Pseudoscience and Social Science in Nineteenth-Century Life and Letters* (Hamden, Conn.: Shoestring Press, 1978), 213.

67. Moncure Daniel Conway, *Autobiography: Memories and Experiences* (Cambridge: Houghton Mifflin, 1904), 1:265. In "Modern Times, New York," Conway describes Mary Chilton as "a person of distinction . . . a woman . . . a little over thirty years of age, [with] an indefinable grace and fine intellectual powers, united with considerable personal beauty . . . She had studied medicine, and was earning her livelihood by medical practice" (Conway, *Fortnightly Review*, 427). For Mary Chilton and Theron C. Leland, with whom she lived at Modern Times before they married, see George E. Macdonald [their son-in-law], *Fifty Years of Freethought*, 1:450–55.

68. Conway, *Pine and Palm*, 236. Conway translated Rabelais's "Thélème" as "Thelema."

9. CHANGING TO BRENTWOOD

1. For the Religion of Humanity and its impact on America, see Richmond Laurin Hawkins, *Positivism in the United States 1853–1861* (Cambridge, Mass.: Harvard Univ. Press, 1938), which examines Edger and Modern Times in depth. The best study of Edger and his crusade in Robert E. Schneider, *Positivism in the United States: The Apostleship of Henry Edger*, previously cited.

2. Hawkins, *Positivism*, 170.

3. Ibid., 190, quoting Comte to Edger, 9 Archimedes 69 [3 Apr. 1857]. Years on the Positivist calendar starting from Bastille Day, 14 July 1789, had thirteen months of four weeks each; every week, month, and day bore the name of a sage or prophet. Convinced that Jesus was a dangerous radical, Comte acknowledged Paul as the founder of Christianity; among 558 notables in the calendar, Jesus' name did not appear (ibid., 189). See Henry Edger, *The Positivist Calendar: Or, Transitional System of Public Commemoration Instituted by Augustus Comte, Founder of the Positive Religion of Humanity, With a Brief Exposition of Religious Positivism; and an Appendix, Containing I. A Concordance of the Calendars; II. The Positivist Library; And III. Narrative of the Rise and Progress of Positivism. Diis extinctis, Deoque, successit Humanitas* (Modern Times [Thompson], Long Island: the author, the 68th Year of the Great Crisis [1856]), "the most profound work on positivism . . . ever published" (Comte to Edgar, 17 Frederick 68 [20 November 1856] (Hawkins, *Positivism*, 180). Comte read a canto of Dante's *Divine Comedy* and a chapter of Thomas à Kempis's *Imitation of Christ*, his personal favorites, every day; the 150 books listed in his *Positivist Library* were the required and only reading allowed to the faithful.

4. Ibid., 54–55.

5. Hawkins, *Positivism*, 103.

6. Next to J. S. Mill, Lewes "was the most influential of the British writers who early sought to create a favorable reception for Comte," but Mill, Lewes, and Martineau rejected the polity and religion superimposed by Comte upon his philosophy (Hawkins, *Positivism*, 8); see John Stuart Mill, "Part II: Later Speculations of Auguste Comte," in *Auguste Comte and Positivism* (1865; reprint, Ann Arbor: Univ. of Michigan Press, 1961), 125–200; the failure of a mind that was so strong in middle ages distressed Martineau (Hawkins, *Positivism*, 18, 22).

7. Hawkins, *Positivism*, 103.

8. Conway, "Modern Times," 426.

9. Edger to Comte, Modern Times, Thompson's Station, Long Island, N.Y.: Juvenal 19, Homer 66 [16 Feb. 1854], in Hawkins, *Positivism*, 130. Edger's sixteen letters to Comte are in the archives of the Société Positiviste in Paris. For Comte's twelve letters to Edger, see *Lettres d'Auguste Comte à divers* (Paris: 1902–1905), and elsewhere. For Edger's letters and most of Comte's answers, see Hawkins, *Positivism*, 128–203.

10. Edger to Comte, Modern Times, 6 Dante 66 [21 July 1854], in Hawkins, *Positivism*, 133.

11. Comte to Edger, 20 Dante 66 [4 Aug. 1854], and 17 Frederick 68 [20 Nov. 1856], in Hawkins, *Positivism*, 138, 181.

12. Ibid., 134 n. 1. Edger's journal entry for 16 Charlemagne 66 [3 July 1854] mentioned Mary Wait (of whom no other record exists) as present, in addition to those named by Hawkins (Schneider, *Henry Edger*, 48).

13. Edger to Comte, Modern Times, 7 Descartes 67 [14 Oct. 1855], in Hawkins, *Positivism*, 163–64; Comte to Edger, 26 Descartes 67 [2 Nov. 1855], ibid., 166. The nine positivist sacraments are presentation (baptism), initiation (candidacy, at the age of 28), admission (apprenticeship, as a vicar, at the age of 35), destination (priesthood, at the age of 42), marriage, retirement, transformation (death), and incorporation (into the secular sainthood). Priests could not receive salaries or hold political office; to experience the salutary influence of woman, they had to marry (ibid., 139, 150).

14. Comte to Edger, 26 Descartes 67 [2 Nov. 1855], in Hawkins, *Positivism*, 16. With John Metcalf and Mrs. Richard Parker as godparents, and with Comte's written permission and reminder to wear the sacerdotal green ribbon around the middle of his right arm, Edger presided at the "presentation" of the infant named for two of Comte's three "guardian angels"–Sophie (Bliot), Comte's housekeeper, and Clotilde (De Vaux), his lost love and "Madonna"; the third was Rosalie Boyer, his mother. Comte was "touched" by the choice of the name, "and Sophie is delighted" (Comte to Edger, 11 Dante 67 [26 July 1855], ibid., 159).

15. Ibid., 134 n. 1.

16. Metcalf to Comte, 5 Homer 68 [2 Feb. 1856], and Comte to Metcalf, 3 Aristotle 68 [28 Feb. 1856], in Hawkins, *Positivism*, 203–5. Comte's four letters to Metcalf are in *Lettres d'Auguste Comte & Henry Edger et à John Metcalf* (Paris: Apostolat positiviste, 1889); Metcalf's first letter to Comte (2 Feb. 1856) and summaries of his other three and of Comte's letters to him are in Hawkins, *Positivism*, 203–7.

17. Hawkins, *Positivism*, 199.

18. Schneider, *Henry Edger*, 107.

19. Spurlock, *Free Love*, 157, 161; for Berlin Heights see Stoehr, *Free Love*, 441–87, and passim.

20. Harvey Wish, "Stephen Pearl Andrews, American Pioneer Sociologist," *Social Forces* 19 (May 1941): 481, citing Andrews, *Basic Outline of Universology*, 210. During the 1870s, Andrews and Edger talked and corresponded cordially, searching unsuccessfully to link their universologies (Schneider, *Henry Edger*, 140–54).

21. Codman, "Modern Times," 9–10.

22. Comte to Edger, 11 Dante 67 [26 July 1855], in Hawkins, *Positivism*, 160.

23. Edger to Comte, 11 Aristotle 69 [8 Mar. 1857] and Comte to Edger, 9 Archimedes 69 [3 Apr. 1857], in Hawkins, *Positivism*, 187–89.

24. Codman, "Modern Times," 10.

25. "In Memoriam–Emily Codman 1826–1886" funeral service held 5 July 1886 (Brentwood, N.Y., Modern Times Collection, Brentwood Public Library, Brentwood, N.Y. An English positivist reported that during a visit to the United States he met

"a Mr. Codman, of Modern Times, one of the original 'Edger Positivists' of Long Island . . . whose wife was buried with Positivist rites twenty-five years ago" (Frederick Harrison, *Autobiographic Memoirs* [London: Macmillan, 1911], 2:215).

26. Comte to Edger, 15 Aristotle 67 [12 Mar. 1855], in Hawkins, *Positivism*, 150; Comte to Edger, 3 Archimedes 68 [17 Mar. 1856], ibid., 172; Comte to Edger, 17 Frederick 68 [20 Nov. 1856], ibid., 181; and Comte to Edger, 10 Charlemagne 68 [26 June 1856], ibid., 176–77. Comte designated John Fisher and Richard Congreve as Edger's colleagues on the British Positivist Committee; because of a dearth of members, their jurisdiction included all of the United States. "Comte's Occidental Positive Committee, or Permanent Council of the New Church, was to be composed of 8 Frenchmen, 7 Englishmen, 6 Germans, 5 Italians, and 5 Spanish" (ibid., 176). Latin America, Brazil in particular, was the only part of the world receptive to Comte's religion; elsewhere the response was negative. The "rich patron" was the wealthy potential sponsor (perhaps the reformer, Gerrit Smith) hoped for by Edger, much as Fourier waited in vain for the backer who never materialized.

27. Schneider, *Henry Edger*, 94.

28. "Comtean Atheism," *American Quarterly Church Review and Ecclesiastical Registry* 20 (July 1868): 179.

29. Edger, "Journal," 21 Dante 68 [14 Aug. 1856], in Schneider, *Henry Edger*, 99, 77–78.

30. Edger to Comte, 21 Descartes 68 [27 Oct. 1856), in Hawkins, *Positivism*, 178.

31. Schneider, *Henry Edger*, 108.

32. Edger to Comte, 10 Moses 69 [10 Jan. 1857], Hawkins, *Positivism*, 186; Comte to Edger, 9 Homer 69 [6 Feb. 1857], ibid.; Edger to Comte, 5 Charlemagne 69 [22 June 1857], ibid., 194.

33. Hawkins, *Positivism*, 202.

34. Schneider's research in England convinced him her name was Milliscent, not Melliscent, or Melicent [the incorrect spelling on her headstone in Brentwood Cemetery]. Milliscent Hobson Edger (1816–1870) was born in the Northamptonshire village of Wellingborough not "Irthlingboro," the name Hawkins contrived by misreading Edger's handwriting (Schneider, *Henry Edger*, 21).

35. Ballou, *Hopedale Community*, 350. Brook Farm went belly-up at the age of six, the North American Phalanx at twelve, and Hopedale at fifteen.

36. Bailie, *Josiah Warren*, 77.

37. Warren, *Practical Applications*, 15. For a similar description by Cubberly of his use of equity commerce to build a house cheaply and well, see Warren, *Peaceful Revolutionist* 2 (May 1848): 10–11.

38. Warren, *Practical Applications*, 15–16.

39. Ibid., 16.

40. Ibid., 26.

41. Warren, *Periodical Letter* 1 (Feb. 1855): 98–99.

42. Kanter, *Commitment and Community*, 245.

43. Bailie, *Josiah Warren*, 63.

44. Warren, *True Civilization*, 52.

45. Ibid.

46. Ibid., 171.

47. Ibid., 171–72.

48. See Truman Nelson, ed., *Documents of Upheaval: Selections from William Lloyd Garrison's* The Liberator, *1831–1865* (New York: Hill & Wang, 1966), 202.

49. Ibid., 203–4.

50. Noyes to Garrison, 22 Mar. 1837, in Schuster, *Native American Anarchism*, 54.

51. Adin Ballou, quoted in *Patterns of Anarchy: A Collection of Writings on the Anarchist Tradition*, eds. Leonard I. Krimerman and Lewis Perry (Garden City, N.Y.: Doubleday, 1960), 143–44.

52. Warren, *Equitable Commerce*, 61.

53. Warren, *Periodical Letter* 1 (Mar. 1855): 127–28.

54. Conway, "Modern Times," 434.

55. Dyson, *Century of Brentwood*, 67.

56. Stern, *The Pantarch*, 86.

57. Codman, "Modern Times," 23. Warren composed, performed, led bands and orchestras, and taught music all his life; he invented a shorthand for musical notation on the order of Andrews's system for transcribing words (see pp. 15, 197 n. 43, above). The "South Bay Quickstep" is no longer extant.

58. For the roster of Suffolk County soldiers, see Richard M. Bayles, "History of Suffolk County," in Munsell, *History of Suffolk*, 70–79.

59. Ibid., 72.

60. Codman, "Modern Times," 24.

61. Codman, "Modern Times," 24. Dr. William H. Ross, to whom Codman turned over his manuscript, inserted the parenthetical reference to Antietam.

62. Bayles, "History of Suffolk County," in *History of Suffolk*, 72–79.

63. Codman, "Modern Times," 13.

64. *Census of the State of New York for 1865*, Third Election District, Town of Islip, 52.

65. Ibid.

66. Ibid.

67. Ibid., First Election District, 63.

68. Ibid., Second Election District, 40.

69. Warren, *Practical Applications*, 53.

70. Warren, *True Civilization*, 171.

71. Spurlock, *Free Love*, 137.

10. LOOKING BACKWARD

1. Noyes, *History of American Socialisms*, 42, 94.

2. *Certificates of Incorporation, Book B*, Office of the Suffolk County Clerk, Riverhead, N.Y., 72.

3. Ibid., 74.

4. Ibid., 79.

5. Ibid., 100. Ellen Lazarus Allen, now married to Walter W. Shutt, completed her metamorphosis from Brook Farm to equitable commerce to the Religion of Humanity, to final membership in Christ Episcopal Church of Brentwood, for which she deeded the land (Dyson, *Century of Brentwood*, 120).

6. "Minute Book of School District 12, 1853–1890," Office of Superintendent of Schools, Brentwood, N.Y.

7. Ibid., meeting of 13 Oct. 1868.

8. Dyson, *A Century of Brentwood*, 153.

9. *Liber of Deeds* 115:596.

10. Dyson, *Century of Brentwood*, 154–56. The mansion is no more, but Olmstead's park is well maintained as the grounds of the Mother House, Convent, and Academy of its owner, the Congregation of the Sisters of Saint Joseph; see Sister Mary Ignatius Meany, C.S.J., *By Railway or Rainbow: A History of the Sisters of St. Joseph of Brentwood* (Brentwood, N.Y.: Pine Press, 1964).

11. Ibid., 157.

12. Warren, *Practical Applications*, 21–22.

13. Bailie, *Josiah Warren*, 78–79. There were *four* survivors when Bailie wrote: Codman, Jennie Dame, James Hilton, and Frank Blacker (Peter and Abigail's son). An example of a Massachusetts-born Modern Timer who sank his roots in Long Island and stayed there for the rest of his life, Frank Blacker served Modern Times–Brentwood as Civil War soldier, postmaster, railroad clerk, school board official, and nurseryman.

14. Codman, "Modern Times," 25–26.

15. Ibid., 26–27.

16. Warren, *Practical Applications*, 22.

17. Arthur Bestor, "Patent-Office Models of the Good Society: Some Relationships Between Social Reform and Westward Expansion," *American Historical Review* 53 (Apr. 1953): 505–26.

18. Prime, *Long Island*, 2:408–9.

SELECTED BIBLIOGRAPHY

PUBLIC DOCUMENTS, COLLECTED PAPERS, AND LETTERS

Beers, F. W. *Atlas of Long Island, New York*, New York: Beers, Comstock & Cline, 1873.

Brentwood, N.Y. Office of Superintendent of Schools. "Minute Book of School District 12, 1853–1890."

"Brentwood School District No. 12, History of." In *Directory and Year Book of Public Schools, Second Supervisory District, 1929–1930*, 117–18.

Chace, J., Jr. *Map of Suffolk County, Long Island, N.Y. from Actual Survey by J. Chace, Junior*. Philadelphia: John Douglass, 1858.

Codman, Charles A. "A Brief History of 'The City of Modern Times' Long Island, N.Y.—and A Glorification of Some of Its Saints" (Brentwood, N.Y., ca. 1905). Modern Times Collection, Suffolk County Historical Society. Pencilscript.

Hawkins, Ebenezer. "Map of the City of Modern Times." *Libers of Maps* 34:19. Suffolk County Clerk, Riverhead, N.Y. Made 20 Mar. 1851; recorded 18 Jan. 1859.

"In Memoriam–Emily Codman, 1826–1886." Brentwood, N.Y., 1886 [funeral service, 5 July 1886]. Modern Times Collection, Brentwood Public Library, Brentwood, N.Y.

Islip, N.Y. Office of Islip Town Clerk. "Minutes of Town Meetings, 1720–1875."

New Harmony Manuscripts. Workingmen's Institute Library, New Harmony, Ind.

New York, State of. *Census of the State of New York for 1855*. Albany, 1855. KTO Microform, Millwood, N.Y.

———. *Census of the State of New York for 1865; Manuscript Census of Population, 1865, County of Suffolk, Town of Islip*. Albany, 1867. Suffolk County Cooperative Library System, Bellport, N.Y. Microfilm.

Suffolk County, N.Y. Office of Suffolk County Clerk, Riverhead, N.Y. *Certificates of Incorporation, Book B*.

———. *Libers of Deeds, Town of Islip*.

————. *Libers of Maps.*

————. *Libers of Mortgages.*

U.S. Bureau of the Census. *Eighth Census of the United States, 1860.* Washington: NARS Microfilm, 1967.

Warren, Josiah. Josiah Warren Papers. Labadie Collection, Univ. of Michigan Library, Ann Arbor.

————. Letters to Stephen Pearl Andrews, 1850–1852. John Ishill Collection, Houghton Library, Harvard University, Cambridge, Mass.

————. Letters to Stephen Pearl Andrews, 1852. Ewing Cannon Baskette Collection on Freedom of Expression, Univ. of Illinois Library, Urbana-Champaign.

————. Warren Manuscripts. Workingmen's Institute Library, New Harmony, Ind.

Wheeler, Samuel, surveyor. *A Map of the Township of Islip.* Islip, N.Y., 1 Jan. 1798.

LONG ISLAND HISTORY

Aldridge, Alfred Owen. "Mysticism in Modern Times, Long Island." *Americana* 36 (Oct. 1942): 555–70.

American Institute. *Sixth Annual Report of the American Institute of the City of New York, Made to the Legislature, March 25, 1848.* Albany, 1848.

Armbruster, Eugene L. *The Ferry Road on Long Island.* New York: The author, 1919.

Bailey, Paul, ed. *Long Island—A History of Two Great Counties, Nassau and Suffolk.* 3 vols. New York: Lewis Historical Publishing Co., 1949.

Bailey, Rosalie Fellows. "The Nicoll Family and Islip Grange, An Address Delivered before the Order of Colonial Lords of Manors in America, April 21, 1938, with Additions." New York: Publications of the Order of Colonial Lords of Manors in America, 1940.

Bayles, Richard M. *Historical and Descriptive Sketches of Suffolk County with a Historical Outline of Long Island.* 1874. Reprint. Port Washington, N.Y.: Ira J. Friedman, 1962.

Bi-Centennial History of Suffolk County, Comprising the Addresses Delivered At the Celebration of the Bi-Centennial of Suffolk County, N.Y., in Riverhead, November 15, 1883. Babylon, N.Y., Budget Steam Print, 1885. Reprint. Suffolk County Tercentenary Commission, 1983.

Breen, T. H. *Imagining the Past, East Hampton History.* Boston: Addison, Wesley, 1989.

Bunce, James E., and Richard P. Harmond, eds. *Long Island as America–A Documentary History*. Port Washington, N.Y.: Kennikat Press, 1977.

Conway, Moncure Daniel. "Modern Times, New York." *Fortnightly Review* 1 (July 1865): 421–34.

———. *Pine and Palm, A Novel*. New York: Henry Holt, 1887.

Cory, David M. "Brooklyn and the Civil War." *Journal of Long Island History* 2 (Spring 1962): 1–15.

Denton, Daniel. *A Brief Description of New York Formerly Called New Netherlands* [sic]. London, 1670. In *Historic Chronicles of New Amsterdam, Colonial New York, and Early Long Island*, edited by Cornell Jaray. Port Washington, N.Y.: Ira J. Friedman, 1968.

Dickerson, Charles. *A History of the Sayville Community Including: Bayport, Bohemia, West Sayville, Oakdale, and Fire Island*. Sayville, N.Y.: Suffolk County News, 1975.

Dugan, J. Frederick. "Land Values Through 300 Years." *Long Island Forum* 10 (Mar. 1947): 41–58.

Dunbaugh, Edwin L. "New York to Boston Via the Long Island Railroad." In *Evoking A Sense of Place*, edited by Joann P. Krieg, 75–84. Interlaken, N.Y.: Heart of the Lakes Publishing, 1988.

Richard S. Dunn, *Puritans and Yankees: The Winthrop Dynasty of New England 1630–1717*. New York: W. W. Norton, 1962.

Dwight, Timothy. *Travels; In New-England and New-York*. 4 vols. New Haven: the author [posthumous], 1822.

Dyson, Verne. *A Century of Brentwood*. Brentwood, N.Y.: Brentwood Village Press, 1950.

———. *Supplement and Index: An Afterpiece to A Century of Brentwood*. Brentwood, N.Y.: Brentwood Village Press, 1953.

Edger, Henry. *Modern Times, the Labor Question and the Family. A Brief Statement of Facts and Principles*. New York: Calvin Blanchard, 1855.

Flick, Alexander C. *History of the State of New York*. Vol. 6, *The Age of Reform*. New York: Columbia Univ. Press, 1934.

French, J. H. *Gazetteer of the State of New York 1860*. Syracuse: R. Pearsall Smith, 1860.

Gabriel, Ralph Henry. *The Evolution of Long Island: A Story of Land and Sea*. 1921. Reprint. Port Washington, N.Y.: Ira J. Friedman, 1968.

Gardiner, Sarah D. "The Sagtikos Manor 1697, An Address Read before the Annual Meeting of the Order of Colonial Lords of Manors in America on April 26, 1934." New York: Publications of the Order of Colonial Lords of Manors in America, 1935.

Hazelton, Henry Isham. *The Boroughs of Brooklyn and Queens, Counties of Nas-*

sau and Suffolk, Long Island. 5 vols. New York; Lewis Historical Publishing, 1925.

History of Queens County, New York, with Illustrations, Portraits, and Sketches of Prominent Families and Individuals. New York: W. W. Munsell, 1882.

History of Suffolk County, New York, with Illustrations, Portraits, and Sketches of Prominent Families and Individuals. New York: W. W. Munsell, 1882.

Horton, H. P. "The Story of 'Modern Times.'" *Long Island Forum* 7 (Feb. 1944): 23–25.

Jaray, Cornell, comp. *The Mills of Long Island.* Port Washington, N.Y.: Ira J. Friedman, 1962.

Kammen, Michael. *Colonial New York: A History.* New York: Charles Scribner's Sons, 1975.

Lewis, G. P. "Long Island Farming," *American Agriculturist* 6 (Sept., Dec. 1925), 281–372.

Lightfoot, Frederick S., Linda B. Martin, and Bette S. Weidman. *Suffolk County, Long Island in Early Photographs 1867–1951.* New York: Dover Publications, 1984.

Linton, Edward F. "Remarks of Edward F. Linton at the Village Cemetery at Brentwood, Long Island, 'Decoration Day,' May 30th, 1905." In *1855 – Fifty Years After at Brentwood Long Island, May 30th, 1905.* Brooklyn: Eagle Press, 1905.

Long Island Railroad Company: *Diamond Jubilee (1834–1909): Celebration of Its Seventy-Fifth Anniversary Friday, April 22, 1910* (Jamaica, N.Y.: Long Island Railroad, 1910.

———. *The Long Island Railroad: 100th Anniversary. (1834–1934)* Jamaica, N.Y.: Osborne Co., 1934.

McCullough, David. *The Great Bridge.* New York: Simon & Schuster, 1972.

MacKay, Robert B., Geoffrey L. Rossano, and Carol A. Traynor, eds. *Between Ocean and Empire: An Illustrated History of Long Island.* Northridge, Calif.: Windsor Publications, 1985.

McManus, Edgar J. *A History of Negro Slavery in New York.* Syracuse: Syracuse Univ. Press, 1966.

McPherson, James M. *Battle Cry of Freedom: The Civil War Era.* New York: Oxford Univ. Press, 1988.

———. *The Negro's Civil War: How American Negroes Felt and Acted During the War for the Union.* New York: Pantheon Books, 1965.

Marcus, Grania Bolton. *A Forgotten People: Discovering the Black Experience in Suffolk County.* Setauket, N.Y.: Society for the Preservation of Long Island Antiquities, 1989.

Matthiessen, Peter. *Men's Lives: The Surfmen and Baymen of the South Fork.* New York: Random House, 1986.

Meany, Sister Mary Ignatius, C.S.J. *By Railway or Rainbow: A History of the Sisters of Saint Joseph of Brentwood.* Brentwood, N.Y.: Pine Press, 1964.

Murphy, Robert Cushman. *Fish-Shape Paumanok: Nature and Man on Long Island.* Philadelphia: Philosophical Society, 1964.

The New Long Island: A Hand Book of Summer Travel Designed for the Use and Information of Visitors to Long Island and its Watering Places. New York: Rogers & Sherwood, 1879.

Newton, David F. *The Pine Barrens Long Island Wilderness.* Riverhead, N.Y.: Cooperative Extension, Suffolk County, n.d. Pamphlet.

Lawrence G. Paul. *The Pine Barrens of Ronkonkoma: A Guide for the Hiker to the Long Island Pine Barrens.* New York: New York–New Jersey Trail Conference, 1986.

Peck, Edgar Fenn, M.D. *Description of the Lands On Long Island.* Brooklyn: the author, 1858.

————. "Edgar Fenn Peck, M.D. to R. M. Bayles, Brooklyn, L.I., 8 October 1873." Appendix to Richard M. Bayles, *Historical and Descriptive Sketches of Suffolk County.* 1873. Reprint. Port Washington, N.Y.: Ira J. Friedman, 1962.

————. "Edgar Fenn Peck" [autobiographical sketch]. In *Civil, Political, Professional and Ecclesiastical History and Commercial and Industrial Record of the County of Kings and the City of Brooklyn, N.Y. from 1683 to 1884,* edited by Henry R. Stiles, 1:40a–46a. New York: W. W. Munsell, 1884.

Poor, Henry Varnum. *History of the Railroads and Canals of the United States of America.* 3 vols. New York: John H. Schultz & Co., 1860.

Prime, Nathaniel S. *A History of Long Island, from Its First Settlement by Europeans, to the Year 1845, with Special Reference to Its Ecclesiastical Concerns.* 2 parts. New York: Robert Carter, 1845.

Rayback, Robert J., ed. *Richards' Atlas of New York State.* Phoenix, N.Y.: Frank & Richards, 1957–1959.

Ross, Peter. *A History of Long Island from Its Earliest Settlement to the Present Time.* 3 vols. New York: Lewis Publishing Co., 1902.

Ross, William H., M.D. "A Study of the Climate of Long Island." *Brooklyn Medical Journal* 18 (Mar. 1904): 81–84.

Seyfried, Vincent. *The Founding of Garden City 1869–1893.* Garden City, N.Y.: the author, 1969.

————. *The Long Island Rail Road.* 6 vols. Uniondale, N.Y.: Salisbury Printers, 1961–1966.

Smith, Mildred H. *Early History of the Long Island Railroad: 1834–1900.* Uniondale, N.Y.: Salisbury Printers, 1958.

Spaulding, E. Wilder. *New York in the Critical Period, 1783–1789.* Port Washington, N.Y.: Ira J. Friedman, 1963.

Starace, Carl A., ed. *Book One of the Minutes of Town Meetings and Register of Animal Ear Marks of the Town of Islip 1720–1851.* Smithtown, N.Y.: Town of Islip, 1982.

Stiles, Henry R., ed. *The Civil, Political, Professional, and Ecclesiastical History and Commercial and Industrial Record of the County of Kings and the City of Brooklyn, N.Y. from 1683 to 1884.* New York: W. W. Munsell, 1884.

Studley, G. B. *Brentwood Long Island In the Heart of the Pine Belt.* Brentwood, N.Y.: Brentwood Sanitarium Corp., 1899. Booklet.

Taylor, Lawrence J. *Dutchmen on the Bay: the Ethnohistory of a Contractual Community.* Philadelphia: Univ. of Pennsylvania Press, 1983.

Thompson, Benjamin Franklin. *History of Long Island from Its Discovery and Settlement to the Present Time.* 3rd ed., revised and enlarged with additions and a biography of the author by Charles J. Werner. New York: Robert H. Dodd, 1918.

Tooker, William Wallace, *The Indian Place-Names on Long Island and Islands Adjacent with Their Probable Significance.* New York: G. P. Putnam's Sons, 1911.

Tredwell, Daniel M. *Personal Reminiscenses of Men and Things On Long Island.* 2 parts. Brooklyn: Charles Andrew Ditmas Publisher, 1912 and 1917.

Treistman, Judith. "What is a Bayman?" *Suffolk Maritime Folklife.* Hauppauge, N.Y.: Suffolk County Office of Cultural Affairs, 1981.

Vagts, Christopher R. *Suffolk: A Pictorial History.* Huntington, N.Y.: Huntington Historical Society, 1983.

Watson, Winslow C. "The Plains of Long Island." In *New York State Agricultural Society, Proceedings for 1859,* 485–505. Albany: Charles Van Benthuysen, 1860.

Weeks, George Lewis. *"Isle of Shells" (Long Island).* Islip, N.Y.: Buys Bros., 1965.

––––––. *Some of the Town of Islip's Early History.* Bay Shore, N.Y.: Consolidated Press, 1955.

Weidman, Bette S., and Linda B. Martin. *Nassau County, Long Island in Early Photographs, 1869–1940.* New York: Dover Publications, 1981.

Whitman, Walt. *Complete Poetry and Collected Prose.* Edited by Justin Kaplan. New York: Literary Classics of the United States, 1982.

Wines, Richard A. "The Nineteenth-Century Agricultural Transition in An Eastern Long Island Community." *Agricultural History* 55 (Jan. 1981): 50–63.

Wood, Clarence Ashton. "First Train to Greenport, 1844." *Long Island Forum* 6 (Nov. 1943): 203–17.

Wunderlich, Roger, "An Island of Mine Owne: The Life and Times of Lion Gardiner, 1599–1663." *Long Island Historical Journal* 2 (Fall 1989): 3–14.

————. "Scale Model of Liberty: The Thirteen Years of Modern Times, 1851–1864." *Long Island Historical Journal* 3 (Fall 1990): 29–47.

Ziel, Ron. *The Long Island Railroad in Early Photographs.* New York: Dover Publications, 1990.

Ziel, Ron, and George Foster. *Steel Rails to the Sunrise.* New York: Duell, Sloane, & Pierce, 1965.

BOOKS, ARTICLES, AND PAMPHLETS

Adams, Grace, and Edward Hutter. *The Mad Forties.* New York: Harper & Brothers, 1942.

Albertson, Ralph. "A Survey of Mutualistic Communities in America." *Iowa Journal of History and Politics* 34 (Oct. 1936): 375–444.

Albin, Mel, and Dominick Cavallo. *Family Life in America 1620–2000.* St. James, N.Y.: Revisionary Press, 1981.

Andreano, Ralph, ed. *The Economic Impact of the American Civil War.* 1962. Reprint. New York: Cambridge Univ. Press, 1967.

Andrews, Edward Deming. *The People Called Shakers: A Search for the Perfect Society.* 1953. Reprint. New York: Dover Publications, 1963.

Andrews, Stephen Pearl. *The Basic Outline of Universology. An Introduction to the Newly Discovered Science of the Universe; Its Elementary Principles, and the First Stages of That Development in the Special Sciences.* New York: Dion Thomas, 1872.

————. *Love, Marriage, and Divorce, And The Sovereignty of the Individual: A Discussion between Henry James, Horace Greeley and Stephen Pearl Andrews, and a Hitherto Unpublished Manuscript Love, Marriage, and the Condition of Woman by Stephen Andrews.* 1853. Reprint. Introduction by Charles A. Shively. Weston, Mass.: M & S Press, 1975.

————. *The Science of Society.* New York: Fowlers & Wells, 1852. Reprint. Introduction by Charles A. Shively. Weston, Mass.: M & S Press, 1970. [Combined edition of two works on Josiah Warren's philosophy: *The Science of Society. No. 1. The True Constitution of Government in the Sovereignty of Democracy and Socialism; and The Science of Society, No. 2. Cost the Limit of Price; A Scientific Measure of Honesty in Trade as one of the Fundamental Principles in the Solution of the Social Problem*].

Arndt, Karl J. R. *A Documentary History of the Indiana Decade of the Harmony Society, 1814–1824,* 2 vols. Indianapolis: Indiana Historical Society, 1975.

————. *George Rapp's Harmony Society, 1785–1847.* Rev. ed. Rutherford, N.J.: Fairleigh Dickinson Univ. Press, 1972.

————. *George Rapp's Successors and Material Heirs, 1847–1916*. Rutherford, N.J.: Fairleigh Dickinson Univ. Press, 1972.

Arrington, Leonard J. *Great Basin Kingdom: An Economic History of the Latter-Day Saints*. Cambridge, Mass.: Harvard Univ. Press, 1958.

Aspinwall, Bernard. "Social Catholicism and Health: Dr. and Mrs. Thomas Low Nichols in Britain." In *The Church and Healing: Papers Read at the Twentieth Summer Meeting and the Twenty-First Winter Meeting of the Ecclesiastical History Society*, edited by W. J. Sheils, 249–70. Oxford: Basil Blackwell, 1982.

Bailie, William. *Josiah Warren, The First American Anarchist: A Sociological Study*. Boston: Small, Maynard & Company, 1906.

Ballou, Adin. *Autobiography of Adin Ballou 1803–1890. Containing An Elaborate Record and Narrative of His Life From Infancy to Old Age*. Edited by William S. Heywood. 1896. Reprint. Philadelphia: Porcupine Press, 1975.

————. *History of the Hopedale Community, From Its Inception to Its Virtual Submergence in the Hopedale Parish*. 1897. Reprint, Philadelphia: Porcupine Press, 1972.

————. *Practical Christian Socialism: A Conversational Exposition of the True System of Human Society; in Three Parts, Viz: I. Fundamental Principles. II. Constitutional Polity. III. Superiority to Other Systems*. Hopedale, Mass.: the author; New York: Fowlers & Wells, 1854.

Barker-Benfield, G. J. *The Horrors of the Half-Known Life: Male Attitudes Toward Women and Sexuality in Nineteenth-Century America*, 175–88. New York: Harper & Row, 1976).

Barthel, Diane L. *Amana–From Pietist Sect to American Community*. Lincoln: Univ. of Nebraska Press, 1984.

Basch, Norma. *In the Eyes of the Law: Women, Marriage, and Property in Nineteenth-Century New York*. Ithaca, N.Y.: Cornell Univ. Press, 1982.

Bassett, T. D. Seymour. "The Secular Utopian Socialists." In *Socialism and American Life*, edited by Donald Egbert and Stow Persons, 1:155–211. Princeton: Princeton Univ. Press, 1952.

Benedict, J. *Benedict's Treatise: Containing a Summary of the Jurisdiction, Powers, and Duties of Justices of the Peace in the State of New York*. 4th ed. Albany: W. C. Little, 1858.

Bestor, Arthur E. *Backwoods Utopias: The Sectarian Origins and the Owenite Phase of Communitarian Socialism in America: 1663–1829*. Philadelphia: Univ. of Pennsylvania Press, 1953. Reprint. Philadelphia: Univ. of Pennsylvania Press, 1981.

————. "Patent-Office Models of the Good Society: Some Relationships Between Social Reform and Westward Expansion." *American Historical Review* 58 (Apr. 1953): 505–26.

―――. "The Evolution of the Socialist Vocabulary." *Journal of the History of Ideas* 9 (June 1848): 259–302.

Billington, Ray Allen, ed. *The Frontier Thesis: Valid Interpretation of American History?* New York: Holt, Rinehart & Winston, 1966.

Bliss, William D. P. *The Encyclopedia of Social Reform*. New York: Funk & Wagnalls, 1897.

―――. *A Handbook of Socialism*. New York: Charles Scribner's Sons, 1907.

―――. *The New Encyclopedia of Social Reform*, 3d ed. New York: Funk & Wagnalls, 1910.

Bole, John Archibald. *The Harmony Society—A Chapter in German-American Culture History*. Philadelphia: American Germanica Press, 1904.

Brisbane, Albert. *Association: or, A Concrete Exposition of the Doctrine of Association, or Plan for the Reorganization of Society*. New York: Greeley & McElrath, 1843.

―――. *Social Destiny of Man*. Philadelphia: C. F. Stollmeyer, 1840.

Brown, Richard D. *The Transformation of American Life. 1600–1865*. New York: Hill & Wang, 1976.

Buber, Martin. *Paths in Utopia*. 1949. Reprint. Boston: Beacon Press, 1960.

Butler, Ann Caldwell. "Josiah Warren: Peaceful Revolutionist." Ph.D. diss., Ball State Univ., 1979.

Calverton, Victor F. [pseud.]. *Where Angels Dared to Tread*. Indianapolis: Bobbs-Merrill, 1941.

Carden, Maren Lockwood. *Oneida: Utopian Community to Modern Corporation*. 1969. Reprint. New York: Harper & Row, 1971.

Chandler, Alfred D., Jr. *The Visible Hand: The Managerial Revolution in American Business*. Cambridge, Mass.: Harvard Univ. Press, 1977.

Clay, James Arrington. *A Voice from the Prison, or, Truths for the Multitude, and Pearls for the Truthful, by James A. Clay, Written During His Confinement in Augusta (Me.) Jail*. Boston: Bela Marsh, 1856.

Codman, John Thomas. *Brook Farm: Historic and Personal Memoirs*. 1894. Reprint, New York: AMS Press, 1971.

Cominos, Peter. "Late Victorian Sexual Respectability and the Social System." *International Review of Social History* 8 (1963): 18–48, 216–30.

Commons, John R., and Associates, eds. *A Documentary History of American Industrial Society*. 10 vols. 1910–11. Reprint. New York: Russell & Russell, 1958.

―――. *History of Labor in the United States*. 4 vols. New York: Macmillan, 1935–1946.

"Comtean Atheism." *American Quarterly Church Review and Ecclesiastical Registry* 20 (July 1868): 169–83.

Conway, Moncure Daniel. *Autobiography: Memories and Experiences.* 2 vols. Boston: Houghton Mifflin, 1904.

———. "Esperanza: My Journey Thither and What I Found There." *The Dial* 1 (May 1860): 325–26.

———. *Life of Nathaniel Hawthorne.* London and New York: Walter Scott, 189?).

Cott, Nancy F., and Elizabeth H. Pleck, eds. *A Heritage of Her Own: Toward a New Social History of Women.* New York: Simon & Schuster, 1979.

Creese, Walter. "Fowler and the Domestic Octagon." *Art Bulletin* 28 (June 1846): 89–102.

DeLeon, David. *The American As Anarchist: Reflections on Indigenous Radicalism.* Baltimore: Johns Hopkins Univ. Press, 1978.

DeMaria, Richard. *Communal Love at Oneida: A Perfectionist Vision of Authority, Property, and Sexual Order.* New York: Edwin Mellen Press, 1978.

Ditzion, Sidney. *Marriage, Morals and Sex in America: A History of Ideas.* New York: Bookman Associates, 1953.

Dixon, William Hepworth. *Spiritual Wives.* Philadelphia: J. B. Lippincott, 1868.

Duberman, Martin, ed. *The Antislavery Vanguard: New Essays on the Abolitionists.* Princeton: Princeton Univ. Press, 1965.

Dunn, Jacob Piatt. "New Harmony." Chap. 19 in *Indiana and Indianans: A History of Aboriginal and Territorial Indiana and the Century of Statehood,* 2:1071–1120. Chicago and New York: American Historical Society, 1919.

Edger, Henry. *The Positivist Calendar: Or, Transitional System of Public Commemoration Instituted by Augustus Comte, Founder of the Positive Religion of Humanity. With a Brief Position of Religious Positivism; and an Appendix, Containing I. A Concordance of the Calendars; II. The Positivist Library, and III. Narrative of the Rise and Progress of Positivism. Diis extinctis, Deoque, successit Humanitas.* Modern Times (Thompson, L.I.): the author, the 68th Year of the Great Crisis (1856).

———. *The Positivist Community: Glimpse of the Regenerated Future of the Human Race. A Sermon Preached at Modern Times, Long Island, on Saturday, 24th Gutemberg [sic] 75, [5th September, 1863], Being the Sixth Anniversary of the Death (Transformation) of Auguste Comte, Founder of the Religion of Humanity.* Modern Times, N.Y.: the author, Year of the Great Modern Crisis 76 [1864].

Egbert, Donald, and Stow Persons, eds. *Socialism and American Life.* 2 vols. Princeton: Princeton Univ. Press, 1952.

Ellis, John B. [pseud.]. *Free Love and Its Votaries, or, American Socialism Unmasked.* New York and Cincinnati: U.S. Publishing Co., 1870.

Ely, Richard T. *Recent American Socialism*. Baltimore: Johns Hopkins Univ., 1885.

Emerson, Ralph Waldo. "Fourierism and the Socialists." *Dial* 3 (July 1842): 86–89.

———. *Self-Reliance* [1841]. In *The Works of Ralph Waldo Emerson*. Edited by James Elliot Cabot, 3:47–87. 14 vols. Cambridge, Mass.: Houghton Mifflin, 1883.

———. *The Works of Ralph Waldo Emerson*. Edited by James Elliot Cabot. 14 vols. Cambridge, Mass.: Houghton Mifflin, 1883.

Engels, Friedrich. *The Housing Question*. 1872. Reprint. New York: International Publishers, n.d.

———. *Socialism, Utopian and Scientific*. Translated by Edward Aveling. 1892. Reprint. New York: International Publishers, 1932.

Fast, Howard. *The Selected Works of Tom Paine and Citizen Tom Paine*. New York: Random House, 1945.

Fellman, Michael. *The Unbounded Frame — Freedom and Community in Nineteenth-Century American Utopianism*. Westport, Conn.: Greenwood Press, 1973.

Filler, Louis. *The Crusade Against Slavery 1830–1860*. 1960. Reprint. New York: Harper & Row, 1963.

Fish, Carl Russell. *The Rise of the Common Man 1830–1860*. Chicago: Quadrangle Books, 1927.

Fisher, Marvin. *Workshops in the Wilderness: The European Response to American Industrialism 1830–1860*. New York: Oxford Univ. Press, 1967.

Fishman, Robert. *Urban Utopias in the Twentieth Century — Ebenezer Howard, Frank Lloyd Wright and Le Corbusier*. New York: Basic Books, 1977.

Fogarty, Robert S. *American Utopianism*. Itasca, Ill.: F. E. Peacock, 1972.

———. *Dictionary of American Communal and Utopian History*. Westport, Conn.: Greenwood Press, 1980.

Foner, Eric. *Free Soil, Free Labor, Free Men: The Ideology of the Republican Party before the Civil War*. New York: Oxford Univ. Press, 1970.

———. *Politics and Ideology in the Age of the Civil War*. New York: Oxford Univ. Press, 1980.

Foster, Lawrence. *Religion and Sexuality: Three American Communal Experiments of the Nineteenth Century*. New York: Oxford Univ. Press, 1981. Reprinted with identical pagination as *Religion and Sexuality: The Shakers, the Mormons, and the Oneida Community*. Urbana: Univ. of Illinois Press, 1984.

Fourier, Charles. *Harmonian Man: Selected Writings of Charles Fourier*. Edited by Mark Poster. Garden City, N.Y.: Doubleday, 1971.

———. *The Utopian Vision of Charles Fourier*. Edited by Jonathan Beecher and Richard Bienvenu. Boston: Beacon Press, 1971.

Freelance, Radical [pseud.]. *The Philosophers of Foufouville by Radical Freelance.* New York: G. W. Carelton, 1868.

Freud, Sigmund. *Civilization and Its Discontents.* New York: W. W. Norton, 1962.

Gorb, Peter. "Robert Owen as A Businessman." *Bulletin of the Business Historical Society* 25 (Sept. 1951): 127–48.

Gordon, Linda. *Woman's Body, Woman's Rights: A Social History of Birth Control in America.* New York: Grossman Publishers, 1976.

Graham, Walter. *English Literary Periodicals.* 1930. Reprint. New York: Octagon Books, 1966.

Greeley, Horace. *Hints Toward Reforms,* in *Lectures, Addresses, and Other Writings.* New York: Fowlers & Wells, 1853.

———. *Recollections of A Busy Life.* 2 vols. 1868. Reprint, Port Washington, N.Y.: Kennikat Press, 1971.

Hale, Sarah Josepha. *Woman's Record, or, Sketches of All Distinguished Women, from the Creation to A.D. 1848.* New York: Harper & Brothers, 1855.

Hall, Bowman N. "The Economic Ideas of Josiah Warren, First American Anarchist." *History of Political Economy* 6 (1974): 95–108.

Haller, John S., and Robin M. Haller. *The Physician and Sexuality in Victorian America.* New York: W. W. Norton, 1974.

Haraszti, Zoltan. "Brook Farm Letters." *Bulletin of the Boston Public Library* 12 (Feb., Mar. 1937): 49–68, 93–114.

Hardy, Dennis. *Alternative Communities in Nineteenth-Century England.* London: Longman Group, 1979.

Harrison, Frederick. *Autobiographical Memoirs.* 2 vols. London: Macmillan, 1911.

Harrison, John F. C. *Quest for the New Moral World: Robert Owen and the Owenites in Britain and America.* New York: Charles Scribner's Sons, 1969.

Hawkins, Richmond L. *Auguste Comte and the United States (1816–1853).* Cambridge, Mass.: Harvard Univ. Press, 1936.

———. *Positivism in the United States (1853–1861).* Cambridge, Mass.: Harvard Univ. Press, 1938.

Hayden, Dolores. *Seven American Utopias–The Architecture of Communitarian Socialism, 1790–1975.* Cambridge, Mass.: MIT Press, 1976.

Heilbronner, Robert L. *The Worldly Philosophers: The Lives, Times, and Ideas of the Great Economic Thinkers.* New York: Simon and Schuster, 1961.

Hersh, Blanche Glassman. *The Slavery of Sex: Feminist-Abolitionists in America.* Urbana: Univ. of Illinois Press, 1978.

Hillquit, Morris. *History of Socialism in the United States.* New York: Funk & Wagnalls, 1906.

Hinds, William A. *American Communities.* 1878. Reprint. Secaucus, N.J.: Citadel Press, 1973.

Hofstadter, Richard. *Social Darwinism in American Thought.* 1944. Rev. ed. Boston: Beacon Press, 1967.

Holloway, Mark. *Heavens on Earth: Utopian Communities in America 1680–1880.* New York: Dover Publications, 1966.

Howard, Ebenezer. *Garden Cities of Tomorrow.* 1902. Reprint. Cambridge, Mass.: MIT Press, 1965.

Jacker, Corinne. *The Black Flag of Anarchy: Antistatism in the United States.* New York: Charles Scribner's Sons, 1968.

Johnson, Alexander Bryan. *A Treatise on Language, or, the Relation which Words Bear to Things, in four parts.* New York: Harper & Brothers, 1836. Originally published as *Philosophy of Human Knowledge, or, A Treatise on Language* (New York: G & C Carvill, 1826).

Johnson, Christopher J. *Utopian Communism in France: Cabet and the Icarians, 1839–1851.* Ithaca: Cornell Univ. Press, 1974.

Kanter, Rosabeth Moss. *Commitment and Community – Communes and Utopias in Sociological Perspective.* Cambridge, Mass.: Harvard Univ. Press, 1972.

Kern, Louis J. *An Ordered Love: Sex Roles and Sexuality in Victorian Utopias – the Shakers, the Mormons, and the Oneida Community.* Chapel Hill: Univ. of North Carolina Press, 1981.

Krimerman, Leonard I., and Lewis Perry, eds. *Patterns of Anarchy: A Collection of Writings on the Anarchist Tradition.* Garden City, N.Y.: Doubleday, 1966.

Kring, Hilda Adam. *The Harmonists – A Folk-Cultural Approach.* Metuchen, N.J.: Scarecrow Press, 1973.

Kropotkin, Peter. *Kropotkin's Revolutionary Pamphlets: A Collection of Writings by Peter Kropotkin.* Edited by Roger N. Baldwin. 1927. Reprint. New York: Dover Publications, 1970.

Kubler, George L. *History of Stereotyping.* Brooklyn: Brooklyn Eagle Commercial Printing Division, 1927.

Lane, Charles. "Brook Farm." *The Dial* 4 (Jan. 1844): 351–57.

Leopold, Richard W. *Robert Dale Owen: A Biography.* Cambridge, Mass.: Harvard Univ. Press, 1940.

Levitas, Irving. "The Unterrified Jeffersonian: Benjamin R. Tucker. A Study of Native American Anarchism as Exemplified in His Life and Times." Ph.D. diss., New York Univ., 1974.

Locke, John. *Second Treatise of Government.* Edited by C. B. Macpherson. Indianapolis: Hackett Pub. Co., 1980.

Lockwood, George B. *The New Harmony Communities.* Marion, Ind.: Chronicle Co., 1902.

Macdonald, A. J. "Materials for a History of Ideal Communities." The Yale

Collection of American Literature, New Haven: Beinecke Rare Book and Manuscript Library, Yale Univ.

Macdonald, George E. *Fifty Years of Freethought: Being the Story of the Truth Seeker, with the Natural History of Its Third Editor.* 2 vols. New York: Truth Seeker Company, 1929–1931.

McNiff, William J. *Heaven on Earth—A Planned Mormon Society.* 1940. Reprint. Philadelphia: Porcupine Press, 1972.

Macpherson, C. B. *The Political Theory of Possessive Individualism: Hobbes to Locke.* New York: Oxford Univ. Press, 1962.

McWatters, George S., ed. *Detectives of Europe and America, or Life in the Secret Service, A Collection of Celebrated Cases in Great Britain, France, Germany, Italy, Spain, Russia, Poland, Egypt, and America* (Hartford, Conn.: J. B. Burr, 1881).

Mannheim, Karl. *Ideology and Utopia: An Introduction to the Sociology of Knowledge.* New York: Harcourt, Brace & World, 1936.

Manuel, Frank. *The Prophets of Paris.* Cambridge, Mass.: Harvard Univ. Press, 1962.

Marcus, Steven. *The Other Victorians—A Study of Sexuality and Pornography in Mid-Nineteenth-Century England.* 1974. Reprint. New York: New American Library, 1977.

Martin, James J. *Men Against the State: The Expositors of Individualist Anarchism in America, 1827–1908.* 1953. Reprint. Colorado Springs: Ralph Myles Publisher, 1970.

Marx, Karl, and Friedrich Engels. *The Communist Manifesto.* 1848. Reprint, edited by Samuel H. Beer. New York: Appleton-Century-Crofts, 1955.

Marx, Leo. *The Machine in the Garden, Technology and the Pastoral Ideal in America.* London: Oxford Univ. Press, 1974.

Masquerier, Lewis. *Sociology, or, the Reconstruction of Society, Government, and Property.* 1877. Reprint. Westport, Conn.: Greenwood Press, 1970.

Meyers, Marvin. *The Jacksonian Persuasion: Politics and Belief.* New York: Random House, 1957.

Mill, John Stuart. *Auguste Comte and Positivism.* 1865. Reprint. Ann Arbor: Univ. of Mich. Press, 1961.

———. *The Autobiography of John Stuart Mill.* Edited by John Jacob Coss. 1873. Reprint. New York: Columbia Univ. Press, 1924.

———. *Utilitarianism, on Liberty, and Considerations on Representative Government.* London: J. M. Dent & Sons, 1922.

Miller, David. *Anarchism.* London: J. M. Dent & Sons, 1984.

Miller, Perry. *Errand Into the Wilderness.* 1956. Reprint. New York: Harper & Row, 1964.

Montgomery, David. *Beyond Equality: Labor and the Radical Republicans 1862–1872.* 1967. Reprint. Urbana: Univ. of Illinois Press, 1981.

Mumford, Louis. *The Culture of Cities.* New York: Harcourt, Brace & Co., 1938.

Muncy, Raymond L. *Sex and Marriage in Utopian Communities—19th Century America.* Bloomington: Indiana Univ. Press, 1973.

Myerson, Joel, ed. *Brook Farm: An Annotated Bibliography and Resources Guide.* New York: Garland Publishing, 1978.

Nelson, Thomas, ed. *Documents of Upheaval: Selections from William Lloyd Garrison's The Liberator 1831–1865.* New York: Hill & Wang, 1966.

Newberry, Edward. *Human Perfectability: Individually and Sociologically Considered.* Brentwood, N.Y.: the author, 1878. Booklet.

Nichols, Mary Sargeant Gove. *Mary Lyndon, or, Revelations of A Life: An Autobiography.* New York: Stringer & Townsend, 1855.

————. *Reminiscences of Edgar Allan Poe.* 1863. Reprint. New York: Union Square Bookshop, 1931.

Nichols, Thomas Low. *Esoteric Anthology (The Mysteries of Man): A Comprehensive and Confidential Treatise On the Structure, Functions, Passional Attractions, and Perversions, True and False Physical and Social Conditions, and the Most Intimate Relations of Men and Women.* 1853. Reprint. New York: Arno Press, 1972.

————. *Forty Years of American Life, 1821–1861.* 1864. Reprint. New York: Stackpole Sons, 1937.

————. *Woman In All Ages and Nations: A Complete and Authentic History of the Manners and Customs, Character and Condition of the Female Sex, in Civilized and Savage Countries, from the Earliest Ages to the Present Time.* New York: Fowlers & Wells, 1854.

Nichols, Thomas Low, and Mary Gove Nichols. *Marriage: Its History, Character and Results: Its Sanctities and Its Profanities, Its Science and Its Facts Demonstrating Its Influence As A Civilized Institution, and the Happiness of the Individual and the Progress of the Race.* Cincinnati: Valentine Nicholson & Co., 1854.

Nissenbaum, Steven. *Sex, Diet, and Debility: Sylvester Graham and Health Reform.* Westport, Conn.: Greenwood Press, 1980.

Noever, Janet Hubley. "Passionate Rebel: The Life of Mary Gove Nichols." Ph.D. diss., Univ. of Oklahoma, 1983.

Nordhoff, Charles. *The Communistic Societies of the United States, from Personal Visit and Observation.* 1875. Reprint. New York: Dover Publications, 1966.

North, Douglass C. *The Economic Growth of the United States 1790–1860.* New York: W. W. Norton, 1966.

Notable American Women 1627–1950: A Biographical Dictionary. 3 vols. Cambridge, Mass.: Belknap Press, 1971.

Noyes, John Humphrey. *History of American Socialisms.* 1870. Reprint. New York: Hillary House, 1961.

Noyes, Pierrepont. *My Father's House: An Oneida Boyhood.* New York: Farrar & Rinehart, 1937.

Orvis, Marianne Dwight. *Letters from Brook Farm 1844–1847.* 1938. Reprint. Philadelphia: Porcupine Press, 1972.

Owen, Robert. *The Life of Robert Owen, Written by Himself with Selections from his Writings and Correspondence.* 2 vols. 1857–1858. Reprint. New York: Augustus M. Kelley, 1967.

———. *Robert Owen in the United States.* Edited by Oakley Johnson. New York: Humanities Press, 1970.

Owen, Robert Dale. *Threading My Way: An Autobiography.* 1874. Reprint. New York: Augustus Kelley, 1967.

Paine, Thomas. *The Age of Reason* [1794–1795]. In Howard Fast, *The Selected Work of Tom Paine and Citizen Tom Paine.* New York: Modern Library, 1943.

———. *Common Sense and The Crisis.* Garden City, N.Y.: Doubleday, 1960.

———. *Rights of Man* [1791–1792]. In Howard Fast, *The Selected Work of Tom Paine and Citizen Tom Paine.* New York: Modern Library, 1943.

Pare, William. "Equitable Villages in America." *Journal of the Statistical Society of London,* Series A. 19 (June 1856): 127–43.

———. "Triallville [sic] and Modern Times." *Chambers's Edinburgh Review* 18 (18 Dec. 1852): 395–97.

Perry, Lewis. *Radical Abolitionism: Anarchy and the Government of God in Antislavery Thought.* Ithaca: Cornell Univ. Press, 1973.

Pessen, Edward. *Most Uncommon Jacksonians: The Radical Leaders of the Early Labor Movement.* Albany: State Univ. of New York Press, 1967.

Podmore, Frank. *Mediums of the 19th. Century.* 2 vols. New Hyde Park, N.Y.: University Books, 1963. Originally published as *Modern Spiritualism* (London, 1902).

———. *Robert Owen: A Biography.* 1906. Reprint. New York: D. Appleton, 1924.

Poe, Edgar Allan. "The Literati of New York City." *Godey's Magazine and Lady's Book* (May 1846), 157–62.

Quint, Howard. *The Forging of American Socialism: Origins of the Modern Movement.* 1953. Reprint. Indianapolis: Bobbs-Merrill, 1964.

Records, Thomas W. "The Old Printing Office in New Harmony." *Indiana Magazine of History* 33 (Dec. 1937): 428–34.

Reed, James. *From Private Vice to Public Virtue: The Birth Control Movement and American Society Since 1830.* New York: Basic Books, 1978.

Reichert, William O. *Partisans of Freedom — A Study in American Anarchism.* Bowling Green, Ohio: Bowling Green Univ. Press, 1976.

Resseguie, Harry E. "Alexander Turney Stewart and the Development of the Department Store, 1823–1876." *Business History Review* 39 (Autumn 1965): 301–22.

Rexroth, Kenneth. *Communalism: From Its Origins to the Twentieth Century.* New York: Seabury Press, 1974.

Robbins, Roy M. "Horace Greeley: Land Reform and Unemployment, 1837–1862." *Agricultural History* 7 (1933): 18–41.

———. *Our Landed Heritage: The Public Domain, 1776–1970.* Lincoln: Univ. of Nebraska Press, 1976.

Rocker, Rudolph. *Pioneers of American Freedom: Origin of Liberal and Radical Thought in America.* Los Angeles: Rocker Publications Committee, 1949.

Rosenberg, Nathan. *Technology and American Economic Growth.* New York: Harper & Row, 1972.

Russell, Bertrand. *Freedom and Organization — 1814–1914.* 1934. Reprint. London: George Allen and Unwin, 1952.

Sachs, Emanie L. [pseud.]. *"The Terrible Siren": Victoria C. Woodhull, (1838–1927).* New York: Harper & Brothers, 1928.

Sams, Henry W., ed. *Autobiography of Brook Farm.* Englewood Cliffs, N.J.: Prentice-Hall, 1958.

Schneider, Robert E. *Positivism in the United States: The Apostleship of Henry Edger.* Rosario, Argentina: the author, 1946 [Ph.D. diss., Columbia Univ., n.d].

Schuster, Eunice M. *Native American Anarchism: A Study of Left-Wing American Individualism.* 1932. Reprint. New York: Da Capo Press, 1970.

Sears, John Van Der Zee. *My Friends at Brook Farm.* New York: Desmond Fitzgerald, 1912.

Semmel, Bernard. *John Stuart Mill and the Pursuit of Virtue.* New Haven: Yale Univ. Press, 1984.

Shelley, Percy Bysshe. *Hellas, A Lyrical Drama* [1821]. In *The Complete Poetical Works of Percy Bysshe Shelley.* Edited by Newell F. Ford. Boston: Houghton Mifflin, 1974.

Smith, Henry Nash. *Virgin Land: The American West As Symbol and Myth.* Cambridge, Mass.: Harvard Univ. Press, 1950.

Soltow, Lee. *Men and Wealth in the United States, 1850–1870.* New Haven: Yale Univ. Press, 1975.

Spann, Edward K. *Brotherly Tomorrows: Movements for A Cooperative Society in America, 1829–1920.* New York: Columbia Univ. Press, 1989.

Spencer, Herbert. *Social Statics or the Conditions Essential to Human Happiness Specified, and the First of Them Developed.* London: John Chapman, 1851.

Spurlock, John C. *Free Love: Marriage and Middle-Class Radicalism in America, 1825–1860.* New York: New York Univ. Press, 1988.

Stearns, Bertha-Monica. "Memnonia: The Launching of a Utopia." *New England Quarterly* 15 (June 1942): 280–95.

————. "Two Forgotten New England Reformers." *New England Quarterly* 6 (Mar. 1933): 59–84.

Stern, Madeleine. *The Pantarch: The Biography of Stephen Pearl Andrews.* Austin: Univ. of Texas Press, 1968.

Stevens, Abram Walters. "Josiah Warren: Remarks Made at the Funeral of Mr. Warren, Friday, April 17 [1874]." *The Index* 5 (23 Apr. 1874): 198.

Stoehr, Taylor. *Free Love in America — A Documentary History.* New York: AMS Press, 1979.

————. *Hawthorne's Mad Scientists: Pseudo-science and Social Science in Nineteenth-Century Life and Letters.* Hamden, Conn.: Archon Books, 1978.

————. *Nay-Saying in Concord: Emerson, Alcott, and Thoreau.* Hamden, Conn.: Archon Books, 1979.

Swan, Norma Lippincott, ed. *Exposé of the Condition and Progress of the North American Phalanx in Reply to the Inquiries of Horace Greeley, with an Introduction by N. L. Swan and Appendices by Frederika Bremer and Charles Sears.* 1853. Reprint. Philadelphia: Porcupine Press, 1975.

Swartz, Clarence Lee. *Josiah Warren, the First American Anarchist.* 1906. Reprint. Berkeley, N.J.: Oriole Press, 1955 [a review of *Josiah Warren* by William Bailie].

Swift, Lindsay. *Brook Farm, Its Members, Scholars, and Visitors.* 1908. Reprint. New York: Corinth Books, 1967.

Symes, Lillian, and Travers Clement. *Rebel America: The Story of Social Revolt in the United States.* 1943. Reprint. Boston: Beacon Press, 1972.

Taylor, Anne. *Visions of Harmony: A Study in Nineteenth-Century Millenarianism.* Oxford, U.K.: Clarendon Press, 1987.

Taylor, George Rogers. *The Transportation Revolution 1815–1860.* 1951. Reprint. Armonk, N.Y.: M. E. Sharpe, 1977.

Taylor, Graham R. *Satellite Cities, A Study of Industrial Suburbs.* New York: Appleton, 1915.

Temin, Peter. *Causal Factors in American Economic Growth in the Nineteenth Century.* London: Macmillan, 1975.

Ten, C. L. *Mill on Liberty.* New York: Oxford Univ. Press, 1980.

Thomas, Robert David. *The Man Who Would Be Perfect — John Humphrey*

Noyes and the Utopian Impulse. Philadelphia: Univ. of Pennsylvania Press, 1977.

Thomson, David. *England in the Nineteenth Century (1815–1914).* 1950. Reprint. New York: Penguin, 1981.

Thoreau, Henry David. *Henry David Thoreau: The Major Essays.* Edited by Jeffrey L. Duncan. New York: E. P. Dutton, 1972.

————. *Thoreau: Man of Concord.* Edited by Walter Harding. New York: Holt, Rinehart & Winston, 1960.

————. *Thoreau: People, Principles, and Politics.* Edited by Milton Meltzer. New York: Hill & Wang, 1963.

————. *Walden: or, Life in the Woods.* 1854. Reprint. Mount Vernon, N.Y.: Peter Pauper Press, n.d.

Tipple, John. *The Capitalist Revolution: A History of American Social Thought 1890–1919.* New York: Western Publishing Co., 1970.

Tocqueville, Alexis de. *Democracy in America.* 1835. Reprint. New York: Random House, 1945.

Trowbridge, John Townsend. "A Reminiscence of the Pantarch." *The Independent* 58 (26 Feb. 1903): 497–501.

Turner, Frederick Jackson. *Frontier and Section: Selected Essays of Frederick Jackson Turner.* Edited by Ray Allen Billington. Englewood Cliffs, N.J.: Prentice-Hall, 1961.

Tuveson, Ernest. *Redeemer Nation: The Idea of America's Millennial Role.* Chicago: Univ. of Chicago Press, 1968.

Tyler, Alice Felt. *Freedom's Ferment: Phases of American Social History from the Colonial Period to the Outbreak of the Civil War.* 1944. Reprint. New York: Harper & Row, 1962.

Wagenen, Jared van, Jr. *The Golden Age of Homespun.* 1953. Reprint. New York: Hill & Wang, 1963.

Walters, Ronald G. *American Reformers 1815–1860.* New York: Hill & Wang, 1978.

————. *Primers for Prudery: Sexual Advice to Victorian America.* Englewood Cliffs, N.J.: Prentice-Hall, 1974.

Ware, Norman. *The Industrial Worker 1840–1860: The Reaction of American Industrial Society to the Advance of the Industrial Revolution.* 1924. Reprint. Chicago: Quadrangle Books, 1964.

Warren, Josiah. *Equitable Commerce, a New Developement [sic] of Principles, as Substitutes for Laws and Governments, for the Harmonious Adjustment and Regulation of the Pecuniary, Intellectual, and Moral Intercourse of Mankind, Proposed as Elements of New Society.* New Harmony, Ind.: the author, 1846. Rev. ed. New York: Fowlers & Wells, 1852. Reprint. New York: Burt Franklin, 1967.

————. *Labor Prices*. New Harmony, Ind.: the author, 1842. Warren MSS, Workingmen's Institute Library, New Harmony, Ind. Leaflet.

————. *Manifesto*. New Harmony, Ind., 1841. Reprint. Berkeley Heights, N.J.: Oriole Press, 1952.

————. *Modern Education*. Modern Times, N.Y.: the author, 1861. Brochure.

————. *Positions Defined*. Modern Times, N.Y.: the author, 1853. Leaflet.

————. *Practical Applications of the Elementary Principles of "True Civilization" to the Minute Details of Every Day Life, Being Part III, the Last of the "True Civilization" Series, and the Facts and Conclusions of Forty-Seven Years of Study and Experiments in Reform Movement through Communism To and In Elementary Principles, Found in a Direction Exactly Opposite to and Away from Communism, But Leading Directly to All the Harmonic Results Aimed at by Communism*. Princeton, Mass.: the author, 1873.

————. *Practical Details in Equitable Commerce, Showing the Workings, in Actual Experiment, During a Series of Years, of the Social Principles Expounded in the Works Called "Equitable Commerce," by the Author of This, and "The Science of Society," by Stephen Pearl Andrews*. New York: Fowlers & Wells, 1852.

————. *True Civilization an Immediate Necessity and the Last Ground of Hope for Mankind. Being the Results and Conclusions of Thirty-Nine Years Laborious Study and Experiments in Civilization As It Is, and in Different Enterprises for Reconstruction*. Boston, 1863. Reprint. New York: Burt Franklin, 1967.

Weisbrod, Carol. *The Boundaries of Utopia*. New York: Pantheon, 1980.

Williams, Aaron. *The Harmony Society at Economy, Penn'a, Founded by George Rapp in A.D. 1805*. 1866. Reprint. New York: Augustus M. Kelley, 1971.

Williams, Mentor. "Paulding Satirizes Owenism." *Indiana Magazine of History* 44 (Dec. 1948): 355–65.

Williams, Raymond. *Keywords: A Vocabulary of Culture and Society*. New York: Oxford Univ. Press, 1976.

Wish, Harvey. "Stephen Pearl Andrews, American Pioneer Sociologist." *Social Forces* 19 (May 1941): 447–82.

Woodcock, George, ed. *Anarchism: A History of Libertarian Ideas and Movements*. Cleveland: World Publishing, 1962.

NEWSPAPERS AND PERIODICALS

The Dial. Boston, 1840–1844.

The Free Enquirer. New Harmony, Ind., and New York, 1828–1835.

The Harbinger. New York and Boston, 1845–1849.

The London *Leader*. London, 1850–1860.

The Long Islander. Huntington, N.Y., 1839–1936.

The New-Harmony Gazette. New Harmony, Ind., 1825–1828.

New York Observer. New York, 1823–1912.

New York Tribune. New York.

Nichols' Journal of Health, Water-Cure, and Human Progress. New York, 1853–54.

Nichols Monthly, a Magazine of Social Science and Progressive Literature. Cincinnati, 1854–1856.

The Peaceful Revolutionist, vol. 1. Cincinnati, 1833.

The Peaceful Revolutionist, Devoted to the Practical Details of Equitable Commerce, vol. 2. Utopia, Ohio, 1846.

The Periodical Letter on the Principles and Progress of the "Equity Movement," to Those Who Have Not Lost All Hope of Justice, Order, and Peace on Earth. Modern Times, N.Y., and Boston, 1854–1858.

The Phalanx. New York, 1843–1845.

The Practical Christian. Milford, Mass., 1840–1860.

The Scrub Oak. Brentwood, N.Y., ca. 1879–1880.

Woodhull and Claflin's Weekly. New York, 1870–1876.

Equitable commerce, 3, 11, 15, 18, 21,
    22, 90, 107, 125, 126–27, 130–33,
    144, 182; Stephen Pearl Andrews,
    defended by, 128–33; Stephen Pearl
    Andrews defined by, 3, 125; at Ber-
    lin Heights, Ohio, 125, 166, 189; in
    England, 142–45, 164; problems of,
    127, 132–33, 172–74, 175, 188–90;
    George Ripley, critique of, 125–27;
    Josiah Warren defined by, 3, 16, 47.
    See also Warren, Josiah, Equitable
    Commerce; Warren, Josiah, Practical
    Details in Equitable Commerce

Fish, Henry, 43, 50, 51, 86, 179; Fish-
    Seaver scandal, 61–62, 83, 134, 135–
    36
Fish, Malinda (wife of Henry), 61, 83
Fish, Myndert M., 40, 46, 85, 119
Fisher, Sumner, 85
Fisher, Mrs. (wife of Sumner?), 84, 85
Fleet, Catherine, 28–29, 31, 32
Fleet, Samuel (husband), 10, 28
Foster, Lawrence, 55, 59
Fourier, François Marie Charles, 125,
    141, 143–44, 168, 224n. 26; Fourier-
    ism in United States, 21, 30, 95–96,
    138–39, 155, 156, 164, 171; on mar-
    riage, 53–54, 63–64, 80; program of,
    47, 96, 105–6, 130, 135, 176, 206n. 26.
    See also Associationism; Andrews,
    Stephen Pearl; Bowles, Benjamin
    Franklin; Emerson, Ralph Waldo;
    Greeley, Horace; Ripley, George;
    Thoreau, Henry David; Warren,
    Josiah
Fowlers and Wells, 20, 21, 28, 29, 30,
    199n. 62, 210–11n. 106
Free love, 3, 53–91; at Berlin Heights,
    Ohio, 166; defined, 53, 77; and
    Modern Times, 3, 22, 53, 60,
    65–66, 73–79, 81, 166–67, 182, 184;
    and Mary Gove Nichols, 58, 69–72,

    74–78, 159, 208–9n. 70; at Oneida
    Community, 54–59; and Victoria
    Woodhull, 207n. 55, 208–9n. 70. See
    also Codman, Charles A.; Warren,
    Josiah
Freud, Sigmund, 106, 206n. 34
Fuller, Margaret, 125, 157, 158, 159, 160

Garrison, William Lloyd, 71, 76–77, 87,
    96
George, Thomas C., 51, 179–80
Gibson, Isaac, 38–39, 40, 45, 51, 185,
    211n. 3; death of, 180, 202n. 33
Gove, Hiram, 70, 83
Gove, Mary Sargeant. See Nichols,
    Mary Sargeant Gove
Gray, Robert, 32, 34, 86, 91, 128,
    202n. 18
Great South Bay, 1, 13, 110, 111, 112,
    123, 187; baymen of, 117–18,
    215n. 26
Greeley, Horace, 128–29, 159; and
    Fourierism, 30, 63, 201n. 9; and
    Homestead Act, 30; Modern
    Times, purchase of land at, 28, 30–
    31, 201n. 12; New York Tribune de-
    bate with Andrews and Henry
    James, Sr., 62–70
Grubbing, 11, 40

Haines, Isaac, 39, 40, 115, 179
Harmonists. See Harmony
Harmony (Harmonists), 2, 3, 16, 22–
    23, 123–24, 130, 174, 197–98n. 47.
    See also Rapp, Geroge
Hawkins, Richmond Laurin, 162
Hawthorne, Nathaniel, 153, 156, 158,
    159–60
Hayward, Mrs. Sophia E., 29, 34, 83,
    165
Hayward, William (brother-in-law), 28,
    29, 186–87, 208n. 58

Non-Resistance (*continued*)
Garrison, William Lloyd; Practical Christian Republic

North American Phalanx, 106, 138, 163, 201n. 9; demise of, 171, 224n. 35

Noyes, John Humphrey, 15; and "Battle-Axe Letter," 55; and Bible communism, 55–56, 58, 124; on Brook Farm, 156–58; and free love, 54–59; *History of American Socialisms*, 56, 104, 138–39, 156, 184, 200n. 2; on Modern Times, 18–19, 74, 184; and the Nicholses, 74; and Oneida Community, 54–59, 124; and Perfectionism, 56, 57, 58, 177; on Practical Christian Republic, 139; on Second Coming, 56; and "stirpiculture," 57, 59, 203n. 46; on U.S. government, 176–77

Octagon buildings. *See* Modern Times, octagons at

Olivieri, Anna, 51

Olmstead, Frederick Law, 186

Oneida Community, 2, 3, 122, 203n. 46; "complex marriage" at, 55–59; and free love, 54–59; "male continence" at, 57; John Humphrey Noyes, role of, 55–59, 216n. 11. *See also* Noyes, John Humphrey

O'Rourke, Brian "Barney," 40, 51, 115

Orvis, Clark, 40, 41, 51, 159, 169

Osborne, Clara Christiana (wife of John Metcalf), 166, 167, 170

Owen, Robert, 15, 130, 138, 145, 163, 168; Declaration of Mental Independence of, 74; and labor notes, 47, 145; on marriage, 53–54, 74; National Labour Exchange bazaars, 47–48, 144–45; New Harmony, 16–20, 174, 184; New Lanark, 16–17; and socialism, 122, 124–25, 130;

and Warren, Josiah, 17–19, 74, 143–45, 184, 205n. 2

Owram, Joseph, 51, 179

Paine, Thomas, 27, 93; *Age of Reason*, 106; *Common Sense*, 109, 149; and deism, 107–8; *Rights of Man*, 108

Pantarch, Pantarchy. *See* Andrews, Stephen Pearl

Pare, William, 142–44, 219n. 1

Peaceful Revolutionist. See Warren, Josiah

Pearsall, Elizabeth (wife), 186

Pearsall, Robert W., 185–87

Peck, Edgar Fenn, 11, 14, 38; and pine barrens, 6–9; and New York City investors, 10, 50, 51, 195nn. 14, 15

Perfectionism. *See* Noyes, John Humphrey

Periodical Letter. See Warren, Josiah

Phelps, Elizabeth B. (mother of Elizabeth Pearsall), 186

Phrenology, 41–42, 73

Pine and Palm, A Novel. See Conway, Moncure Daniel

Pine barrens, 4, 6–11, 110, 180, 186, 189

Piper, Lizzie, 43, 85

Poe, Edgar Allan, 70–71

Practical Christian, 60, 123

Practical Christian Republic, 60, 133–41, 216n. 6; anarchist aspect of, 62, 135–36, 140; and "Christian Chastity," 61–62; and Civil War, 140; constitution of, 134–35; failure of, 138, 171; Fish-Seaver scandal, 61–62, 134, 135–36; and Modern Times, 133–41; Non-Resistance at, 96, 134, 219n. 56; Noyes, John Humphrey on, 139

Prantz, Mary Jane "Jenny" (wife of William U. Dame), 39, 199n. 62, 202n. 34, 226n. 13

UTOPIANISM and COMMUNITARIANISM

LYMAN TOWER SARGENT and GREGORY CLAEYS
Series Editors

This new series offers historical and contemporary analyses of utopian literature, communal societies, utopian social theory, broad themes such as the treatment of women in these traditions, and new editions of fictional works of lasting
value for both a general and a scholarly audience.

Other titles in the series include:

The Concept of Utopia. Ruth Levitas
Unveiling a Parallel. Alice Ilgenfritz Jones and Ella Merchant
*Women, Family, and Utopia: Communal Experiments of the Shakers, the Oneida
Community, and the Mormons.* Lawrence Foster

LOW LIVING AND HIGH THINKING AT MODERN TIMES, NEW YORK
was composed in 11 on 13 Goudy Old Style on Digital Compugraphic equipment
by Metricomp;
printed by sheet-fed offset on 50-pound, acid-free Glatfelter Natural Hi Bulk,
Smyth-sewn and bound over binder's boards in Holliston Roxite B,
and with dust jackets printed by
Braun-Brumfield, Inc.;
and published by

SYRACUSE UNIVERSITY PRESS
SYRACUSE, NEW YORK 13244-5160